On Track

The complete Caribbean guide to Health, Physical Education and Sports

Kirk Bizley

Advisor: Andrea R. Nichols

First published by Pearson Education Limited
Published from 2015 by Hodder Education,
An Hachette UK Company
Carmelite House
50 Victoria Embankment
London EC4Y 0DZ
www.hoddereducation.com

© Hodder & Stoughton Limited 2012

All rights reserved. Apart from any use permitted under UK copyright law, no part of this publication may be reproduced or transmitted in any form or by any means, electronic or mechanical, including photocopying and recording, or held within any information storage and retrieval system, without permission in writing from the publisher or under licence from the Copyright Licensing Agency Limited. Further details of such licences (for reprographic reproduction) may be obtained from the Copyright Licensing Agency Limited, www.cla.co.uk

Hachette UK's policy is to use papers that are natural, renewable and recyclable products and made from wood grown in well-managed forests and other controlled sources. The logging and manufacturing processes are expected to conform to the environmental regulations of the country of origin.

Orders: please contact Hachette UK Distribution, Hely Hutchinson Centre, Milton Road, Didcot, Oxfordshire, OX11 7HH. Telephone: +44 (0)1235 827827. Email education@hachette.co.uk Lines are open from 9 a.m. to 5 p.m., Monday to Friday. You can also order through our website: www.hoddereducation.com

First published 2012

23
IMP   10 9 8 7 6 5

ISBN: 978-0-4350-4965-2

Designed by Juice Creative
Original illustrations © Hodder & Stoughton Limited 2012

Picture Credits

The publisher would like to thank the following for their kind permission to reproduce their photographs:

(Key: b-bottom; c-centre; l-left; r-right; t-top)

ActionImages: Jason O'Brien 11br, JJL / HB Reuters 57 (hurdles), Reuters / Andrew Bira 75b, Reuters / Carlos Barria 57 (swimming), Reuters / Kai Pfaffenbach 72bl, Reuters / Mark Blinch 12c, Reuters / Mike Segar 49b, Sporting Pictures / Phil O'Connor 63cl, Sporting Pictures / Tony Marshall 76l, Stephane Kempinaire / DPPI 24t; **Alamy Images:** 1br, 26b, 34t, 40bl, 51 (hand stand), 72bc, 127tr, 1br, 26b, 34t, 40bl, 51 (hand stand), 72bc, 127tr, 1br, 26b, 34t, 40bl, 51 (hand stand), 72bc, 127tr, AlamyCelebrity 132t, apply pictures 166b, Classic Image 144tl, Dan Galic 117tr, Daniel Swee 82t, dbimages 46t, Design Pics Inc 31br, Eileen Langsley 57 (hockey), Form Advertising 119r, GPI Stock 23l, Ian Nellist 153b, Images & Stories 140br, ImageState 33br, Jenny Matthews 75t, marc Arundale 142cr, Mary Evans Picture Library 141tr, Montgomery Martin 60br, Norman Pogson 54c, PCN Photography 149b, Photos 12 145tl, Richard Wareham Fotografie 51 (scrum), Roger Bamber 161b, Russell Mills 116br; **Bigstock:** Image Source 32r; **Corbis:** 18br, 22tc, 58-59c, 66-67c, 126t, 162t, 18br, 22tc, 58-59c, 66-67c, 126t, 162t, Anindito Mukherjee / epa 95bl, Jeff Bachner / Demotix 51 (arm wrestling), Leo Mason 68br, Liu Dawei / xh / Xinhua Press 148b, Matthew Ashton 143tl, Monica M. Davey / epa 131t, Ocean 101t, 101c, Philip Brown / Reuters 94c, Steve Craft 59c, Tibor Illyes / epa 170t, Tom Bean 48c; **Fotolia.com:** 111br; **Getty Images:** 9c, 52-53c, 70t, 72br, 79br, 91t, 121b, 145br, 171bl, AFP 15br, 20c, 114b, 157b, 175tr, Bongarts 77c, Chris Clinton 4b, FIFA 30t, Jupiterimages 106tl, PNC 35cr; **Glow Images:** 136, 163b, Jim Cummins 2t; **ICC:** 152tl; **Newspix International:** 90tl, 90tc, 101b; **Pearson Free Image:** 122tl, 123tr; **Reuters:** 13b, 65b, 150t, Ho New 22tr; **Science Photo Library Ltd:** 134t; **Shutterstock.com:** 3t, 16b, 25br, 36tl, 43b

Cover images: *Front:* **Getty Images:** l, r; **Glow Images:** c

All other images © Hodder & Stoughton Limited

Every effort has been made to trace the copyright holders and we apologise in advance for any unintentional omissions. We would be pleased to insert the appropriate acknowledgement in any subsequent edition of this publication.

Printed and bound by CPI Group (UK) Ltd, Croydon, CR0 4YY

Dedication from the author:
This book is dedicated to all my present grandchildren – Lola, Luca, Isabelle, Florence, Oliver and Harry.
Enjoy reading this when you can! Love from Granddad.

Contents

	How to use this book	iv
1	Acquisition of skill	1
2	Tactics and teamwork	8
3	Formations and strategies	11
4	Officials	15
5	Rules	18
6	Planning, performing and evaluating	21
7	Practices and drills	25
8	Organising and running sports events	28
9	Health and hygiene	31
10	Nutrition and diet	37
11	Diet and physical activity	42
12	Exercise	45
13	Fitness	48
14	Strength	51
15	Flexibility	56
16	Endurance	60
17	Speed and power	64
18	Age	68
19	Somatotype	71
20	Individual differences	74
21	Factors affecting performance	78
22	The skeletal system	83
23	The muscular system	88
24	The nervous system	93
25	The circulatory system	97
26	The respiratory system	103
27	The digestive system	107
28	The principles of training	110
29	Training sessions	113
30	Training methods	116
31	Fitness testing	121
32	Injury prevention	128
33	Injury types and treatments	133
34	The history of sport and international sport	140
35	Politics and sport	153
36	Sponsorship	155
37	The media	160
38	Drugs and sport	165
39	Discrimination in sport	173
	Glossary	176
	Index	182

How to use this book

On Track has been developed for use in secondary schools across the English-speaking Caribbean. The chart below demonstrates how the chapters relate to topics covered in syllabuses from Jamaica, Trinidad and Tobago, Barbados and *CSEC*®.

Chapter	Jamaica	Trinidad & Tobago	Barbados	CSEC®
1. Acquisition of skill	✓	✓	✓	✓
2. Tactics and teamwork	✓	✓	✓	✓
3. Formations and strategies	✓	✓	✓	✓
4. Officials	✓	✓	✓	✓
5. Rules	✓	✓		
6. Planning, performing and evaluating			✓	✓
7. Practices and drills	✓	✓	✓	✓
8. Organising and running sports events		✓		✓
9. Health and hygiene	✓	✓	✓	✓
10. Nutrition and diet	✓	✓	✓	✓
11. Diet and physical activity	✓	✓	✓	✓
12. Exercise	✓	✓	✓	✓
13. Fitness	✓	✓	✓	✓
14. Strength	✓	✓	✓	✓
15. Flexibility	✓	✓	✓	✓
16. Endurance	✓	✓	✓	✓
17. Speed and power	✓	✓	✓	✓
18. Age		✓	✓	✓
19. Somatotype		✓	✓	✓
20. Individual differences	✓			✓
21. Factors affecting performance	✓	✓	✓	✓
22. The skeletal system	✓	✓	✓	✓
23. The muscular system	✓	✓	✓	✓
24. The nervous system	✓	✓	✓	✓
25. The circulatory system	✓	✓	✓	✓
26. The respiratory system	✓	✓	✓	✓
27. The digestive system	✓	✓	✓	✓
28. The principles of training	✓	✓	✓	✓
29. Training sessions	✓	✓	✓	✓
30. Training methods	✓	✓	✓	✓
31. Fitness testing	✓	✓	✓	✓
32. Injury prevention	✓	✓	✓	✓
33. Injury types and treatments	✓	✓	✓	✓
34. The history of sport and international sport				✓
35. Politics and sport				✓
36. Sponsorship				✓
37. The media				✓
38. Drugs and sport	✓	✓	✓	✓
39. Discrimination in sport				✓

Chapter features

Each chapter in this book has a variety of features which have been designed to both assist and challenge the readers in various ways.

These include:

Key point

This helps to focus the reader on the topic in question; regarding how the topic needs to be put in perspective with the topic specifically and PE and sport generally.

Did you know?

This feature provides some talking and discussion points regarding the topic. It can relate to some interesting to know facts and further information about the topic which students may even be able to use in question answers as realistic examples.

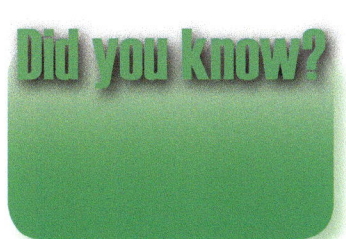

Tasks

These are designed to provide readers/students with some possible extension tasks which can be practical in nature or even involve some degree of further research or written work. These are often individual but there are also examples of some group tasks which can be used.

Performer profile

Various Caribbean performers have been identified to emphasise their particular links to some of the factors which are considered in some chapters where their personal achievements are considered in some depth.

Hints and Tips!

These are designed to put the particular chapter into a more specific focus at the end of each section. They are often linked to questions which could be asked regarding the particular content and they also attempt to sum up the key points of each chapter.

Key questions

These are all linked to the preceding text within each chapter so that each question can be answered by referring to the text. At times these questions extend the readers so that examples and explanations are asked for which, draw on the basic information contained within the text. These questions provide good opportunities for discussion and oral question and answer sessions which can involve the whole teaching group.

Features of the CD-ROM

In the back of this book you will find a CD-ROM. The CD-ROM provides fun and engaging support to complement the course and reinforce key concepts explored in class. It has been designed for use by teachers and students alike.

For *CSEC*®

A full sample exam paper with a matching mark scheme enables students to familiarise themselves with the format of the exam and gain valuable practice in answering CSEC-style questions.

Worksheets

There are various types of practical-based worksheets which refer to specific sports and activities in terms of their playing areas and the basic rules which apply to them. Also included are word searches, crosswords and quiz sheets. The worksheets are suitable for printing for use in class, as homework, and as revision material for concepts covered in an earlier term or form group.

Answers

All worksheets have accompanying answer sheets to enable teachers to easily check progress.

Activities

Fun interactive activities include multiple choice quizzes and true/false questions.

1 Acquisition of skill

One of the most important parts of learning or starting a physical activity is the acquisition of skill. The higher the level of skill that the performers have, the better they will be at their chosen activity. Also, when either helping others to acquire skill or observing their skill levels, it is important to understand skill acquisition fully.

What is skill?

Skill is using knowledge or expertise to succeed efficiently and effectively in achieving a particular objective. In PE, skill is the ability to perform activities or movements with **control** and **consistency**, to bring about a desired result – for example, full control of a ball, a bat or body movements. A skill can be basic or complex, often depending on the type of activity undertaken.

Basic skills

These are usually simple things such as throwing, catching and striking. A key requirement for mastering these basic skills is the control of body movement – **co-ordination**. Performers must be able to fully control their body movements to perform a skill correctly. They must be able to perform basic skills well, before going on to more complicated movements or activities.

Throwing a ball is considered a very basic skill but it is still a very complicated movement. It takes co-ordination between the legs, the arms, the hands and the brain in order to achieve an accurate throw.

Complex skills

These are skills that take a long time to learn because they involve a high level of co-ordination and control. Athletic field events are good examples of using complex skills. The pole vault, in particular, requires a combination of skilled movements for run-up, take off, flight and landing to complete a successful jump.

Nobody could hope to compete in a pole vault competition at even a basic level without gaining a high level of complex skills such as judging the run-up with precise accuracy, carrying and gripping the pole correctly, taking off and rotating in the air, and then landing safely.

All activities have this combination of basic skills leading on to more complex ones and it is the mastery of all of these that leads to a truly skilful performer. Throwing a ball in cricket can be a basic skill but to throw it in from a deep fielding position quickly and accurately to the wicketkeeper behind the stumps is a complex one.

> **Key point**
> Skill has been defined as 'when a predetermined objective is accomplished with a minimum outlay of energy'. Put in simple terms this would mean that it is a combination of knowledge and expertise.

> **Task 1**
> Which parts of the body do you have to move and control when you throw a ball? Watch someone do it and describe fully the movements you see.

Figure 1.1 Some sports require high levels of control and skill

Acquisition of skill 1

Task 2

Choose **three** different sporting activities and for each one name at least one simple and one complex skill that must be learned.

Did you know?

South African golfer Gary Player was once accused of being very lucky by an opponent playing against him in a competition and he replied, 'The more I practise the luckier I get!'

Task 3

Describe a sporting situation where the 'form' of **one** of the players has affected the result.

Figure 1.2 A good pole vaulter must master many complex skills

Practice

Skills can only be acquired through **practice**. To make progress and improve in an activity or event, the performer must be prepared to practise repeatedly certain parts or aspects of that activity over a long period of time. There are no short cuts. A performer must be prepared to start at the very beginning when learning an activity or movement. This means that the basic skills must be acquired first before attempting more difficult or complex skills. Even top-level performers continue to practise and improve the skills they have learned. This is an important part of their **training**.

In most schools, PE lessons will have an initial **warm-up** session followed by a skills practice related to the particular activity students are about to do.

The following factors of form, style and technique are all aspects of performance which are very closely linked to skill acquisition as the basic knowledge regarding how skills are acquired clearly impact upon them.

Form

In relation to physical activities, we talk about performance form and stylised form.

Performance form

This is the level of performance which a player is able to produce when taking part in an activity. It is linked to the likelihood of success in taking part because a player who is 'on form' is more likely to perform well. There does not seem to be any way either to predict or to control whether a performer will be on form. No matter how a person prepares in terms of practice and training, their performance form can change from day to day, game to game and performance to performance.

Players or performers are often selected or dropped from games as a result of their being on or off form.

Acquisition of skill

Figure 1.3 A good warm-up session can help to prevent injury

> **Task 4**
> Describe the contrasting styles of **two** different performers in one activity.

> **Task 5**
> Name both basic and advanced techniques which must be learnt for **two** physical activities.

The following factors seem to have an influence on form.

Confidence – if a performer is well prepared mentally and has a positive belief that they will do well, good form may be maintained. Many successful teams and individuals are referred to as having a 'run of good form'. Clearly, a performer who feels that they have high levels of skill acquisition is more likely to have equally high levels of confidence as well.

Match fitness – regular performance seems to keep people 'sharper' and their form is more consistent if they can react well to the pressure of competing regularly.

Practice – nearly all performers will lose form if they are not practising regularly. These practice sessions will always involve developing and refining skills.

A common saying in physical activities is 'class is forever and form is variable'. This may be true – it does happen that a top performer is beaten by someone who is thought of as a lesser player due to the different levels of form they are able to produce 'on the day'.

Stylised form

This means the performer has to produce a good shape, position, appearance or manner of presentation. Often the activity itself requires them to perform in a particular way and there may even be marks awarded for the form they show. Trampoline is a good example of this because a judge will deduct points from a competitor if there is a loss of form in the movements which are performed. All the movements in a trampoline routine have a set way or shape in which they must be performed and it is fairly easy to see if they are not done correctly.

This kind of form is also very important because someone who uses the correct form is more likely to be performing effectively and safely. There are also accepted ways in which skills need to be performed.

Acquisition of skill

Style

Style is slightly different from form as it is the way in which an individual actually performs a set movement. The movement itself can be a standard one but two people with contrasting styles can present it quite differently. For example, a tennis serve is a set skill movement but different players will have clearly different service actions showing different 'styles'.

Gymnastics is an activity where style is very important as it is something which is judged. The style in which a movement is performed is just as important as how difficult the movement is.

Style can be important in team games, too. Some teams may have a particular style of play which needs to be noted by opponents (cricket is a good example) and tactics may be needed to combat it. Also, style can be very important to spectators who can appreciate a stylish performance as it is pleasing to watch.

Technique

Technique is the manner in which someone performs, or the way in which it is done. It is very closely linked to skill. Any newcomer to an activity should be taught the correct technique for the skills they must learn.

The importance of correct technique

Effectiveness – if a skill or a movement is performed correctly it will be done more successfully. There will be little wasted or inefficient effort. For example, in swimming a poor technique can result in a lot of splashing and little progress whereas good technique results in a smooth, fast, efficient stroke.

Injury prevention – a poor or incorrect technique can often result in injury. A rugby player using the wrong tackling technique can be at risk, as can a trampolinist or a gymnast if they do not use the correct technique in their activity.

Marks – are often awarded for good technique, so in these events this is essential in order to be successful.

Figure 1.4 Gymnastic events require a very high level of skill acquisition

Within one activity there can be basic techniques, advanced techniques and there may even be totally new techniques. Taking the high jump as an example:

basic technique – a simple scissors jump over the bar following a diagonal run

advanced technique – a western roll, rotating over the bar

new technique – the 'Fosbury Flop', devised by Dick Fosbury and used by him in the 1968 Olympics, at which time it was a completely revolutionary new technique. It became so successful that it is now the only advanced technique used by top-class high jumpers.

In all physical activities, performers are always trying to improve their own technique or even to find a new, better way in order to give themselves an advantage in competition

Applying skills

It is one thing to learn or acquire a skill, it is quite another to be able to use that skill at the right time and in the right way. Top performers can be selective and consistent in applying their skills – this is what makes them successful.

At the top level in professional tennis there is very little to choose between the top one hundred players in terms of the skills they possess – it is the ways in which they can apply those skills that makes the difference between winning and losing!

Many skills are similar in different activities and a great deal of **transfer of skills** can take place. For example, a performer who is skilful at throwing and fielding in cricket will find that many of the skills are transferable if they decide to take up rounders or softball. So it is important to concentrate on acquiring a variety of basic skills, as they can often be useful in more than one activity.

Open and closed skills

Some skills are called **open skills**. These show up in situations that are constantly changing. For example, footballers taking part in a match are in a constantly changing environment and may have to change or adapt their skills according to the demands of the game. If a strong wind starts to blow they will have to take this into consideration when passing the ball long distances. Although many situations may arise during the game that are similar in terms of players' positions, passes that could be made or opportunities to shoot, each will be slightly different.

A trampolinist, on the other hand, is performing in an environment that does not change, as the equipment used is always the same and there are set moves, shapes and **routines** to be used. The skills used here, such as somersaults and twists, are called **closed skills**, as these are skills in which the environment does not change.

Not all skills fall neatly into one of these two categories. The skills needed in some activities fall somewhere on the continuum between being open and being closed – because they contain elements of each. For example, a volleyball player uses many skills that are neither fully open nor closed skills.

Task 6
Draw up a list of basic skills and give some examples of activities that may have transferable skills.

Task 7
Give examples of **two** activities that have closed skills and **two** that have open skills. List what those skills are.

Feedback

In order to improve in a skill, performers need a way to judge how well they have already performed. This might be as simple as being told by a teacher or a coach if it was good or bad, and ways of improving. Alternatively, performers may be able to judge for themselves how well they performed the skill. Often it is not just whether it was successful or not, but how it was performed which is important. This information is called **feedback** and there are several types.

- **Continuous feedback** – this is where it is clear to the performer during the performance how well it is going. For example, if a routine is going as it did in practice or if, for some reason, it has broken down.
- **Terminal feedback** – this takes place at the end of a performance.
- **Knowledge of results** – this is a form of terminal feedback at the end of a performance and could be as simple as whether you won or lost.
- **Knowledge of performance** – this concerns how well the performance was done rather than just the end result.
- **Internal/intrinsic feedback** – this is sensed, or felt, by the performer while they are performing.
- **External/extrinsic feedback** – this comes from sources other than the performer, such as sounds or things they can see.
- **Positive feedback** – this is information received regarding successes in the performance.
- **Negative feedback** – this is information about unsuccessful aspects of the performance.

Types of guidance

Most guidance for performers is usually provided either by a teacher or a coach and this is one of the main ways in which a performer receives their knowledge of results.

It is very difficult for any performer to actually watch themselves while they are performing to check for any faults or areas for improvement. This is why nearly all top performers have a coach who will work with them all the time, analysing their performance and reporting back to them. This is especially important during the early stages of learning a skill when there will be a great deal for the coach to comment on.

You may find yourself in this guidance/coaching role as an alternative to performing. It is important to be aware of the responsibilities this role entails and also the amount of useful help you may be able to give to the performer.

Goal setting

One of the important reasons for feedback is to use that information for further goal setting for the performer.

Once a performance (or practice session) has taken place, it should be analysed and then the targets set for the performer.

These are the points to bear in mind when goal setting:

- make sure that you are acting on accurate information from the actual performance(s)
- be realistic with the goals that you are set and do not expect too much too soon
- be aware of the effects of plateauing (see page 27) and be prepared to take your time moving from one stage to another
- be aware that if you do not set yourself goals you are unlikely to make any significant progress.

Mental rehearsal

Many performers and coaches now treat mental rehearsal as an important part of skill acquisition. It involves the performer spending some time, before actually taking part, going through the performance in their mind. This is a technique often used by sprinters before a race. For beginners it can be useful so that there is less wasted effort.

Knowing what you have to do beforehand, and going over it in your mind, makes you better prepared and can also improve your confidence.

Task 8

Choose **two** different activities. For each activity, give examples of knowledge of results you received. Describe the goals you set yourself as a result.

Hints and Tips!

Skill acquisition should always be considered in conjunction with any practical work you do, as how you learn skills, practise or rehearse them and the guidance you receive while you are doing so are the key points you must understand.

Key questions

1. Describe what is meant by a simple and a complex skill and give an example of each.
2. Explain the difference between performance form and stylized form.
3. What is the difference between an open and a closed skill?
4. Identify one fully open skill and one fully closed skill and explain why each skill is classified as open or closed.
5. What types of feedback are there and why are they important in the learning of skills?
6. Describe the types of guidance a performer might receive. Explain who is likely to give guidance to performers.

2 Tactics and teamwork

Games such as soccer, netball, basketball and hockey are called **invasion games** because the aim is to get into the opponents' playing area to score. These are all also team games, and they need **tactics** and **teamwork**. To be successful, a team needs an effective combination of both tactics and teamwork so that all the individuals can work together as one **unit**.

Tactics

These are pre-arranged, thought through and usually rehearsed strategies or methods of play that a team, or individuals, decide to use during a game or match. Tactics must be adaptable so that if they are not proving to be successful the team can turn to a more appropriate alternative. A sporting saying that illustrates this point is: 'Never change a winning game; always change a losing game'.

Many teams adopt a game plan. This is the way they decide to approach a particular game. It may be designed particularly to suit their own strengths or it may be designed to exploit what they see to be the opponents' weaknesses. Either way, it must be carefully considered, discussed and fully understood by all the members of the team if it is to achieve its purpose – to win that particular game!

Tactics can be very basic. For example, they might be as simple as deciding which way to start a match, taking into consideration such things as the strength of the wind, weather conditions, possible pitch slope, surface conditions and bright sunlight. The wind might affect how far a ball is going to travel, as may the slope of the pitch. The sun might be low and shining brightly into an opponent's (or goalkeeper's) eyes, making catching or handling the ball difficult. The surface conditions might be poor, and certain areas may be likely to get worse as the game goes on – this could be particularly vital in cricket! All these factors should be taken into account when deciding which direction to start a match, because it might be possible to use them in your favour during the second period of play.

Tactics can be very complex. They may be designed to exploit one particular weakness in an opposing team, perhaps concentrating on one particular player or even on one part of a team such as a defensive unit or the midfield unit. The more complex the tactic becomes, the more likely it is to fail. Often, the most simple and basic tactics are the most successful and effective ones.

> **Key point**
> Individuals can also use tactics in particular sports, but the greatest variety of tactics becomes available within the team games due to the larger number of players who are involved.

> **Did you know?**
> The England cricket tour to Australia in 1932/33 was known as the 'Bodyline Series' because the England team had decided on a tactic of continuously bowling short-pitched deliveries to rise into the batters' bodies. It was particularly directed at the Australians' leading batter, Don Bradman. The tactic went on to cause an international incident resulting in the laws of the game being changed to stop it happening again!

> **Task 1**
> Give **one** example of a game plan that you have used or seen used, in an invasion game. How effective was it?

Teamwork

For tactics to work there must also be effective teamwork. This involves all the members of a team working together as one, to achieve the same thing. As teams can consist of up to 15 individuals, plus others such as substitutes, this can be very difficult to organise.

Such people as coaches, captains and managers are very important. They have to make sure that a group actually works as a team and that everyone in the team knows what is expected of them.

A well-organised team should beat a team of less well-organised members, even if the skill levels of the two teams are equal. Effective teamwork also needs a great deal of practice. Many hours and days need to be spent going over moves, formations and tactics so that everyone knows what their particular role is. There may also be a great deal of non-playing work such as talking through the strategies to be used, plotting positions on the coach's 'chalkboards', watching videos of opponents and working out plans on paper before actually trying them out in a game.

Reliance on teammates is an essential part of teamwork. Often a successful team builds a great deal of camaraderie both on and off the field.

Did you know?

In ordinary tournaments tennis players are not allowed to receive any advice from coaches. However, in Davis Cup team competitions the team captain is allowed to sit on court with the players and advise/coach them as the match progresses.

Figure 2.1 The defending and attacking teams have both decided on their tactics for this set-play free kick

Task 2

Describe an attacking tactic you could use from a restart position in a particular named sport.

Task 3

Imagine you are the coach for a team. On a sheet of paper draw out the positions for all the players for a set-play tactic. Describe how the tactic should work.

Task 4

Describe a tactic for a set play that could take place in an attacking situation. Then consider how this particular tactic could best be defended against.

Restarts and set plays

One important area of tactics in invasion games includes restarts and **set plays**.

Restarts

Restarts occur when the ball has gone out of play and one team is given the ball to restart the game. This is a free possession of the ball (i.e. the opponents may not challenge for possession); it gives the team with the ball many options. Some restart positions occur in an attacking situation (such as a corner in soccer or hockey or a side line throw-in in basketball), so a team needs tactics already prepared for this situation.

Set play

Set plays occur when one team is given a free play or possession when their opponents have broken the rules. This can result in a **penalty**.

The team is then allowed to make a move without opposition from the opponents. Free kicks, free hits, free passes, penalties and free throws are all examples of these.

In a set play it is vital that the defending team has also previously agreed its tactics to deal with any moves the opponents may make.

Remember that tactics can be both attacking and defensive and for a team to be fully effective they must be totally prepared in both areas.

Hints and Tips!

It is important to be aware of the role tactics and teamwork play in matches and games, as it may be something you are involved in as a player. There is also a possibility that questions could be asked regarding suitable tactics for particular sporting situations.

Key questions

1. Describe what is meant by a tactic in general terms.
2. Explain one particular defensive tactic that could be used in one particular named sport.
3. Explain what is meant by the term 'game plan'.
4. Describe how different weather conditions might influence a particular tactical decision.
5. What is the difference between a restart and a set-play? Give an example for each from two different sports.

3 Formations and strategies

Formations and strategies are usually set by the coach of a team and are vitally important. They are very closely linked to tactics and teamwork (see Chapter 2).

Formations

In team games these are the ways in which a playing area can be covered by the positions the players take up. Team formations are very important in invasion games but they can be equally important in net/wall games and striking games. Any activity that involves two or more players has particular formations that may be used.

Formations are usually either attacking or defensive. This applies in all activities and there is often a need to switch from one to the other very quickly. Many activities have units (particular members of the team) who are responsible for either attacking or defending and they will have set formations within their own unit. In an activity such as American football there is even a specific defensive unit that only comes onto the field of play when the other team has the ball and they have to defend.

In some activities it is not so easy to be flexible with formations. For example, in netball each player must be clearly identified (with a named bib) and is only allowed to play within certain areas of the court. Because of this the basic formation is fairly set and it is not possible to vary it very much.

In cricket, on the other hand, there are 32 clearly named fielding positions for the nine fielders (excluding the bowler and the wicketkeeper), so much more variety is available. With the different formats of the game (5-day test matches, limited over 1-day match and the Twenty20 version) there is an even greater variety of placements.

> **Key point**
>
> Formations and strategies are interconnected, as they are both ways in which players can seek to gain an advantage over their opponents. There are choices performers can make, often with the help of coaches, that can involve all members of a team or specific individuals.

Figure 3.1 The successful Jamaica netball team, known as the 'Sunshine Girls'; the team is currently ranked fourth in the world

Did you know?

The Dutch football team Ajax, and then the Dutch national team, pioneered a formation known as 'total football' (in the 1960s and 1970s) where any outfield player took over the role of any other player within the team as they constantly interchanged positions. The Dutch national team used this approach in the 1974 World Cup, which they narrowly lost to Germany, 2–1.

Task 1

Draw a diagram of a football (soccer) pitch. Add the positions in which each member of a team would stand for the kick-off for one of the above formations.

Formations for major activities

Football/soccer

Although there are only 11 players in a football team there are many different formations that have been devised in soccer. These include:

- **4 – 2 – 4** – consisting of four defenders, two midfield players and four forwards
- **4 – 3 – 3** – consisting of four defenders, three midfielders and three forwards
- **3 – 2 – 5** – consisting of three defenders, two midfielders and five forwards.

As well as these basic formations, teams can also play in a diamond formation or a sweeper system, both of which are slightly different again.

Basketball

Figure 3.2 A zone defence basketball formation

One of the most basic formations in basketball is the zone defence shown in the photo on this page. All five players take up a defensive position around their own key (the marked out defensive area) when they lose possession of the ball. The idea is to keep the opponents out of close scoring positions and force a missed shot from greater distance.

Rugby

In rugby the team is divided into two units – the forwards and the backs. Because of this there are often specific formations that the units take up at certain times. The forwards will have set formations for the scrum and the **lineout** and the backs will have some for **penalty moves** and for defensive situations. There will also be times when the whole team will have to take up a formation when the two units are working together.

Hockey

Most of the formations for hockey are the same as for football, but hockey also makes use of **link players** who will work between the defensive and attacking units.

Badminton

There are two basic formations for doubles in badminton:

- **up and back** – one player towards the front of the court, one towards the back, usually centrally, for an attacking formation
- **sides** – one player on each side of the court, roughly in the middle, for a defensive situation.

For most net or wall games the defensive formation is to the rear of the playing area such as the back of the court in tennis or well back from the table in table tennis. This means that for the attacking formation one of the players moves forward.

Volleyball

In volleyball, all of the players must go to a particular position for the serve and then they can move to either attacking or defensive positions. These have to done very quickly due to the speed of this game so there is a lot of movement.

Figure 3.3 A cricket captain will often discuss fielding placements with the bowler

Task 2

Draw a diagram of a badminton court. On one side of the net add the players in a defensive formation. On the other side add the players in an attacking formation.

Did you know?

Both formations and strategies can vary considerably in the game of cricket depending on the type of game being played. Because of the different formats and length of games (from 20 overs to 5-day tests), different formations and strategies are employed and there are often completely different sets of players who are used as well!

Task 3

Name and describe **one** strategy that could be used in a physical activity of your choice.

Strategies

In some activities it is not possible to make use of formations. Instead, the movement or positioning of the players in the team relies on strategy.

A strategy is a large-scale plan or method of play involving the movement and positioning of the team players. This may take place over a long period of time (for example, in a cricket match it can last up to 5 days) and it is very important in competitions where teams may be involved in a lot of matches.

A tactic is usually set, but strategies can more flexible. This is why tactics are suited to sports that take a long time and are more likely to change. A team will have various strategies to cope with different events that could happen, such as changes in the weather or the success or failure of certain tactics.

A coach may decide a strategy but it is usually the captain of a team who is responsible for putting it into action. As a game or match progresses, different strategies may be brought into play and in a game such as cricket, there is a greater responsibility on the captain, who has to make fielding changes and bowling changes almost constantly. Added responsibility falls on the captain in many activities because the coach is not allowed to give instructions to the team once the game has started.

Hints and Tips!

Being aware of the different options available in terms of formations and strategies is likely to be more important when taking part in physical activities, especially if you have a coaching or captain's role. However, questions relating to the options available are also popular.

Key questions

1. Who is likely to decide on and set formations in a team?
2. What particular role can units within a team play and what examples of these units can you name and describe?
3. Explain one common formation often used in the sport of football (soccer)?
4. Explain and describe a particular formation that is commonly used specifically in the sport of basketball.
5. Define what is meant by the term 'strategy'.

4 Officials

Activity	Number of officials
Football or soccer	3 (4)
Cricket	2 (3)
Lawn tennis	1 (12)
Gymnastics event	5
Volleyball	7
Discus/Shot-put/Javelin	5

Table 4.1 The number of officials per event can vary depending on the activity

Table 4.1 shows how many officials are needed for a small selection of activities. This is just an example of the number of people necessary for a physical activity to take place. In an athletics meeting, there would be considerably more than the five officials for the throwing events. All the track and field events together would require a great many officials.

At most activities many of the officials have organisational roles, as they have to organise the competitors and maintain the smooth running of the tournament or event. Very few officials are actually paid to do their jobs. Most of them are volunteers and only receive their travelling expenses for attending the activity.

In professional sports there are more full-time, paid officials. There are two reasons for this:

- the standards and rewards are high and the players and supporters or fans demand the highest standards from officials
- the sports events earn enough money to be able to pay officials.

In most amateur sports, or activities played at a lower level, officials are not paid. There is simply not enough money available to pay them. Often, activities take place with the bare minimum of officials, or with team members or substitutes taking the place of officials. For example, in many football matches the substitutes act as the referee's assistants (or **linesmen**) and in cricket matches the players often take turns to umpire. In many activities it is not easy to get officials at all and it can be very difficult to get qualified ones.

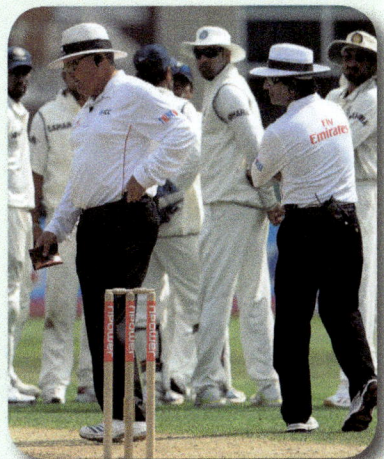

Figure 4.1 Officials are required at many sporting events

Key point

Officials are essential to enable any game or competition to go ahead. Rules exist in all sporting activities and it is vitally important that the official is there to make sure that these rules are applied and respected. Ensuring players'/participants' safety is just about their most important role.

Task 1

Give reasons why, in Table 4.1, there are numbers in brackets for football, cricket and tennis. Who do those numbers refer to?

Did you know?

International football referees are forced to retire at the age of 45! They are not allowed to go on officiating at this level no matter how fit they are!

Task 2

Choose **one** sport. Find out the training/requirements for an official to become qualified in that sport (local competition and International competition).

Task 3

List **two** sporting activities that need a referee, **two** that need a judge and **two** that need an umpire.

Task 4

Choose **one** sport and name an official. List **three** specific responsibilities of that official.

It takes quite a long time to qualify as an official in any recognised sport. This usually means participating in special courses that have to be paid for. It sometimes takes a long time to ascend the different levels as an official. This is because all officials are expected to be experienced before they can take control of an international game/match.

Being an official can sometimes be a thankless task as it is almost impossible to please everyone, but without an official, competitive events cannot take place.

Responsibilities of officials

The main job of the officials is to organise and control the activity. There are two main types of officials. **Senior officials** include:

- referees
- judges
- umpires.

Minor officials include:

- referee's assistants
- timekeepers
- scorers.

All of the officials have to work together doing their various jobs to make sure that the event runs smoothly.

Other responsibilities can include interpreting the rules, laws or regulations of the event/sport, checking the equipment to be used, making sure the correct players are taking part and timing the activity. Each event has its own particular responsibilities.

Figure 4.2 Officials must complete various qualifications to referee at international level

Qualities of officials

The qualities an official must have do not really differ between sports. They may be summarised as follows.

1 A full and thorough knowledge of the rules or regulations of the activity

The officials cannot refer to a rulebook halfway through a game so they must be prepared for, and know how to deal with, any incident that might occur. Some activities have very complicated rules and some have so many it is almost impossible to know them all. In golf, for example, there are even local rules that only apply to a particular golf course! When activities have a complicated system such as this the official in charge may need assistance and rulings can take some time to decide.

2 A fair approach to the game

This means that the official does not favour one of the teams or players but is **impartial**. To make sure of this many activities at international level have **neutral officials** who usually come from a different country to all the participating teams.

3 Good physical condition

This may be as simple as having good eyesight or enough speed to keep up with the play. Some activities make their officials take an annual **fitness** test and some have a maximum age for officials that acts as a retirement age.

4 Firm and decisive

When they are in charge, officials often need to prevent/defuse any arguments during play. Their decision is usually final, so they must be in control of all situations.

Task 5

Choose an activity for which you will officiate as the main official. Prepare for this by making sure you know the qualities you must have as well as making sure you know the rules!

Hints and Tips!

It is important to be aware of the responsibilities and duties of officials – especially those involved in sports in which you participate. It is also useful to be aware of the specific qualities that officials must have. Ask your teacher to give you the opportunity to try officiating – you may like it!

Key questions

1. Why do major competitions insist on having neutral officials in charge of events?
2. What is the difference between a senior and minor official?
3. Why is it important for officials to remain in good physical condition?
4. Why do the numbers of officials for certain events differ?
5. Why is being firm and decisive yet approachable such an important quality for an official?

5 Rules

Most physical activities have rules that say exactly how the activity should be played. Often the rules of an activity are called laws or regulations. Some of the organisations that make the rules for certain sports are listed in Table 5.1.

Sport	Ruling body
Cricket	ICC International Cricket Council
Netball	IFNA International Federation of Netball Associations
Gymnastics	FIG Federation International of Gymnastics
Basketball	FIBA Federation Internationale de Basketball
Athletics	International Association of Athletics Federations

Table 5.1 Ruling bodies in sport

The need for rules

The purpose of rules is to:

- ensure safety
- aid basic organisation
- ease administration
- promote enjoyment.

Most of the rules for the sporting activities enjoyed today have developed over a long period of time. Some very old sports did not have any set rules but it soon became necessary to set out basic guidelines for all the popular sports. One of the most important of these is safety. Many of our present-day sports would be very dangerous if there were not very strict rules about **foul play** and the safety/protective equipment to be used.

The playing area or surface to be used has to be defined and clearly stated, as do, for example, the length of time-periods for the activity, the clothing to be worn and the number of people who can take part.

Key point

Rules exist in all sporting activities and it is essential that anyone participating in any sport has a good basic knowledge of them before they actually take part.

Task 1

Find out who sets the rules for **at least three** other sports.

Did you know?

Leisure activities do not have formal rules.

Figure 5.1 Third officials can be used in sports such as cricket to help make correct decisions

International rules

These are set by the various International Governing Bodies. However, any country's Local Governing Body can set their own rules if they wish to do so. Two examples of Local Governing Bodies are the Caribbean Football Union (CFU) and the West Indies Cricket Board (WICB).

Many activities also have players' organisations that work closely with the ruling bodies, setting rules and often, more importantly, enforcing the rules! These players' organisations are more common in professional sports than they are in amateur ones.

Etiquette

This is an unwritten rule or form of behaviour as opposed to an enforceable or **decreed** rule, law or regulation. It often takes the form of fair play, good manners or good sporting attitude/gestures.

In all sports there is acceptable **etiquette** that is not written down in any rule book. So it is up to the participants to behave in the correct way. The fact that it is not written down means there is no real way to ensure that it happens. However, players can become very unpopular if they do not conform to these acts of etiquette. This is another reason why there are players' organisations in many sports because they will often take action against players who are in breach of etiquette.

Here are some examples of etiquette.

- **Football or soccer** – if an opponent is injured, a player will kick the ball out of play to stop the game to allow treatment. On the restart, the team with the throw-in will throw the ball back to their opponents who originally kicked the ball out of play.
- **Lawn tennis** – at the end of a match, opponents shake hands and also thank and shake hands with the umpire.
- **Cricket** – batters are applauded by the fielding side as they come out to bat and the two teams will line up at the end of a match to shake hands with each other.

Rule changes

Changes are often made to rules. These come about for a number of reasons, including:

- making the activity safer
- making it more exciting, which will attract more players, spectators and sponsors
- keeping up with changes or developments in equipment or materials used.

Often changes are made for particular tournaments or events. Sometimes these are experiments to see what effect the changes will have, so that they can be introduced if they are successful. Many changes were introduced for the football World Cup in America in 1994 and have remained ever since.

Did you know?

Technology has given rise to the most recent rule changes as systems such as 'Hawkeye' and slow motion action replays mean that it is easier for decisions to be checked. This technology can only be used if the rules allow it!

Task 2

Identify both the Regional and Local Governing Body for two of the sports listed in Table 5.1.

Task 3

Name **one** rule change that has been introduced for each of the reasons opposite.

Rule enforcement

Rules have to be obeyed and there is a system in every sport to make sure that this happens. If a player, participant, club or organisation does not abide by (i.e. follow) the rules, action has to be taken against them. This can include:

- temporary suspension during that game/match
- a ban for a stipulated time or number of games/matches
- a monetary fine
- expulsion from further participation in that sport.

All activities have penalties that can apply when the game is in progress, such as the yellow and red card system in football or soccer, the 'sin bin' in ice hockey and rugby league, and the 'fouled out' system in basketball. For more serious offences, action will be taken after the event has ended; this can be for drug taking, extreme foul play, illegal payments or 'bringing the game into disrepute'.

Figure 5.2 It is accepted good etiquette to shake hands at the end of a match

Hints and Tips!

Your knowledge of the rules should always be backed up by being aware of the reasons for the rules existing in the first place and also by knowing what actions are likely to be taken if rules are broken.

Key questions

1. Suggest two reasons why rules are needed in sport.
2. Explain why there might be regional/local rules as well as international ones.
3. What is meant by the term 'etiquette'? Describe two examples of it.
4. What are the main reasons for the possibility of rules being changed?
5. Why is it important for rules to be enforced?
6. Give two examples of the action that might be taken against a player who is in breach of the rules of a sport.

6 Planning, performing and evaluating

Making progress in a physical activity needs careful planning, performing and evaluating in order to ensure that the maximum amount of progress is made. The following are some of the ways in which these can be approached.

Planning

The essential elements for this are listed here.

- Setting realistic goals – these should not be too difficult.
- Predicting likely outcomes – what is likely to result?
- Exploring and selecting options for specialisation and development – what might be the next stage?
- Composing (e.g. dance movements) – planning out moves or routines in advance.

A common method of planning involves setting targets using SMART target setting. SMART stands for:

- S – specific
- M – measurable
- A – achievable
- R – realistic
- T – time-bound.

Performing

Putting planning into effect is the performing stage. The following are factors in this:

- copying experts in the same field
- practising and improving
- participating in suitable events
- repeating, correcting and improving skills
- implementing a plan of action
- refining particular skills
- adapting to achieve a personal style
- identifying weaker areas and improving in them
- improvising.

> **Key point**
> Planning, performing and evaluating form a constant cycle which, if put in place properly, enables individuals to improve their performance in both the short and long term.

> **Did you know?**
> All top-level performers put in many hours of practice in order to be the best they can in their particular sports. Gymnasts, for example, would expect to train for up to 6 hours a day carrying out training and conditioning work as well as working on particular routines for specific apparatus and in preparation for events.

Task 1

Make a copy of Table 6.1. Complete all of the sections for an activity or task that you have either attempted already or are about to attempt. You may find the information in the text helpful.

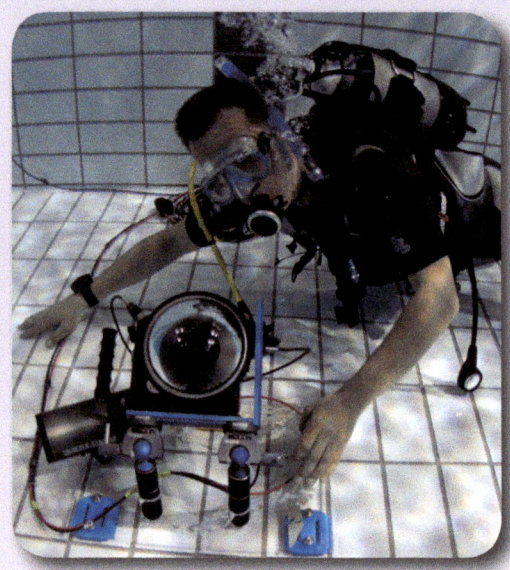

Figure 6.1 These are ways of analysing performances for sporting improvement

Evaluating

This is the third part of the cycle. It is the period of reflection on what has happened and covers:

- describing performance, improvements and targets
- recognising strengths, weaknesses and areas for improvement
- comparing and contrasting your own skills and achievements with those of peers and experts
- analysing what is done well and what needs to be worked on in order to improve
- judging levels of improvement and, areas which need to be developed further
- reviewing progress since the last evaluation.

In all activities it is necessary to go through a process of planning, performing and evaluating using some or all of these suggestions, as this is the main way that improvements and progress can me made. However, there are also two other things to consider:

1. the **difficulty** of the task attempted
2. the **quality** of the task attempted.

Task to be attempted:	Difficulty	Quality
Planning		
Performing		
Evaluating		

Table 6.1 Evaluating for improvement and progress

Did you know?

Top-level performers would not expect to carry out evaluations on their own. They would usually have a team of coaches and advisers who would be observing their practice and performance and feeding back to them (see Chapter 1). They would also make full use of technology to watch their performance using video analysis programmes.

Difficulty

Ways of making a task more difficult include:

- having a greater variety of movements (e.g. adding more movements to a trampoline routine)
- finding different ways to perform a task (e.g. this could be done in any ball game by finding alternative ways to pass or collect the ball)
- transferring skills from one activity area to another (e.g. by applying jumping and **travelling** skills from gymnastics to athletic or dance activities)
- increasing the difficulty or control of balance
- increasing the level of strength, perhaps by increasing personal performance in athletic activities
- improving the co-ordination of movements, for example by combining dance and gymnastic activities
- taking less time in performing effectively in activities requiring quick decision making (this can be done in any game where opponents or team mates are involved)
- allowing fewer options (this could be through playing a conditioned game – see Chapter 7 – for any form of invasion game)
- using smaller targets – this could even mean reducing the size of goals or having smaller racket courts to play on
- moving from single actions to multiple actions (a lay-up shot in basketball is an example of this because it combines the single actions of running, dribbling, jumping and shooting into one smooth action)
- moving from concrete to abstract ideas (this will mainly apply to gymnastic activities where the skills of jumping, turning, gesture and stillness can be used as ways of expressing moods, feelings or ideas by the movements performed)
- moving from simple to complex (more difficult) knowledge of the activity (e.g. by learning more advanced techniques or knowing how to analyse and improve a performance).

Figure 6.2 The final stage of a lay-up shot

Quality

Ways of increasing quality include:

- developing better poise (this can be the ability to keep a balance or a position, or even self-control in a game situation)
- improving form and body tension (this often refers to gymnastic and dance performances but it can equally apply to a 100 metres sprinter as well)
- developing better hand and eye co-ordination in games (especially those that require the use of equipment, such as racket sports)
- working at an increased control of the body (e.g. developing a more efficient and effective swimming stroke)
- increasing knowledge and understanding of the mechanical principles of how movements occur (this involves knowledge of anatomy and **physiology** to know how the body works – see Chapters 22-27).

Planning, performing and evaluating

Task 2

Describe the movements and body actions that take place when performing the long jump.

Figure 6.3 James Beckford – the Jamaican long jumper

Hints and Tips!

Planning, performing and evaluating link very much to personal performance and the ways in which this can be improved. You need to know how important these are and also to be aware of the ways in which you could make use of these concepts when planning a programme for your own personal development.

Key questions

1. What is meant by SMART target setting?
2. Choose three aspects of performing and explain how they are likely to help and improve a performance.
3. For a chosen sport or activity describe three ways in which the levels of difficulty for the activity could be adapted.
4. Choose two specific activities and describe how skills could be transferred from one to another.
5. Describe three different ways in which the quality of tasks could be increased in order to bring about an improvement.

7 Practices and drills

If individuals or teams wish to improve, they must be prepared to spend a great deal of time practising.

Practice sessions

The practice sessions must be well organised if they are to be useful. A typical practice session would be arranged as follows:

1 Warm-up

This is important before the start of any physical activity and it should not be ignored in a practice session. It should include some stretching and flexibility exercises (see Chapter 15) as well as some more energetic exercise aimed at increasing the heart rate (these are often known as 'pulse raisers') and body temperature. If the practice session is going to involve one particular part of the body more than another, that part must be fully prepared during the warm-up. If this is not done properly the performer is more likely to be injured.

Top gymnasts would expect to warm-up for about 15 minutes before they would be ready to go onto the next stage of their practice session (and gymnasts of all standards warm up for at least several minutes).

2 Skills practice

This involves practising the skills particular to the activity. These may be group skills or individual skills. If it is a team-game activity it would be a good idea to practise both to be fully prepared to use them in the game situation. This is a good opportunity to work in groups, practising skills and giving each other feedback on the performance of the skills. It is also an ideal opportunity to co-operate in the learning of a skill by, for example, hand feeding a tennis ball accurately, supporting a partner in gymnastics or just 'shadowing' an opponent in basketball.

These skills practices can be made more useful by having static defenders (people who make no attempt to intercept or interfere with another player) and active opposition (players who take full part as opponents to tackle or dispossess the others). It is a good idea to use a combination of both of these in a practice session.

> **Key point**
>
> Organising practice is important so that it is then fully beneficial. It needs to be considered carefully in order to be manageable, meaningful and, wherever possible, enjoyable. It is the only way in which performers improve!

> **Did you know?**
>
> In all major athletic competitions there is a warm-up track next to the main competition track that the athletes use just before entering the stadium for their event. The organisers would not be allowed to stage the event if they did not make this facility available for the competitors.

Figure 7.1 A group skills practice session

Task 1

Choose an activity. Work out a practice session a coach could use. Give details of the warm-up, skills practice and the game or match session.

Task 2

Talk to a team player and an individual performer. Find out how often they practise their chosen activity.

3 Game situation

The session should finish off with an opportunity to try out the skills that have been practised in a game. This does not have to be an actual game or match because the idea of the session is to improve performance. Instead a **conditioned** game may be more useful. This is a game or match where some new or adapted rules are introduced that could make it easier to play, or even harder to play!

The theme of the practice session (that is, the particular skills that have been practised) can be continued to improve on things that have been tried out earlier. For example, if a basketball session was concentrating on accurate passing, a temporary rule of no dribbling but only passing the ball could be introduced.

All practice sessions should be helpful, but it is very important that they are organised and well thought out. A coach or teacher usually takes a practice session with clear ideas of what they want to achieve.

Frequency of practice

As well as being necessary to improve skills, practice is vital to keep up levels of performance. The amount a person practises will depend on how seriously they take their sport and at what level they play. A professional would expect to practise every day, often for several hours at a time. On the other hand, an amateur may only practise once or twice a week for a total of a few hours.

Practice does not just consist of taking part in the sport itself. There will have to be some training in order to work on fitness (see Chapter 13). A person taking part in an individual activity will probably practise far more than a team player. They have the sole responsibility for their performance and will have to make sure that they are both skilful and on form. It is also far easier to organise one person than it is to organise a whole team, so team training sessions may not be so frequent.

Figure 7.2 Regular practice is very important

Drills

Team players make more use of drills – repeated group practices designed to develop the correct way of doing something. Although these can be very repetitive they are an essential part of practice. Successful performers can get to the level of 'grooved' performance where they have practised something so often that they perform it almost automatically.

What should be practised?

The content of a practice session is clearly very important and will vary between different performers. A beginner will have to start with the basics, while a more experienced performer can work on more advanced skills.

If a skill is constantly practised there will be reinforcement, which means that the performer will become better and more consistent at that skill. A performer may experience different effects when skills are being practised. For example:

- a new skill is learned quickly, then progress slows down – this is called a negative acceleration
- learning a new skill is difficult at first but then progress quickens – known as positive acceleration
- progress is fairly level and consistent – this is known as linear progress
- possibly the most frustrating effect is known as plateauing where a performer appears to be stuck at a certain level and cannot progress beyond it for some time. When practising a skill a performer may plateau at several points and it may be a long time before progress is made. For this reason a performer must be prepared to break skills down into stages in a practice session and be prepared to work at them for some time before mastering them.

> **Task 3**
>
> Choose a team activity. Fully describe **one** drill that can be performed in that particular activity.

Hints and Tips!

This chapter should be read and considered in conjunction with Chapter 28, as there is a great amount of cross-over between them.

Key questions

1. Why is it vital to include a warm-up at the start of a practice session?
2. What do you understand by giving 'feedback' to another performer?
3. What is meant by a conditioned game?
4. What is the difference between static and active opposition?
5. What is meant by:

   a negative acceleration   **b** positive acceleration   **c** linear progress   **d** plateauing?

8 Organising and running sports events

A sports event can be a number of different things and you will first need to decide what sort of event you are planning for. There are then different processes that have to be gone through to make sure the event is a success.

Planning process

This is crucial to the success of any form of event and the various aspects of the planning all need to be carefully considered. It includes the following:

1 The nature of the event

Each different type of event has its own particular requirements and these have firstly to be identified and then addressed. These include:

- **the type of event** – it could be a competition (if so there are various types of these that can be used), a sports festival or even a training day
- **size** – a small-size event has less problems but a large-scale event may create manageability issues
- **location** – this includes issues such as how people are going to get to the event (transport might be an issue) and whether it is to be based inside or outside. An outside event always has weather as a major issue.

2 The timings related to the event

There are many sets of timings that need to be considered:

- **the time of year** – whether a particular sport is played at this time of year may be an issue (is it the playing season?). Different times of the year will have different weather conditions to be considered
- **the day of the week that is most suitable** – weekends may be more suitable for some people as they work throughout the week
- **the time of the day** – does it need to be morning, afternoon, evening (when light may be an issue if it is outdoors) or even all day or over more than one day?
- **start and finish times** – considerations need to be made for the overall start and finish time of the entire event. If there is any form of competition, then the duration of each match or game needs to be considered. A football match can be scheduled to last a specific time but an uneven cricket game can be over very quickly if one team is dominant.

> **Key point**
>
> There are several factors that are key elements in any sports event in terms of organising and running it. It is important to be aware of the processes that are involved and then to consider the content in line with these. The most important process is almost certainly the planning stage.

> **Task 1**
>
> Make a list of the advantages and disadvantages of indoor and outside facilities that could be used as a venue. What sports could only really be competed for outside?

> **Did you know?**
>
> Golf is one sport that has very strict guidelines regarding weather conditions. If a thunderstorm occurs, the event is stopped, and all players and spectators are cleared from the course to prevent the possibility of lightning strikes. This usually happens before the storms have arrived (if a severe weather warning is received), due to the time it takes to get everybody under cover.

3 The responsibilities and roles of those involved

It is likely that an event is going to be organised by a team of people rather than just one person, as there is so much to be done. If this is the case then the following has to be considered:

- organised meetings prior to the event
- keeping a record of meetings, and decisions that may be made in them, so that everyone is aware of their particular role and responsibility.

4 Various other considerations

This is likely to be a very long list! You will need to consider things that could be very specific to particular types of events or particular sports/activities, as the list below shows.

- **Resources that will be needed** – this includes all the equipment, which can include balls, nets, marker cones and bibs.
- **Staffing required** – a competition will require officials/referees/umpires, and you might need marshals to organise both the players and the crowd/spectators.
- **Costings** – there may be a cost involved such as the hire of the facilities or payments to officials.
- **Risk assessment** – this will have to be carried out to make sure the event is safe and full safety measures will need to be in place that will include planning for first-aid facilities and possible medical assistance.
- **Promoting the event** – getting people to attend the event, either as participants or spectators, may be one of your main aims, so this needs to be put in place to ensure it is a success.

Event/competition types

There is no single way or type of competition, but there is a variety to choose from and each has particular advantages and disadvantages. These types include the following:

- **a one-off or one-day league** – here every team plays against every other team until there is an overall winner. Points are then awarded for wins and draws, and there may even be bonus points for particular levels of success
- **knockouts** – only the winners of each game go through to the next round
- **round-robin** – this is a form of mini-league where several groups play in separate leagues, and then the winners usually go through to some form of final
- **combination events** – this can involve any combination of the above formats such as starting with a league and then going through to a knockout format in the final stages.

Running the event

After the planning and organisation comes the actual running of the event. This needs to be considered in three stages.

1 Setting up

It is likely that most of this is going to have to be done on the day of the event. It may be possible to set up some aspects beforehand (such as erecting signs the night before) but the facility/venue must be prepared for play.

All equipment will need to be provided, collected and made available. This could be as basic as setting goal nets up, rolling out netball posts or making sure that bibs and officials' tables are ready for basketball games.

Changing facilities and/or refreshments might need to be provided and made ready for both participants and the spectators – you may even need to think about getting rubbish bags and bins ready to tidy the venue once you have finished.

2 During the event

There will be a need to respond to any unforeseen circumstances such as teams or officials not turning up, and for making sure that everything that has been organised runs smoothly. Teams will need to be in place at the right time and the officials will need to be there as well with someone responsible for collecting scores and supervising specific areas – such as several pitches that might be being used. This is where all of the planning needs to be in place but back-up and contingency plans also need to be considered.

3 Closing down

The site/venue will need to be cleared and all of the equipment that was provided and used needs to be checked back in and put away. A lot of participants/players/spectators may also mean a lot of mess, and this will all have to be cleared up. Any signs that were set up initially will need to be taken down.

Did you know?

The football/soccer World Cup is a combination event that lasts a very long time. Teams from all over the world play in different world zone qualifying leagues to get through to the final stages played at the World Cup venue. They then play initially in leagues with the winners and runners-up going through to the knockout stages right through to the final. Rules even change as the format changes, as draws can occur in the initial leagues. However, in the knockout stage there must be a winner, so extra time is played and then there is a penalty shoot out if the scores are still level!

Figure 8.1 Football World Cup – large events need a lot of organising

Task 2

Make a list of all of the resources you would need to provide for a one-day cricket tournament. This should include equipment as well as personnel.

Task 3

Describe both the advantages and disadvantages of the different competition formats listed above.

Hints and Tips!

Organising and running a sports event is likely to be something you are asked to do rather than be asked questions about. Clearly, the planning process is the most important part (and the part that is going to take up the most time). Failing to do this properly is likely to result in a failed event.

Key questions

1. What types of events could be planned as sporting events?
2. What are the main issues likely to be associated with the location of an event?
3. What are the main disadvantages to staging events in an outdoor setting?
4. Describe three different types of event that could only take place in an indoor venue and explain why.
5. What format of competition would you choose if you were organising a one-day netball competition with six teams? Explain why you would use this format.

9 Health and hygiene

The World Health Organization defines health as:

> a state of complete physical, mental and social well being and not merely the absence of disease or infirmity. Health is one of the fundamental rights of every human being without distinction of race, religion, political belief, economics or social conditions.

It is important that everyone should develop the knowledge and skills that will enable them to understand their own bodies, how to keep them healthy and to have a regard for the health of the community. The following nine components can influence your health.

1. Use and misuse of substances such as alcohol, tobacco, medicines and other drugs.
2. Sex education – the physical, emotional and social aspects of an individual's development as a male or female; personal relationships; responsible attitudes and appropriate behaviour. This factor is very closely linked to the issue of HIV and AIDS.
3. Family life education – the value and importance of the family as a social institution; its contribution to the development of attachment, love and concern in caring for others.
4. Safety – the safety of the individual in different environments, e.g. at home, on the road, at school, at work, during leisure activities.
5. Health-related exercise – the importance of exercise in promoting good health.
6. Nutrition – the association between diet and health; the nutritional value of various foods; the quality of food preparation and handling.
7. Personal **hygiene** – personal cleanliness; avoidance of disease; social considerations.
8. Environmental aspects of health education – the effects of various environments on health: social, physical and economic factors that contribute to health and illness.
9. Psychological aspects of health education – mental health, emotional well being, stress.

Health is very important, and good health is something that everyone wants. There are ways to help maintain your health and there are also many things that can damage your health.

Key point

The World Health Organization definition of health is very important, as it sums up what being healthy is all about and it sets the standards that should be aspired to and met at all times.

Did you know?

It is possible for you to be healthy without necessarily being fit but it is impossible to be fit if you are not healthy!

Figure 9.1 Good health enables you to enjoy your life more

Task 1
Describe some sporting situations where a performer could be put at risk because of the effects of alcohol.

Task 2
Describe ways in which a sportsperson's performance could be affected if they were a regular smoker.

Did you know?
Every cigarette smoked reduces life expectancy by 11 minutes! So, for every carton or packet of cigarettes smoked, a day and a half of life is then lost. Death can start occurring as early as 35 years of age. Half those people who die from smoking-related causes will die in middle age, each losing about 25 years of life expectancy.

Alcohol

Like many other things, moderate amounts of alcohol do not necessarily do any harm. However, if someone drinks too much, then the immediate effect is that they become drunk. This can often lead to violent behaviour. It also causes a lack of co-ordination and usually results in vomiting. If excessive drinking continues over a period of time there can be more serious effects such as:

- damage to the liver, muscles and heart
- damage to the digestive system
- mental illness such as hallucinations, memory loss, depression, brain damage and extreme confusion
- damage to the immune system, leaving the body less able to fight diseases.

Alcohol is a mood-altering drug. Technically, it is a depressant drug as it slows down the action of the brain. Some people think that it is a stimulant, but this is not the case. It only takes a small quantity for some effect to be felt. Any performer in a physical activity would be affected by alcohol and it is for this reason that performers should never drink alcohol before taking part in sport.

Smoking

Packets of cigarettes often carry a health warning, which must be printed by law in many countries. These include, 'Smoking causes cancer' and 'Tobacco seriously damages health'.

There is no dispute about the fact that smoking is harmful, which is why these warnings have to be printed. The dangers caused by smoking are:

Figure 9.2 Alcohol, in moderation, may not be a hazard to health – smoking always is!

- greater risk of serious diseases such as heart disease, lung cancer and chronic bronchitis
- developing a 'smoker's cough'
- frequent sore throats
- shortness of breath
- nose, throat and chest irritation and breathing difficulties
- headaches
- dizziness
- nausea and lack of concentration.

The most dangerous thing about smoking is that it kills. Thousands of people a year die as a result of smoking and it kills more people by causing heart attacks than any other disease.

No one who smokes can expect to be healthy or maintain a good level of **fitness**. Even non-smokers can be affected by **passive smoking** by breathing in other people's tobacco smoke, which can be equally harmful.

Health and hygiene

The only good news about smoking is that something can be done about the harmful effects. A reduction in the number of cigarettes smoked can help. Stopping altogether can enable the body systems to recover, although this may take several years.

The simplest solution seems to be not to start in the first place!

Medicines

Medicines are drugs that are intended to help to keep people healthy, to cure illnesses or to aid recovery. Something as simple as cough medicine can be used easily and safely, and many everyday medicines can be bought from chemists' shops. Other medicines are controlled more carefully and can only be acquired on a **prescription** authorised by a doctor. Again, many of these medicines aid good health, as people with more serious illnesses, such as asthma, need them to control their condition.

A drug is a chemical substance. If it is taken into the body it affects the chemical balance within the body. Because of this serious effect, most drugs are controlled and should only be used on medical advice and with medical supervision, as they can be harmful when not used properly. For many people drugs are essential; they not only keep them healthy but also may even keep them alive. However, drug abuse can be extremely harmful if the drugs are taken for the wrong reasons or in the wrong dosages.

Some drugs are known as **performance enhancing** (see Chapter 38). Their use in physical activity is often illegal (according to the rules of the particular activity) because it can give the people who take them an unfair advantage.

The important thing to remember with all substances is that they can be both used and abused. Any performer taking part in physical activity should be aware of this.

Safety and risk assessment

Safety is particularly important for anyone taking part in physical activity. All activities have some element of risk that can be reduced by taking the necessary precautions.

Many activities, especially games activities, have their own particular safety rules or precautions that players and performers should be aware of and stick to (see Chapter 32).

Some activities, especially outdoor and adventurous ones, can actually take place in a potentially dangerous environment. There is therefore an extra need to make sure that all the necessary safety actions are taken. The challenge element of these activities is what attracts many people, but the safety aspect must not be ignored.

Task 3
Name **three** medicines that can be used to make people healthier.

Task 4
Think of **three** physical activities. For each one, think of **three** different safety precautions that should apply.

Figure 9.3 A challenging activity might be dangerous if safety precautions are not taken

> **Task 5**
>
> List some ways that environmental, social and economic factors could affect someone taking part in physical activities.

Figure 9.4 A careful and correct warm-up is an important safety factor

Some basic safety factors that apply to most activities include:

- lifting correctly (when lifting heavy or awkward loads or weights always keep your back straight and bend your legs)
- wearing the correct clothing/footwear for the activity
- not wearing jewellery
- abiding by the rules of the activity
- checking any of the equipment that is necessary and using it properly
- wearing protective items where it is appropriate
- making sure the activity is properly supervised
- warming up before taking part and cooling down when you have finished.

No activities are guaranteed safe but all of them should be carried out in as safe a manner as possible. In team activities each performer has a responsibility not just for themselves but for all the other performers as well.

Many safety regulations have been tightened up in recent years as a result of accidents. Most schools have very detailed guidelines for trips and physical activities.

Environmental factors

Environmental factors such as where you live can be related to health. In some areas pollution can be a very real problem as it can affect the air or even the water supply. People who live in large cities may have problems caused by car exhaust fumes or factory emissions, both of which can drastically reduce the air quality.

Many people – for example, those who suffer from asthma or hay fever – can be affected by such simple things as high pollen levels during the summer months.

Air quality can also be affected by pressure changes brought about by weather systems. This can result in smog (a mixture of smoke and fog), which can be dangerous for people who have respiratory problems.

Social and economic factors can be just as important and just as damaging. Poor housing, lack of main services such as a clean water supply, heat and light, and lack of support services such as medical help (vaccinations, doctors, nurses and medical centres) can cause health risks. Poverty is also a problem as this can often result in lack of suitable clothing and food.

Hygiene

If you want to remain healthy it is very important that you follow the basic rules of hygiene. This is also linked with risk assessment because following good hygiene guidelines greatly reduces the risk of illness and injury.

Personal hygiene includes:

- washing
- cleanliness
- prevention of disease
- prevention of infection
- food preparation practices
- dental care
- clothing
- **self-esteem** and confidence
- social considerations.

Most of these should be quite obvious, but some need to be considered in more detail.

One of the things you must maintain very carefully is your skin. This is the largest organ of your body and on an adult male it can be about 3 square metres in area. It can be quite a job to look after it all carefully and well.

Washing

You should do this regularly. It should be fairly obvious that if your hands are dirty then you wash them, and this might be necessary several times a day. However, it applies equally to all parts of your body. If you do not wash at all, your skin will soon become dirty and an unpleasant body odour (commonly known as BO) will be produced. Many deodorants and antiperspirants are available to buy but these do not cure the problem, they only cover it up.

The only solution is to wash regularly. Ideally, this should include a bath or a shower where the whole body is thoroughly washed, preferably using soap. It is especially important to bath or shower after physical activity to remove the traces of sweat on the skin. It is just as important to make sure that you dry yourself thoroughly afterwards, especially between your toes, to help prevent **athlete's foot**.

It is also very important to wash your hair as it can quickly become oily or greasy, or you may develop an itchy scalp.

Cleanliness

It is important that anything you come into contact with is as clean as possible. This is obvious for things such as knives and forks but it should apply to any equipment you might be using or wearing, and it is very important if it is clothing.

Clothes should be regularly washed and changed – especially your underwear. You should always change all of your clothes after physical activity, particularly if it has been strenuous. Your clothes could be dirty and will almost certainly be sweaty. They should be washed before being worn again. This is why it is a good idea to have a sports kit that is just worn for a particular physical activity and to change into a clean set of clothes after you have had a shower or bath. If you have a PE kit, make sure that it is washed regularly, preferably after every time you use it.

Nails should be kept clean and toe nails, in particular, should be cut regularly as this can help to prevent **ingrown toe nails**. These can be most uncomfortable and painful, and can stop participation in physical activity.

Ears should be kept clean and if earrings are worn in pierced ears these too must be carefully cleaned and maintained. Remember that earrings should be removed when taking part in physical activity.

Did you know?

About 1.8 million to 2.4 million dead skin cells fall off your body every hour, so billions fall off every day. One of the chief ingredients of household dust is human skin.

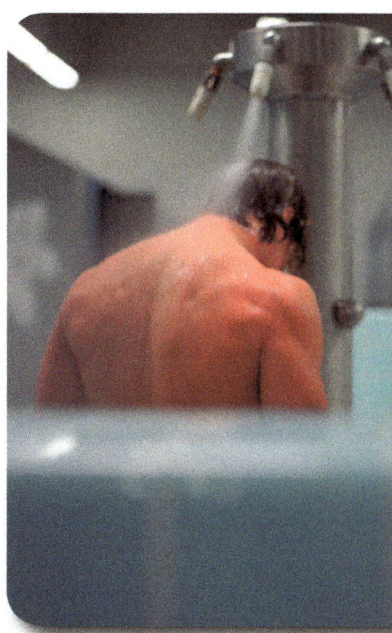

Figure 9.5 Showering after taking part in a physical activity should be encouraged

Task 6

Design a poster that points out the importance of washing and that is designed to encourage people to keep themselves clean.

Figure 9.6 You will probably need to clean yourself and your kit after physical activity

Prevention of disease can be achieved largely by washing and cleaning. Cleanliness can prevent an environment developing where germs can survive and multiply.

Any cuts or wounds should be carefully cleaned and antiseptic should be applied. This can help with the prevention of infection. Another great help is the **immunisation** programme in which young people are **vaccinated** (usually by injections) to prevent them suffering from diseases such as:

- HIB (a type of meningitis)
- whooping cough
- diphtheria
- tetanus
- polio
- measles
- mumps
- rubella (German measles).

Other vaccinations are made available if there is an epidemic of a particular disease.

Dental care is also very important. This doesn't just mean regular and correct brushing of teeth; it also requires regular visits to the dentist for check-ups and any treatment that might be necessary. Tooth decay and gum disease are common and the condition of teeth declines with age, so regular check-ups are essential.

Food preparation must be carried out very carefully on clean surfaces, and with clean hands and equipment. The necessary precautions must be taken both before and during the cooking. These include making sure that foods are stored correctly (fridges or freezers may be necessary), that sell-by dates are checked and that cooking instructions are followed carefully. People who are careful about hygiene may have higher self-esteem and are more likely to be accepted by other people socially than those who are unhygienic.

Task 7

Find out the symptoms and effects of **at least two** of the diseases listed opposite.

Hints and Tips!

Health and hygiene are completely interrelated and it is important to be aware of the relationship that exists between the two. Establishing good hygiene habits is essential to be able to maintain good health.

Key questions

1. What is the World Health Organization's definition of health?
2. Explain two short-term effects of drinking too much alcohol.
3. Describe two long-term effects that can occur through excessive alcohol intake.
4. Describe three particular smoking-related diseases.
5. Explain why is it important to maintain good hygiene habits. What is the relationship between hygiene and health?

10 Nutrition and diet

Everyone needs food to survive. Food provides the body with energy and nutrients. The nutrients in food are:

- carbohydrates
- fats
- proteins
- vitamins
- minerals.

Although not a nutrient, water is essential for life. Dietary fibre is also needed to keep the digestive system in good working order.

No single food provides all the nutrients the body needs, so it is important to eat a variety of foods. Table 10.1 shows the six Caribbean food groups.

Caribbean food group	Examples of food	Main nutrients
Staples	rice, pasta, sweet potato, oats, grains	carbohydrates
Legumes	string beans, cashew nuts, black eye peas	proteins
Food from animals	pork, fish, chicken, milk, eggs, dairy products	proteins
Fruits	bananas, pawpaws, golden apples, guavas	vitamins and minerals
Vegetables	carrots, spinach, tomatoes, okra	vitamins and minerals
Fats and oils	margarine, butter, lard, avocado pears	fats

Table 10.1 Caribbean food groups

It is important to achieve a balanced diet. All the nutrients needed by the body can be obtained by eating a wide range of foods from each of the groups shown in Table 10.1.

Key point

A balanced diet is the correct intake of all of the appropriate amounts of nutrients which provide the body with energy. A balanced diet also provides you with foods to help the body to grow, function normally and stay healthy.

Did you know?

A balanced diet contains: approximately 55 per cent staples/carbohydrates; 30 per cent oils and fat; and 15 per cent foods from animals/protein.

Task 1
Collect labels from a variety of different packaged foods. Compare the energy values of these foods. Which **five** foods contain the most energy and which **five** contain the least? Explain the differences.

Task 2
Suggest ways in which you could cut down on the amount of sugary carbohydrates you eat. How would you change your diet to include more starchy carbohydrates?

Energy

Even when a person is resting, energy is still needed to keep the body functioning. The amount of energy needed for important processes such as breathing and keeping the heart beating is called the **basal metabolic rate** (BMR).

Activity levels also affect a person's energy requirements. A person who has an active job (e.g. working on a construction site or teaching Physical Education) is likely to need more energy than someone who sits at a desk each day (e.g. receptionist or a clerk typist). Physical activities such as football, cycling, cricket, basketball and hockey also increase a person's need for energy.

To keep body weight constant, the amount of energy provided by food needs to match the amount of energy used by the body. If the diet provides more energy than is needed, the extra is stored as fat (or adipose tissue) and weight gain occurs. In the long term, a person may become overweight or **obese**. By contrast, if the diet supplies less energy than is required, stores of adipose tissue are used to provide the extra energy needed and weight loss occurs.

The best way to lose excess body fat is to reduce the amount of energy provided by food while increasing the amount of energy used by the body. So, it is beneficial to everyone to have an active lifestyle.

The components of the diet that provide energy are fats, carbohydrates and proteins. Most foods contain a mixture of these nutrients. The amount of energy provided by a particular food (sometimes called the energy value) depends on the combined amount of energy provided by each of the nutrients. The energy value of a food is usually expressed in kilojoules (kJ) or kilocalories (kcal). In everyday language, most people refer to kilocalories as **calories**.

Carbohydrates

Carbohydrates can be divided into two groups based on the number of sugar units – simple carbohydrates and complex carbohydrates.

Simple carbohydrates consist of one or two sugar units. Types of simple carbohydrate include **glucose**, **sucrose**, fructose (fruit sugar) and lactose (milk sugar). Simple carbohydrates are found in sugar, sweets, chocolates, jam, honey, sweet drinks, cakes, biscuits, milk and fruit. With the exception of milk and fruit, most of these foods are not very nourishing and should not be eaten too often.

Complex carbohydrates (**starches**) consist of hundreds of sugar units. Starchy foods such as bread, pasta, rice, potatoes and pulses are rich sources of complex carbohydrates. These foods contain a wide range of other nutrients and should form the main part of most meals and snacks.

Carbohydrates provide the body with energy, so they are an important part of the diet – particularly for sportspeople and other people who are very active. During digestion, carbohydrates are broken down into single sugar units, such as glucose. Once absorbed, glucose can be used to provide energy. However, if it is not needed immediately it is converted into **glycogen**, which is stored in the liver and muscles. During exercise, the body can use stores of muscle glycogen to provide energy. If glycogen stores are full, glucose will then be used to make fat which is stored as adipose tissue.

Top sports performers have to work out their energy needs very carefully and will sometimes **carbohydrate load** (eat lots of starchy foods) in the week before an important competition or event (e.g. a marathon). Carbohydrate loading increases the amount of glycogen in the muscles, which helps to delay tiredness and may improve performance in the end stages of a competition.

Fats and oils

Fats and oils contain substances called fatty acids. There are three main types:

- saturated fatty acids (**saturates**)
- monounsaturated fatty acids (**monounsaturates**)
- polyunsaturated fatty acids (**polyunsaturates**).

Most fats contain a mixture of different fatty acids. Foods that contain a high proportion of saturates are usually of animal origin such as meat, meat fats such as lard, and dairy products. Some margarines and oils also contain saturates. Monounsaturates are found in many foods – olive oil is a particularly rich source. Foods that contain a high proportion of polyunsaturates include margarines and oils made from seeds and nuts such as sunflower, soya and corn oils. Oily fish such as sardines are also a rich source of polyunsaturates.

Fats are important because:

- they provide a concentrated source of energy
- fat stored under the skin helps to keep the body warm
- fat stored around major organs has a protective effect
- foods with a high fat content contain fat-soluble vitamins
- two fatty acids (called essential fatty acids) cannot be made in the body and must be provided by our food.

Although fats are an important part of the diet, most people should aim to cut down on the total amount of fat they eat. In particular, they should try to reduce their intake of saturates.

Fats can provide the body with energy during exercise, but this depends on the intensity and duration of the exercise, and also on the fitness level of the person taking part. Fat tends to be used to provide energy during light activity and during prolonged periods of exercise. As a person becomes fitter, fat tends to be used to provide energy instead of glycogen.

Proteins

Proteins are made from building blocks called **amino acids**. The body needs 20 different amino acids to make all the proteins needed for good health. Nine of these (called essential amino acids) cannot be made in the body and must be supplied by food. The remaining amino acids (called non-essential amino acids) can be made in the body.

Proteins from animal sources such as meat, fish, eggs, milk and cheese contain all the essential amino acids in adequate amounts. With the exception of soya beans (which also contain all the essential amino acids), proteins from plant foods – such as beans, lentils, breakfast cereals, bread, pasta, rice, nuts and seeds – lack one or more of the essential amino acids.

Proteins are needed:

- for the formation, growth and repair of tissues such as muscle, hair and skin
- to make enzymes and hormones.

In general, proteins only provide the body with energy if the diet contains inadequate amounts of carbohydrates and fats. But during very strenuous activities or prolonged periods of exercise, proteins in muscles may start to be broken down to provide extra energy.

Sportspeople are very active, and so need a very good supply of proteins to ensure that muscles grow, are repaired and kept in good working order. They need more protein when they train hard or for long periods of time. Someone with a lack of proteins could suffer from **malnutrition**.

Vitamins

Vitamins are only needed in small amounts, but they are still essential for good health. Vitamins can be divided into two groups:

- **fat-soluble vitamins** (A, D, E and K) – these can be stored in the body

Task 3

Suggest ways in which you could cut down on the amount of fat your diet provides.

> **Did you know?**
> As each different vitamin was discovered it was given a letter.

- **water-soluble vitamins** (B group and C) – these cannot be stored, so the body needs a constant daily supply.

Vitamins are important because they:

- protect the body and maintain the body's chemistry
- enable growth and maintenance of bones, teeth, skin and glands (this is especially important in young children because of the growth process)
- help with digestion, the stability of the nervous system and tissue growth, and resistance to bacteria and disease.

Although **vitamin supplements** are widely available, it is far more important to meet requirements for vitamins by eating a balanced diet. If a wide variety of foods are eaten every day, vitamin supplements are not necessary.

Compared with inactive people, individuals who exercise regularly or spend a lot of time training may have slightly greater needs for certain vitamins. For example, some of the B-group vitamins convert nutrients in food into energy.

During exercise, the body uses more energy and so the need for some of the B-group vitamins increases slightly, but vitamin supplements, taken in excess of a person's need, are unlikely to improve performance.

> **Task 4**
> Find out the names of **three** diseases that are caused by vitamin deficiencies. Explain the symptoms of each disease and state how these deficiencies can be prevented.

Minerals

As with vitamins, minerals are necessary for the efficient working of the body. Some minerals are needed in smaller amounts than others. These are called trace elements.

The human body takes in minerals from a variety of vegetables and meats. For example, calcium is obtained from milk, cheese, yoghurt and bony fish (e.g. mackerel); iron is found in red meat, liver, eggs and dark green vegetables (e.g. spinach).

> **Task 5**
> Compare the different vitamin and mineral supplements available at a large supermarket. Consider the nutrient content and cost of each type.

Minerals:

- help to build tissues (zinc)
- are constituents of bones and teeth (calcium and fluorine)
- help to release and use energy in the body (potassium helps with heart and muscle contraction)
- provide soluble salts in the body fluids and cells (sodium) to maintain the fluid balance in the body and encourage the correct functioning of cells and muscles.

Requirements for minerals can be met with a varied diet, but as with vitamins, the need for some minerals may increase if a person exercises or trains regularly. Similarly, mineral supplements taken in excess of need are unlikely to improve performance. A mineral deficiency can result in stunted growth, damaged eyesight or weak, malformed bones.

Figure 10.1 Runners may need to replace fluids lost when taking part in a race

Fibre

Fibre is needed to keep the digestive system healthy. A good intake of fibre or roughage helps to prevent constipation and may reduce the risk of developing conditions such as **bowel** cancer. Most people should eat plenty of fibre-rich foods. Good sources are wholemeal bread and pasta, wholegrain cereals, brown rice, pulses, fruits and vegetables (especially where skins can be eaten), nuts and seeds.

Water

Water makes up about two-thirds of body weight and is essential for good health. Water is lost from the body in urine, sweat, expired air and faeces. An average-sized man loses about 2.5 litres of water from his body every day. If this is not replaced, **dehydration** occurs.

During exercise, more water is lost from the body than at rest. Some of this extra water is lost in sweat, and some is lost as water vapour when a person breathes out. The amount of water lost depends on the:

- intensity of exercise
- duration of exercise
- temperature and humidity of surroundings.

In general, more fluid is lost when a person exercises vigorously, for a long time, or in a hot environment.

Task 6

Suggest ways in which you could increase the fibre content of your diet.

Hints and Tips!

You should be aware that people need to have a balanced diet and know which nutrients make up one. You should be able to outline briefly what all of the essential nutrients are, what they consist of and the types of food that are rich in them.

Key questions

1. Name all the nutrients that together make up a balanced diet.
2. What are the two carbohydrate groups? Give both of the terms for them.
3. Name the three main types of fats. Why do you need fats in a balanced diet?
4. What are proteins made from? Name two things they are needed for.
5. Why is fibre needed in a balanced diet?
6. What problem can arise through a lack of, or shortage of, water?
7. What do the 'energy equation' and 'basal metabolic rate' mean?

11 Diet and physical activity

Everyone needs to follow a balanced diet to make sure they stay in good health. It is even more important that sportspeople consider their diet carefully. Often their choices can make the difference between success and failure in competition.

Different activities may require different diets but individual needs also vary greatly. Dietary needs can be affected by age, activity and weight.

Age

Younger people experience various periods of rapid growth when they need a greater amount of food to enable their bodies to cope with the demands put upon them. As they get older, however, the demand for food decreases and tends to level out.

The trend seems to be that as we get older we need to regulate our food intake and our weight more. This is almost certainly linked with the fact that we tend to take less exercise as we get older.

The amount and type of activity undertaken

People taking part in different physical activities may need different diets depending on the activities they choose to do.

- **Gymnasts** need to remain fairly small and light, so need to avoid very fatty foods that could lead to an increase in body weight. They need strength and energy to keep going so they need a good balance of carbohydrates, proteins and fats. They need to monitor their body weight regularly.
- **Football players** don't need to be particularly light or heavy to take part in their activity but they do need energy to keep going in matches and training. Body weight is not a major concern but players would have to monitor it if excess weight caused them to slow down during games. They need a fairly normal diet with sufficient carbohydrates, proteins and fats to supply their energy needs.
- **Weightlifters** need to have a great deal of body weight and may even need to increase it if they wish to get into a certain body weight category (there are ten of these ranging from 52 kg to 110+ kg). Because of this, weightlifters may eat to increase **bulk** so the quantities consumed would be large, with carbohydrates and fats as a priority. They also need to increase strength, so proteins are needed to help with muscle development.

As shown in the examples above, quantities eaten can be just as important as the types of food.

> **Key point**
> Sports performers need to consider their diet very carefully, taking into account their age and the type of activity in which they participate.

> **Did you know?**
> Men need to consume about 3000 kcal a day (for women it is 2200). This needs to be doubled if you are particularly active or train regularly.

> **Task 1**
> Think of **two** other types of performer. What sort of diet will they need for their sport?

Dietary needs

Performers also need to pay particular attention to their dietary needs at particular times, such as:

- before activity
- during activity
- after activity.

Before activity

This is always a period of preparation for performers and they must make sure that they are as ready as they can be to take part. If their activity requires them to be particularly light, or even large, this has to be planned out and maintained over quite a long period of time. Their diet would become a routine with some adjustments from time to time.

Top performers adjust their diets for up to a week before an important event. Many long-distance runners decrease the amount of carbohydrates at the start of this period and then increase it substantially towards the end, especially the night before (carbohydrate loading). The timing of this is important. It can be dangerous to eat within 2 hours of an event because the body finds it very difficult to cope with digesting food and meeting the demands that the increased amount of exercise makes. Fats and meat are particularly difficult to digest so they should not be eaten for several hours before an event. Liquids can be taken just before an event without causing the same problems.

During activity

No food should be eaten during activity because the digestive system would not be able to cope and it could cause extreme discomfort or even illness. What is important is that the performer replaces lost fluids and drinks enough to prevent dehydration.

Failing to take in enough liquid, especially in hot climates like the Caribbean, can lead to collapse and, in extreme cases, hospital treatment may be required to replace the fluids.

Figure 11.1 Replacing fluids lost during exercise is important to prevent dehydration

> **Did you know?**
> Extreme stomach cramps and pain can be felt if you eat too much either just before, or just after, vigorous exercise.

After activity

When an activity is over, the performer must replace all the energy that has been used up. This should not be done immediately – it is unlikely that the desire to eat will be felt anyway (remember that exercise can suppress the appetite). It is possible to take liquids and fruit almost straight away and many track athletes can be seen doing this immediately after a race.

At least 2 hours should be left before any substantial amounts of food are eaten and then the cycle of eating, following the correct diet, can start again, ready for the next performance or event.

Possible dietary problems

Being underweight can be just as unhealthy as being overweight. In some cases a person may be anorexic. **Anorexia** is a psychological illness that results in someone refusing to eat. The person may suffer a loss of appetite or may appear to follow a normal diet but then force themselves to vomit later (called anorexia bulimia). This results in them being extremely thin and **undernourished**. It is a very serious condition, and if left untreated, can lead to death.

Obesity is the opposite condition. Being extremely fat and greatly overweight can also be very dangerous as it puts a great strain on the heart, joints and muscles.

> ### Task 2
> Using the information in this chapter, choose a physical activity and consider the dietary needs for a performer. Design **three** meal plans before, during and after that activity.

> ### Hints and Tips!
> You need to be able to link the information you have about nutrients and a balanced diet and apply it to the specific requirements of particular performers. This is often easier to do if you consider two extremes such as a weightlifter and gymnast.

> ### Key questions
> 1. Compare two different performers in two different activities and describe the dietary requirements of each.
> 2. If you were the trainer of a marathon runner, what sort of dietary needs would you suggest in the following three stages:
>   - in the long-term period building up to a race
>   - during the race
>   - the period immediately after the race?
> 3. Why is it important for sports performers to maintain adequate fluid levels?

12 Exercise

The most basic way to be physically active is to exercise or to experience 'healthy physical exertion'. Exercise is something everyone should take part in. It does not have to be particularly strenuous and the amounts of exercise will vary from person to person. Some people exercise to maintain their general good health and wellbeing. Others exercise to achieve a very high level of fitness (see Chapter 13).

We have seen that exercise plus a balanced diet can help to keep body weight down (see Chapter 11). However, exercise has other benefits, such as:

- improving your body shape
- helping with the relief of tension and stress
- helping you to sleep better
- reducing the chances of getting illnesses and disease
- giving you a physical challenge to aim for
- toning up the body and the muscles, which leads to an improvement in **posture**
- increasing your basic levels of strength, stamina and flexibility.

Exercise can also be a very social thing, as it can involve joining clubs and associations and starting up new friendships.

Physical activity is important for everyone because it improves our general health. Many jobs require a good level of strength and stamina in order to manage tasks like stacking shelves or standing on one's feet all day. Other jobs, called **sedentary** jobs, involve sitting down for long periods with little regular body movement, so it is very important for these people to exercise.

How much exercise is necessary?

This very much depends on two things:

- the physical condition of the person
- the long-term aims of the person.

Physical condition

If someone is not very healthy or has not been exercising regularly they should see their doctor before they decide how much exercise to do. This would also be a particularly good idea if the person were middle-aged or older because the advice would be to start off with fairly gentle exercise and then to increase it gradually. You do not have to join expensive

> **Key point**
> Exercise can be considered to take place on two levels. The basic level is to maintain good health, and a higher level is aimed for by performers who need to achieve specific targets in their chosen sports.

> **Did you know?**
> You must exercise your body to some degree daily or your muscles can literally waste away. This is known as atrophy.

> ## Task 1
> Breathlessness or panting after a brisk walk or short jog, stiffness in muscles and feeling tired are all signs of lack of exercise. List as many more signs as you can think of that indicate the need for an increase in exercise.

clubs or gyms to maintain good physical condition. There are many parks, beaches and public spaces where people are easily able to engage in 'social sporting activities'.

Figure 12.1 Caribbean beaches provide a variety of excellent ways to get daily exercise

Many doctors are now prescribing exercise instead of drugs, and many have arrangements with local sports facilities providers so that people can go there to exercise.

Long-term aims

Exercise has to be done regularly to enjoy the benefits, and the amount of exercise can be increased gently. A long-term aim can be to move on from the gentle levels of exercise that are appropriate when you begin, to much higher levels. After a while you could reach the level that a person who takes part in regular, quite strenuous physical activity would need.

Many sports have playing seasons and 'closed seasons' when the sport is not played competitively. Performers in these sports would therefore need to plan their exercise around this and carry out exercise training during the closed season. Some performers even travel abroad to do this where the climate is better – if they can afford it!

> ## Task 2
> List some other simple exercise habits you can start.

Good exercise habits

Here are some simple and easy ways to increase the amount of exercise you can take.

- Don't drive, or be driven, short distances; walk instead.
- Try to walk at least part of a journey. This is easy to do if you travel by bus.
- Use a bicycle.
- Walk up stairs rather than using an escalator or a lift.
- Do some simple stretching or **flexibility** (see Chapter 15) exercises at various times daily.

Exercise guidelines

The following are some general guides to the type and quantity of exercise advisable.

- Being slightly breathless is not a bad sign but if you are unable even to talk when exercising you have probably overdone it.
- Try to exercise for periods of 15–20 minutes about four or five times a week.
- Exercise until you are pleasantly tired; do not overdo it. 'No pain no gain' is not necessarily a good slogan.
- Go for good all-round exercise. Swimming is particularly good because it includes some stretching movements, allowing the muscles to move freely, without straining the body.
- Establish an exercise routine that becomes a regular part of life. Joining a club is a good idea as it can help organise your exercise routine.

Effects of exercise

The long-term effect of exercise is the enjoyment of all the benefits that have been listed. There are also some short-term effects that occur as exercise takes place.

- The rate at which the heart beats (the pulse rate) will increase.
- The rate of breathing will increase.
- The body temperature increases and sweat appears on the surface of the skin.
- Skin will appear to redden, especially on the face.
- There may be a feeling of tiredness or 'heaviness' in some muscles that are being used.

Task 3

Observe someone who is exercising. As the exercise continues, note down the differences in: pulse rate, skin colour, amount of sweat and breathing rate. What changes have you listed?

Hints and Tips!

Exercise makes you fitter in the long term but it is also important to be aware of the immediate effects it has when exercise is actually being taken.

Key questions

1. Describe the main benefits of exercising regularly.
2. What guidelines should someone consider when they are planning to start exercising?
3. Are there cases where a person would be advised not to exercise? Give an example.
4. Why do doctors 'prescribe' exercise to some of their patients?
5. What special considerations should someone who has a sedentary job take into account when planning a basic exercise programme?
6. What are the main short-term effects that exercising can have on the body?

13 Fitness

It is important to keep a level of both physical and mental fitness relative to your needs and requirements.

A basic level is always necessary, but you may have to work very hard to achieve high levels. Fitness can only be achieved through hard work and it is relative to the standard at which you perform. Some of the factors related to fitness are:

- age
- sex
- somatotype
- strength
- power
- flexibility (also known as suppleness or mobility)
- endurance (also known as stamina)
- speed.

The first three are different because an individual does not have any real control over them. They will be dealt with later (see Chapters 18, 19 and 20). The other factors can be changed. The ways in which they are important will be dealt with in this chapter.

> **Key point**
> 'Fitness is available on prescription but it is not in tablet form.' This means it is possible to reach a high level of fitness but that there are no short cuts – fitness can only be achieved by working at it.

> **Task 1**
> Make a list of **five** physical activities that require only a general fitness level.

Figure 13.1 Some activities only require a level of general fitness

So what is fitness? Basically, it is having a highly efficient body that can cope with a high level of physical demand. We have seen the importance of being healthy (Chapter 9) and the way in which physical activity and exercise can help (Chapter 12). Both of these are vital if a high level of fitness is to be achieved. It is possible to be healthy without being fit, but it is not possible to be fit without being healthy.

There are two different levels of fitness depending on the type of physical activity being undertaken. They are general fitness and specific fitness.

General fitness

For general fitness, individuals need to be in good health and be able to carry out everyday tasks comfortably. They should also take part in a number of physical activities at a low level of performance. Some individuals may be able to compete at a relatively high level in a particular sport due to natural ability or because they have acquired a high skill level in that physical activity.

Specific fitness

This is necessary if the physical activity in which the individual takes part is particularly demanding or if they are competing at a high level. It is therefore an extension of general fitness because the physical demands require that the individual must prepare very carefully for the specific needs of that sport. Natural ability and skill alone will not be enough to compete at the highest level, where specific fitness is essential.

Achieving specific fitness

Clearly, the first thing needed is a good level of general fitness. This can be achieved by following the exercise guidelines in Chapter 12. It would be very dangerous to do too much too soon because you could make demands on your body that it might not be able to cope with.

The activity for which a person is trying to get specifically fit will dictate the amount and type of training needed (see Chapter 28). This training will, in some way, aim to improve:

- strength
- flexibility (suppleness, mobility)
- endurance (stamina)
- speed
- agility.

Did you know?

Some of the fittest professional sportspeople are Formula 1 Grand Prix drivers! Although they are seated for the entire race they can lose up to 3.5 litres of fluid in a 2-hour race. A loss of just 1 per cent of body fluid is enough to cause serious lapses in concentration.

Task 2

Make a list of **five** physical activities that require a specific fitness level.

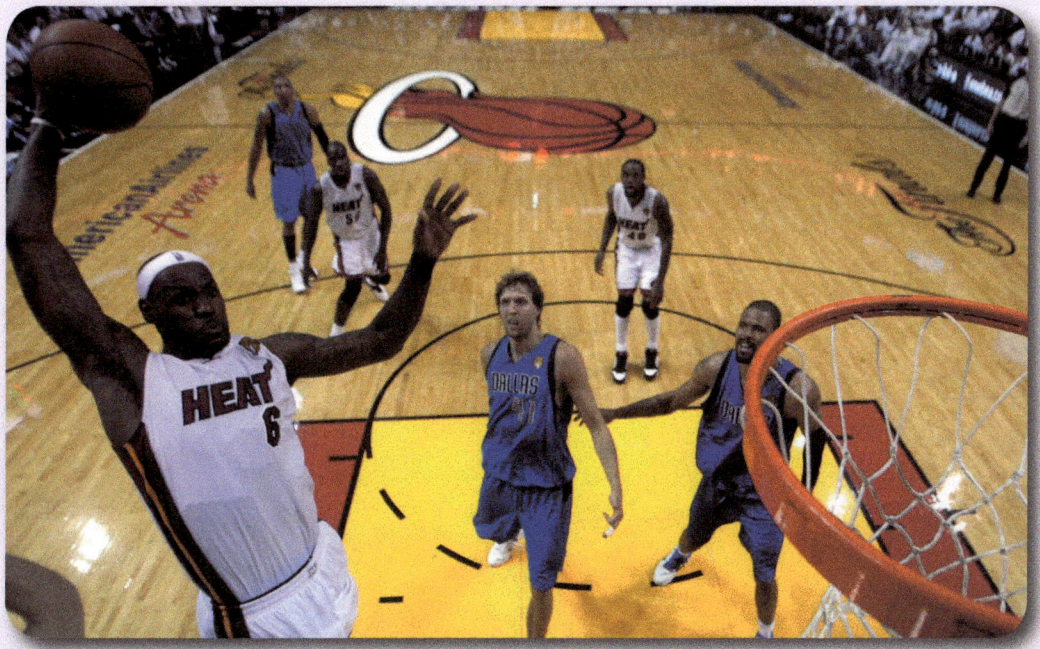

Figure 13.2 High-level activities require a high level of specific fitness

Task 3

Choose **two** different physical activities and list, in order of importance, the factors needed to achieve specific fitness for them.

This does not mean that you will only need to consider one aspect, as all of them need to be considered to some degree. What is important is that certain physical activities need greater concentration in one area than in others, and it is important to be able to identify these and work on them specifically. All of the factors can be identified and all of them can be improved so it is important to recognise them and look at ways of improving them.

It is also important to remember there are factors that, if not carefully considered, can have a damaging effect on fitness. Not all of them can be controlled but they must be noted.

- **Physical disability** – this can limit fitness in certain areas, depending on the severity of the disability, but many people with disabilities concentrate on particular aspects of fitness for their chosen sport and reach high levels, often using adapted training equipment. They may have to accept a limitation on the activities that are available, considering their particular disability, but the variety and standard of sports for disabled people shows that these barriers can be overcome.
- **Illness, injuries and medical conditions** – little can be done about these. Short-term illnesses or injuries such as broken bones may mean only a temporary reduction in fitness levels. If the illness or medical condition is fairly serious, it could greatly restrict the level of fitness that can be achieved.
- **Diet** (see Chapters 10 and 11).
- **Drugs, alcohol and smoking** (see Chapter 9).
- **Weight, height and somatotype** (see Chapters 19 and 20).
- **The stress and pressures of competition** – many performers will be trying to become fit in order to compete. The pressures they experience both before and during competition are very high and can be damaging. These psychological factors can prevent fitness being achieved or maintained (see Chapter 21).

Hints and Tips!

It is important to be aware of both the differences and links between general and specific fitness, and also to be aware of all the factors that can be linked to making someone fit.

Key questions

1. Describe three factors affecting fitness over which an individual does not have any real control.
2. Give a basic definition of fitness.
3. Describe what is meant by general fitness.
4. What is the link between general fitness and specific fitness?
5. How can specific fitness be achieved and maintained?
6. Describe two factors that could have a damaging effect on fitness.

14 Strength

There are different types of strength, each one having a different effect on the efficiency of the body. Muscular strength consists of:

- static strength
- explosive strength
- dynamic strength.

Performers can use different methods to improve their strength. The method they choose may depend on which particular type of strength they want to develop.

Static strength

This is the greatest amount of force that can be applied to an immovable object. It is very important in any activity where you have to brace yourself against another performer or some object or weight.

Arm wrestling requires static strength. A member of the pack in a rugby scrummage needs it to be able to push against opponents. Sometimes it will be used just to stay still and sometimes to push the other pack backwards. A gymnast uses static strength to keep upright and motionless in a handstand position.

Figure 14.1 Three examples of static strength

Key point

Different types of strength can be identified, but it is very likely that all of the different ones will be used at some time in any particular activity or performance. It is also a factor that can be adapted and improved.

Did you know?

There is often a debate about what being strong involves. One argument is that it is related to whoever can lift the largest amount of weight. The other is that it should be about how strong someone is in relation to their bodyweight.

Task 1

Identify **at least two** other sporting situations that require a great deal of static strength.

Explosive strength

This is muscular strength used in one short, sharp movement. A sprinter leaving the starting blocks uses a great deal of explosive strength to push forwards and upwards as quickly as possible. A great deal of explosive strength is needed in the leg muscles for this.

Strength, in general terms, is defined as the maximum force in a muscle or a group of muscles during a single maximal contraction. However, it is very difficult to accurately measure it by using one particularly method which fully takes into account the different types of strength which exist.

One method of measurement which is used is the hand held dynamometer. This is a device which is squeezed in the hands with maximum effort for five seconds and a reading is shown on a calibrated dial. However, this only really tests the strength in the forearms so it does not represent the strength present in other muscles. Another common measurement is performing 'chin-ups' on a bar which is above the stretch height of an individual, but this can advantage shorter, lighter people over taller, heavier ones.

Task 2

Name **two** other sporting situations that require a great deal of explosive strength.

Did you know?

The 'Worlds Strongest Man' events are very common and are often competed for on an annual basis. However, each competition has to have a variety of different events to help to choose the eventual winner as there is no one test which anyone can agree upon as being both fair and accurate. These competitions also have to take place over a number of days in order for the competitors to 'recover' sufficiently to take the next test.

Performer profile

Ato Bolden (born 1973 in Port-of-Spain, Trinidad) won two gold medals in the 100 and 200 metres in the World Junior Championships – a feat never performed before! In the 1996 Olympic Games he won bronze medals in both the 100 and 200 metres. The following year he won the World Championship gold in the 200 metres. By 1998 he had run more times under 9.90 seconds than any other sprinter when he notched up his fifth one. In the 2000 Olympics he won a silver and bronze medal to take his total Olympic tally to four before retiring from competition in 2004.

Task 3

Decide upon **three** different ways of testing strength (such as maximum number of chin-ups performed) and test them with a group. Make sure that you test different muscles/muscle groups each time so that the specific muscles do not get fatigued completely and affect the results. See if the same individuals are the 'strongest' in each of the different tests and discuss within the group which method of testing for strength appears to be the best one.

Dynamic strength

This is the muscular strength sportspeople need to support their own bodyweight over a prolonged period of time. It also refers to the muscular strength needed to be able to apply force against some type of object.

This type of strength is very closely linked with **endurance** (see Chapter 16) because the muscles need to work continuously, moving and supporting the body. Compare this with explosive strength, which only occurs for a short space of time and you can see the difference. A gymnast performing on the rings or the pommel horse needs a lot of dynamic strength to be able to complete a routine.

Sportspeople, or performers, will always require some degree of static strength, explosive strength and dynamic strength to be able to take part in their chosen physical activity. They must be able to identify the most important type and the ones they need to work on most as part of their training programme.

Sometimes it is easy to see the types of strength which top sportspeople have developed. Speed skaters have very well-developed muscles at the tops of their legs as they need explosive power to accelerate, and they will work on these muscles specifically. Many male gymnasts need considerable arm strength, especially for the rings exercise, and they have very clearly defined arm muscles.

Figure 14.2 An example of modern weight-training equipment

54 | Strength

How can strength be increased?

Developing and increasing strength is relatively easy, as long as you follow the right training programme and understand the principles of training (see Chapter 28).

In recent years there has been an increase in the number of gyms where strength can be improved. This has been helped by the improvements in the equipment and facilities available. Previously, the only way to 'weight train' was to use weights on bars. These would have to be frequently changed, and it was necessary to work with others who could help to load and unload and also to supervise the lifting.

The new, purpose-built equipment means that people can now train individually, using equipment that is safe, and easily and quickly adjusted. The new equipment can also be much more specific to certain muscles, or muscle groups, so it is easier to work on the areas you want to.

Although free weights (bars with weights which can be added or subtracted) are still used, by far the most popular method of training is to use multi-gyms or gyms fitted with weight-training stations.

Task 4
With a partner/group, write down other sporting situations that require a great deal of dynamic strength. Compare your answers with those of another group and see which team identified the most situations.

Task 5
Identify a physical activity that you do. Try to work out when you are using static, explosive or dynamic strength. Which type of strength do you use most? Which muscles do you use most?

Task 6
Give **three** advantages that multi-gyms have over free weights as a method of improving strength?

Hints and Tips!
You need to be able to distinguish between muscular endurance (the ability of a muscle to keep working against a resistance) and muscular strength (the ability to overcome a force or resistance). The main difference is clearly that of the time element.

Key questions
1. Define what is meant by strength.
2. Name three specific types of strength and for each one give an example of when it could be used in a sporting situation.
3. What is the difference between muscular strength and muscular endurance?
4. Explain how it is possible for strength to be increased.

15 Flexibility

The advantages of flexibility

The amount you can bend and stretch your joints is very important when you are taking part in physical activities. Every sportsperson should work to improve flexibility. It is something that is often ignored by performers who might not realise all the advantages that increased flexibility can bring.

Less chance of injury

Most physical activities require performers to reach or stretch. Serious injuries can occur if you stretch too far. A hooker in rugby needs flexibility in the shoulders to bind on to the prop forwards; a tennis player needs it to be able to stretch and reach for shots; and a cricket player needs it to be able to bend and stretch when fielding.

Preparing the body for performance

If flexibility exercises are carried out immediately before taking part in a physical activity, as part of the warm-up, it not only reduces the chances of an immediate pull or strain but also means that the performer is properly prepared for taking part.

Improving body posture

Good posture means that the muscles are holding the body in position correctly and that there are no over-tight muscles that can cause aches and pains.

Better, more efficient performance

With a full range of movement at the joints all performances will be improved. In many activities you cannot perform some of the movements without good flexibility. In others, you become more efficient. Tackling in hockey and performing the butterfly stroke in swimming are good examples of where a high level of flexibility is an asset to performers.

Gymnastics and dancers will be able to provide a more pleasing performance because increased flexibility will enable them to be more expressive.

Some events have scores awarded for how well certain movements are performed and for events such as hurdling, a flexible athlete is able to clear the hurdles far more efficiently.

Flexibility occurs around joints. The main joints involved in movement are as follows.

> **Key point**
> There is no downside to increasing your flexibility. The listed advantages can only help you in any sport you choose to take up!

> **Task 1**
> List some physical activities for which flexibility is important in reducing the chances of injury.

> **Task 2**
> Name some activities in which marks would be awarded for performing movements that require a lot of flexibility.

> **Did you know?**
> There is no such thing as being double jointed! Joints only move in one direction and it is the high degree of flexibility that gives this illusion!

- **Shoulders and arms** – where the flexibility occurs at the shoulder joint and also at the elbow and the wrist. Most people have quite a good range of movement in all these areas as they are used all of the time in many everyday activities. Just putting on clothes requires quite a lot of flexibility in these joints. Shoulder and arm flexibility is used in any activity requiring lots of arm movements such as throwing or swimming.
- **Back** – the majority of movements require some flexibility in the back and it is an area that is often ignored in flexibility exercises. Very few people have much range of movement here which is why it is an area prone to injury (bowlers in cricket are a good example).
- **Hips** – lots of movements involve bending at the hip joint, where it is possible to have a very large range of movement in various directions. Any form of leg raising or lowering requires flexibility here. Any movement from the waist involves a combination of hip and back flexibility. This is an area where many people do not have a particularly good range of movement and it is a good area to test for flexibility (see Chapter 30).
- **Legs** – movement is mainly in the knee and ankle joints. Many people have a fairly good range of movement here because they are areas that are used often. Any walking or running movements, and certainly any kicking movements, require full flexibility.

If joints are not regularly used and exercised flexibility decreases quite rapidly, so it is very important to carry out flexibility exercises regularly for all areas and concentrate particularly on those areas you use in any chosen activities.

Figure 15.1 Hurdling is more effective with good levels of flexibility

Figure 15.2 Butterfly stroke and tackling in hockey can be improved by increased levels of flexibility

Performer profile

Melanie Walker (born 1983 in Kingston) is a former pupil of St Jago High School. When she won the gold medal in Beijing she set the Olympic championship record time of 52.64 secs. She also won the World Championship in 2009 with the second fastest time in history of 52.42 secs. Melanie was also a successful junior performer as she won a silver medal in 200 metres in the World Junior Championships in 1998 before winning the silver in the 2002 Junior Championships in the 400 metres hurdles.

Ways of improving flexibility

All flexibility exercises need the joints to be moved as far as possible, but this can only happen if the muscles surrounding them contract (see Chapter 23) and if they are able to work against some kind of resistance (some force which is pushing back against the muscles). Here are some examples.

- **Passive or isometric contraction** – this is where you bend or stretch as far as possible pushing against something. Then you try gradually to push farther and farther to increase the range. Sometimes a coach or training partner can help you to push but this must be done very carefully.
- **Active or dynamic contraction** – this is where you get into a stretched position, as far as possible, and then bounce or bob further. This must be carried out very carefully. Some coaches advise against it, as it can cause a sudden strain that can damage muscles.

Task 3
Name an activity you take part in and describe how improved flexibility could improve your performance.

Figure 15.3 Fully stretching before performing helps to improve flexibility

Hints and Tips!

Stretching should always be included as part of a warm-up – mainly to help prevent injuries. It should also be included in the cool-down to help to remove the lactic acid from the muscles.

Key questions

1. Explain what is meant by flexibility.
2. How could flexibility help a performer in a sporting situation or named event?
3. Suggest one activity for improving flexibility.

16 Endurance

Endurance is probably the most important aspect of fitness and most training usually concentrates on improving this. It is important for all performers to be able to keep going with a movement or activity for as long as possible, or at least as long as is necessary. Endurance is also called stamina and there are very few physical activities for which it is not a priority.

Muscular endurance

Muscular endurance is the ability of the muscles, or a group of muscles, to keep working against a resistance. The amount of dynamic strength you have (see Chapter 15) relates to the amount of muscular endurance you have. When a muscle is no longer able to continue working properly, **muscular fatigue** takes place and the muscle will literally not be able to work against, or hold, a load any longer.

Signs of lack of muscular endurance can soon set in. Muscles begin to ache and feel tired, limbs feel heavy and even the most determined performer has to stop. The only way to improve muscular endurance is to increase dynamic strength. This can be done by using weight-training methods (see Chapter 30).

Your ability to improve muscular endurance can be affected by the different muscle fibre types which you have in your body. There are two types.

- **Slow-twitch fibres** contract slowly. They can keep doing so for quite long periods of time and they are essential for endurance.
- **Fast-twitch fibres** contract quickly so they also tire quickly. They are therefore more suited to speed and power.

Different individuals have different quantities of these fibres. Performers are more likely to be able to improve their muscular endurance if they have a greater proportion of slow-twitch fibres in their muscles.

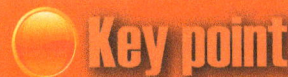

Key point

It is essential to be able to understand endurance in the two specific categories of muscular endurance and cardiovascular endurance. Both are very important to all performers but they are distinctly different and must be considered as such.

Cardiovascular endurance

Cardiovascular endurance is the ability of the heart and lungs to keep supplying oxygen in the bloodstream to the body to provide the energy to sustain physical movement. In any activity that requires you to keep moving for quite long periods of time you will be far more effective if you have a high level of cardiovascular endurance.

Figure 16.1 You can use press-ups to test your muscular endurance

Anyone who has felt out of breath while performing an activity has felt the effect this activity has had on their heart and lungs. When at rest (this can mean just sitting or standing but not doing anything strenuous) the average person has a heartbeat of about 72 beats per minute and a breathing rate of about 14–16 breaths per minute. That is enough to keep your body working efficiently as enough oxygen will be available to satisfy your needs.

As soon as your body starts to exercise there is a greater demand for oxygen as your body is working harder. The heart rate goes up and so does the breathing rate and if you are performing strenuous activity for long periods it goes up quite considerably. Your ability to keep going at this high level of demand is a measure of your level of cardiovascular endurance.

It is important to be able to monitor heart rate, as this is one of the basic ways of measuring and testing endurance. You can check your heart rate (commonly called **pulse rate**) by placing your fingers on the inside of your wrist or on your neck. Use your fingers rather than your thumb, because there is a pulse in your thumb that can give you a false reading. Simply count the number of beats you can feel in 1 minute and this will give you your pulse rate. The most accurate measure of your **resting pulse rate** can be obtained if you take your pulse as soon as you wake up in the morning before you actually get out of bed.

Chapter 12 describes the effects of exercise. It is very easy to experience the effect exercise can have upon the pulse rate. Once you have learned how to find your pulse you can check it after several minutes' exercise and you can see for yourself how much higher it is.

There are now watches and chest monitors that have sensors which can give a very accurate pulse reading, and many sportspeople use them. These monitors are also used to help you to improve your level of endurance. Unlike muscular endurance, you cannot exercise your heart and lungs on weight-training machines to make them more efficient. To improve them you have to make them work harder by working your body hard. This increases pulse and breathing rates. It is most important to keep them at a high level for some time. The graph below gives you an indication of the levels the pulse should be relative to age.

On the graph:

- **maximum pulse** is worked out by taking your current age away from 220 (e.g. if you are 15 your maximum pulse would be 205); this is the absolute highest level that you should achieve
- **training zone** is the level to which your pulse should be raised and maintained for maximum benefit (see page 119)
- **aerobic zone** is from 60 to 80 per cent of your maximum pulse and also benefits increased endurance levels but is not as intensive, or beneficial, as the training zone.

Did you know?

Cyclist, and five-time Tour de France winner, Miguel Indurain, had a resting heart rate of 28 beats per minute which is one of the lowest ever recorded!

Task 1

Count your own resting pulse rate for 1 minute and write it down. Practise to make sure that you can locate your pulse quickly and easily.

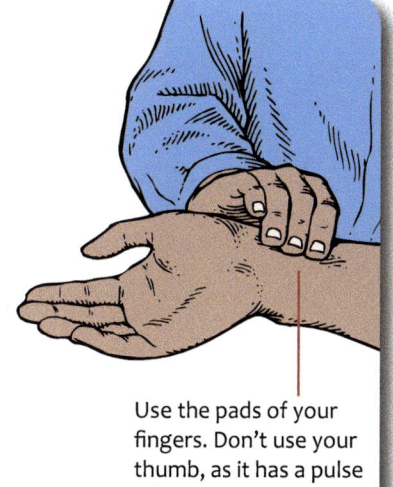

Use the pads of your fingers. Don't use your thumb, as it has a pulse of its own.

Figure 16.2 Locating pulse and pulse rate graph

Endurance

Task 2

Work out your training zone and see if you can exercise at that level comfortably for a period of time. (Only build up to longer periods if you are able to.) Try to do this regularly and keep a record of your progress.

Task 3

Before exercising, or taking part in a physical activity, check your resting pulse rate. Afterwards, record how long it takes your pulse rate to return to normal after you have finished. Try to do this regularly and keep a record of the results.

Improving levels of endurance

To be able to benefit fully from exercise in terms of improving endurance it is necessary to work at a high level (aerobic zone and training zone) for at least 15 minutes. This is a long time to work at such a high level so it is very important that you build up gradually to this standard.

No one should attempt to exercise at high levels or in a strenuous way unless they have carefully built up to it. If you are in any doubt you must seek medical advice. Excessive exercise can be just as harmful as a lack of exercise.

Chapter 30 looks at ways of training and Chapter 31 looks at ways of testing. These are very closely linked to improving endurance. If you want a simple way of exercising in your training zone then jogging, cycling, swimming or running on an exercise treadmill (if you have access to one) are good ways to do this.

Pulse recovery rate

This is another way to check endurance levels. It involves taking your resting pulse before you begin to exercise, raising it to a high level and then recording how long it takes to return to normal. The quicker it returns to normal, the higher your level of cardiovascular endurance and the fitter you are considered to be.

Specific tests (see Chapter 31) can be used to check recovery rates, but it is easy to check your own recovery rate after any period of strenuous exercise.

If you regularly exercise using the guidelines set out you will be able to reduce your resting heart/pulse rate and you will have made your heart more efficient. Reducing your resting pulse rate by ten beats a minute (and this is quite possible) means that your heart beats five and a quarter million times less in a year.

Top sportspeople who have a great deal of cardiovascular endurance have a very low resting pulse rate.

Oxygen uptake

As the cardiovascular system is concerned with the heart and the lungs it is important to consider the amounts of oxygen your body needs when exercising, as well as the heart rate.

Oxygen uptake is the total amount of oxygen that the body needs and takes in at any time. It is also referred to as **VO_2**. Obviously this increases when you exercise, as the body needs to take in more oxygen to produce energy. This cannot go on indefinitely so the maximum amount that a person can take in is known as **VO_2 maximum**.

It is possible to test a person's VO_2 maximum. The higher it is, the greater their level of endurance.

Just as there is a level of heart rate to aim for during exercise in order to improve your level of endurance there is also a level to which your VO_2 should be raised. This should be between 55 and 75 per cent of your VO_2 maximum. One simple way of recognising when you are working at this level is that you will not be able to carry out a conversation with anyone, as you will not have enough breath to do so. The oxygen system is sometimes referred to as the aerobic system. (Do not confuse this with 'aerobics', which simply refers to a method of exercising that affects the aerobic system.) There are two terms that relate to it.

- **Anaerobic energy** is used when physical activity is carried out without the use of oxygen. In this case oxygen is not used to generate the energy; it is in fact ATP (to be precise: adenosine triphosphate). This can only be used in short bursts and for short periods.
- **Aerobic energy** is used when the body is continuing with activity for a long period of time and the energy to do so is produced with oxygen.

Chapter 26 looks at the respiratory system in more detail and the way in which oxygen is converted to energy.

If you work very hard during a physical activity you may find that you are out of breath for quite a time after you have finished. This is because your body has needed more oxygen than you were able to supply and you have experienced **oxygen debt**. Your body has managed to keep working by using the **lactic acid system** where glucose is broken down in the muscles. Too much lactic acid can lead to fatigue and tiredness and even stiffness in the muscles after exercise.

The feeling of being short of breath after exercising is not unusual, but you need to repay the oxygen debt and you also need to be able to disperse the lactic acid that has built up. One of the best ways to do this is to exercise lightly after you have finished. This is called the cool-down (or sometimes the **warm-down**) because this helps to remove that lactic acid.

Did you know?
Lactic acid is actually a mild poison. It contributes to the burning sensation often felt in the muscles when exercising vigorously, but it is essential to help the muscles contract more efficiently.

Figure 16.3 Cyclists often have low resting pulse rates

One important thing to remember about endurance is that most physical activities require a high level of both muscular endurance and cardiovascular endurance. It is only very specialist activities that require just one.

In any activity there are often times when muscular endurance is needed and then cardiovascular endurance takes over. This often works in cycles.

Task 4
Choose a sporting activity (preferably one you take part in) and analyse a specific performance to see how and when it requires each type of endurance.

Hints and Tips!
You should be able to distinguish between the two types of endurance and also explain what each one consists of. The ways in which these types of endurance can be both improved and tested is also important.

Key questions
1. Define what is meant by muscular endurance.
2. Explain how muscular endurance can be developed or improved.
3. Identify a sporting situation where muscular endurance is required. Explain how and when it is used (or needed).
4. Describe how levels of cardiovascular endurance can be increased.
5. What is the relationship between pulse recovery rate and levels of fitness?
6. State the difference between aerobic and anaerobic energy.

17 Speed and power

Speed

Two factors contribute to this.

- **Reaction time** is how quickly a performer can respond to something. It could be a sprinter reacting to the gun or a tennis player reacting to a tennis ball coming towards them.
- **Movement time** is how quickly a performer can carry out the actual movement. For example, it could be how long it takes the sprinter to run 100 metres or the tennis player to play and follow through their stroke.

The total speed of a performer is the combination of reaction time and movement time, so clearly reaction time is very important. It can certainly mean the difference between a winning or losing performance, especially in events that last a short time.

A 100-metre sprint race takes less than 10 seconds at the top level, so sportspeople who react to the gun and are out of the starting blocks quickly will have a considerable advantage.

Because of the importance of this and the advantage it can give, there are sensors in the starting blocks, linked electronically to the starting gun, to check how quickly the sprinter has reacted to the gun. If it is too quick it will register as a false start and the race is restarted. Top performers react so quickly that electronic checking is the only way of knowing for sure.

Although it is possible to train to improve speed there may be restrictions on how effective this may be.

- **Inherited factors.** In Chapter 16 we saw that a high proportion of fast-twitch fibres can help to improve speed. If you have inherited a lower quantity your chances of substantially improving your speed are reduced.
- **Body shape and size.** Because of body weight, muscle size and bone structure you may not be able to increase speed.
- **Duration and distance of the event.** It is not possible to maintain speed indefinitely. Sprinters will slow down progressively the farther they go. Distances up to 400 metres are considered sprint events and even then sprinters cannot maintain the speed at which they can run 100 metres.

> **Key point**
> Speed is basically how quickly you can move part, or all, of your body. Power is the combination of speed and strength. There is a very close link between both of these factors.

> **Did you know?**
> Speed in sport is measured in metres per second and a 60-metre sprint is the standard measure.

However, speed can be improved by:

- increasing strength, particularly in the main muscles required
- developing action and style for your activity or event
- making speed-work part of your training programme – this involves ways of training the muscles to contract quickly.

Another factor often thought to be a part of fitness is **agility**. This is a combination of flexibility and speed as it is the ability to move quickly, changing direction and speed whenever necessary.

Being agile can be a great advantage in a great many physical activities. The way to improve it is quite straightforward – you should practise the particular aspect of the sport that requires agility. For example, soccer and hockey goalkeepers will regularly practise saving footballs fed to them from different angles and heights, as well as at different speeds.

Power

Power is the combination of the maximum amount of speed with the maximum amount of strength.

There is a very strong link between power and explosive strength (see Chapter 14), and there are a great many physical activities that require power, although not necessarily all the time, as Table 17.1 on page 67, shows.

> **Task 1**
> Name parts of three physical activities needing agility and describe a practice for each that could improve it.

Figure 17.1 Yuderquis Contreras of the Dominican Republic (note that for safety there is usually a spotter nearby)

Performer profile

Usain Bolt (born 1986 in Trelawny, Jamaica) is the son of a grocery store owner. He attended Waldensia Primary School and later went on to William Knibb High School. He won his first major gold medal in the 2002 World Junior Championships for the 200 metres, which he won again the following year. As a senior performer he won a silver medal in the 2007 World Athletics Championships. In a 2008 Grand Prix event, Usain broke the world 100-metre record with a time of 9.72 seconds. Later in the year, at the Beijing Olympics, he won gold medals in the 4 × 100 metres, the 200 metres (setting a world record of 19.30 seconds) and the 100 metres, breaking his own recent world record with a time of 9.69 seconds. In the 2009 World Athletics Championships he not only won the gold again in the 100 metres but also broke the record for the third time when he ran 9.58 seconds – the fastest time ever run!

Activity	Power required for
Tennis	Serving and smashing
High jump	Take-off phase
Rugby	Scrummaging
Golf	Driving
Soccer/football	Shooting
Cricket	Fast bowling and batting
Athletics	Throwing events, sprints
Hockey	Hitting/shooting
Table tennis	Smashing

Table 17.1 Power required for different activities

Power is not something that can be maintained for long periods. The table includes sports that would not normally be considered 'power events'. This is because power is only used in short bursts. It is impossible to sustain it for long.

Events such as weightlifting and power lifting only require the performer to use power for a very short time. In weightlifting the power is needed to lift the weight above the head then control it for a few seconds.

It is clear that you do not have to be particularly strong to have effective power. Table 17.1 includes several examples of activities where strength is not a priority. What is important is the combination of strength and speed, but there are other factors that also help.

- **Co-ordination** – you must be able to link all the parts of a movement into one efficient, smooth movement.
- **Balance** – being in control of your movement is vital; without it power will be reduced.

Did you know?

Power generated by sports performers is measured in watts. An example of this would be an average cyclist who generates 100 watts, whereas Lance Armstrong, when riding in the Tour de France, averaged 400 watts over the final hour of a racing stage.

Hints and Tips!

It is important to be able to learn the definitions for speed, power and agility as a great many movements require the combination of all three of these. It is also important to be able to identify when each of the factors is being used primarily.

Task 2

Make a list of other events, or stages in a physical activity, where it is important to have power.

Key questions

1. What are the two factors that combine to make up speed?
2. Define speed.
3. Describe three ways in which speed can be improved or developed.
4. Explain what is meant by agility.
5. What is meant by power?
6. What are the other two factors that can combine with power and speed to enable an efficient movement or performance?

18 Age

Age constantly affects a person's level of fitness in varying ways. It is a factor to be considered for young people as well as older people. For all forms of competitive sport there are various age divisions – usually junior, youth and then senior. These exist because of the great effect age can have.

Within these age divisions there are usually subdivisions. For example, typical age divisions that a tennis club might use for its annual championships would be:

- under 10
- under 14
- under 18
- veterans (40+)
- under 12
- under 16
- seniors
- super veterans (50+).

Some sports would have even more categories.

Why are age divisions necessary?

Practising and learning

Very young people are not able to cope with too much information, especially if it is quite complicated. They may simply not understand how to do things, so tasks must be kept simple.

Flexibility

This decreases with age. People are usually at their most flexible in their teens. This is one of the reasons why gymnasts, especially girls, tend to be at their best in their early teens when they are able to perform really well. The decline in flexibility tends to be more noticeable after the age of 30, although it can start in the 20s.

Figure 18.1 Former gymnast Nadia Comaneci

Key point

As a person's age increases so the different physiological effects associated with it are more likely to take effect. The most crucial ages that need to be considered are at the lower end and higher end of the age range, as this is where the effects are most noticeable.

Task 1

Choose **one** sport and find out the different age groups that exist for competitions.

Strength

A young person will not achieve their maximum strength until they are fully grown. Muscle mass starts to increase in the mid-teens. Up to the age of 20 the body is still growing and developing in terms of bone size and muscle. Therefore, young people should not start weight training until their mid- to late teens. Doing so before this could cause problems.

During a person's 20s and 30s, there is ample growth hormone so strength tends to peak at this age. There is a loss of protein over the next 40 years and there can be a decline in strength of up to 40 per cent.

Diet

The body's metabolism slows down as people get older, so weight is likely to be gained. This tends to occur in the 40s when the body also loses lean muscle mass, so fewer calories are needed than before and the extra may turn to fat. As you get older, you preserve less fluid so there is a tendency to dehydrate quicker.

Oxygen capacity

This reduces with age; a 50-year-old has a reduced capacity compared to a 20-year-old.

Injury and disease

The older people get, the more likely they are to suffer injuries (and the longer it takes to recover from them). There is also an increased chance of disease. For instance, there is a far greater chance of heart disease among older people.

Reaction time

This decreases with age; the very young have been tested as having very good reaction times.

Skill

This can improve due to growth (high jumpers may appear more skilful as they get taller, so might basketball players). However, experience is an invaluable asset which can only be gained over a period of time.

Some of the ways in which age affects our bodies are more important than others because there is little that can be done about them. For example, it is not possible to prevent protein loss as this is just a part of the ageing process, but it is possible to improve or maintain flexibility by regularly performing flexibility exercises. It is also possible to regulate the diet to take account of the changes in the metabolism. If you are aware of the effects of ageing, there are steps you can take to lessen them.

Age and physical activity

Some activities are regarded as young people's sports and some are regarded as old people's sports. Sometimes there are good reasons for this and sometimes there is no real need for it to be true.

If an activity requires a great deal of physical exertion, then it will become more difficult to compete at a high level as you get older for all the reasons already mentioned. There is no need for an age bias for activities that are less strenuous.

Did you know?

Nadia Comaneci was only 14 years old when she scored the first ever perfect 10 in the 1976 Montreal Olympics. The scoreboard was not set up to display a 10 score, so it was reported on the boards as a 1.00 score overall! She won three gold medals at these Olympics.

Task 2

In which sports would you expect players to be in their:
- teens
- 20s
- 30s?

Did you know?

Once professional golfers have reached the age of 50 they can switch to the Seniors tour where they still compete professionally (and for prize money), but they play a total of three rounds instead of four.

In many professional sports there are few performers under age 16 who have not at least left school or college. Tennis has been an exception to this several times in the past, when female players appeared to mature earlier than males. In most activities top performers do not seem to be able to master the range of skills necessary until their late teens or early 20s. Their 'playing career' quite often only lasts between 10 and 15 years due to the very demanding nature of playing full-time sport at the top level. Veteran players in these sports are the exception rather than the rule.

Figure 18.2 Many female tennis players play at their highest level while still in their teens

Hints and Tips!

Age has to be considered in line with the particular demands that an activity might be putting on it. For example, cricket could be played by any age group but a powerlifter would have to be fully physically developed before they could take part in their sport.

Key questions

1. Identify two functions that could deteriorate as a person gets older.
2. At what age should a person first start taking part in weight training? Give a reason for your answer.
3. Explain what happens to a person's body metabolism as they get older.
4. Name two sports or activities that do not have age divisions.
5. Name three sporting activities considered to be suited to younger performers only. In each case give a reason for your answer.

19 Somatotype

The description '**somatotype**' refers to the structure or build of a person, especially the extent to which it exhibits the characteristics of an ectomorph, an endomorph, or a mesomorph. They were first identified by an American called W.H. Sheldon. The drawings in this chapter show three different somatotypes (or body types).

Your body type is something you are born with because it is determined genetically. Body shape can be improved but you cannot make drastic changes such as increasing your height or your basic bone structure.

The three classified groups: are (a) ectomorph (thin); (b) mesomorph (muscular); and (c) endomorph (fat). These drawings show the extremes of the three body types.

- **Ectomorph** – this body type is relatively short with thin arms and shoulders. Ectomorphs often have a small head with a long neck, a short waist and long legs.
- **Mesomorph** – this body type is a basic Y-shape, well muscled with wide flexible shoulders, long arms and hands, a narrow waist and lightweight legs.
- **Endomorph** – this body type is short and rounded with a tendency to gain fat. Endomorphs have short legs in relation to their trunks.

Not many people fall clearly into one of these categories, as most people are a mixture of all three. To classify body type, Sheldon used a scale of 1–7 for each somatotype, giving 7 points for an extreme somatotype. To work out your body type give yourself a mark somewhere between 1 and 7 for each of the three types, depending on how close you are to the extreme of the type.

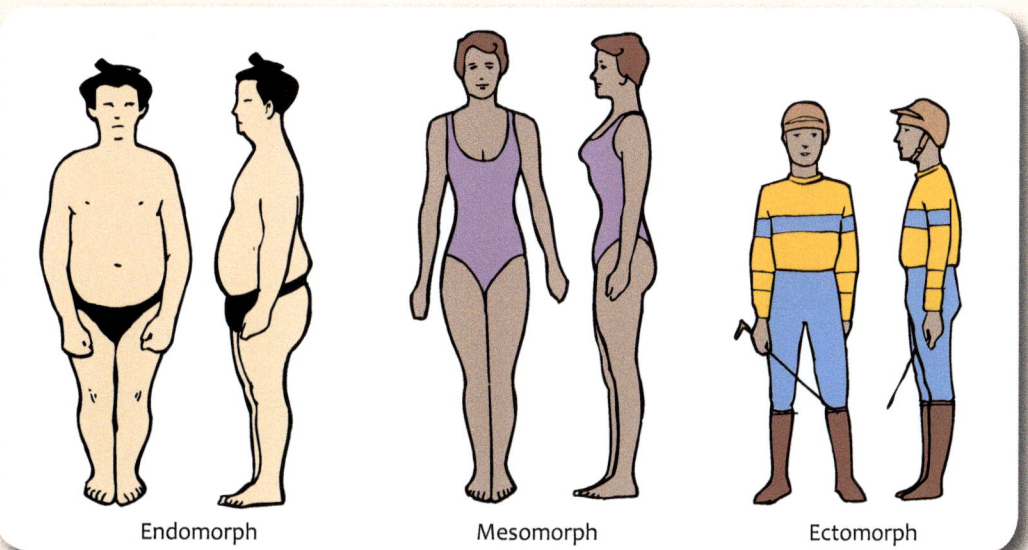

Figure 19.1 An endomorph, mesomorph and ectomorph body type

Key point

The definitions and drawings of somatotypes are examples of extremes and there are very few people who will fall completely into any particular category. However, it must be remembered that somatotype is a factor that cannot be changed as it is an individual's basic body shape and type.

Did you know?

There are no Olympic standard high jumpers less than 1.83 metres (6 feet tall) and many of them are much taller still. This is because they have a higher centre of gravity in their bodies, which gives them an advantage when jumping over the bar.

Task 1

Attempt to give a somatotype rating either for yourself or a sports player of your choice. How does this body shape make the person you have rated especially suited to a particular sport or activity?

Task 2

Choose an activity or game and identify **at least one** somatotype. Explain the advantages that type would have in a particular position.

Somatotype and sport

Somatotype is a very important factor in physical activities because it may mean that you are particularly well suited to one sport or that you are particularly unsuited to another.

It makes a lot of sense to identify the activities you are suited to, with your natural advantages, rather than trying to overcome the limitations your body type might impose.

In Australia in the 1990s, there was a national programme called Sport Search. Schoolchildren were measured in an attempt to match them to particular sports. Somatotype characteristics were not the only things tested; factors related to fitness were also taken into account.

In the past, many Eastern European countries used similar programmes to try to identify potential sportspeople. Female gymnasts are at an advantage if they are extreme ectomorphs. This means that very young children were sometimes selected and sent to specialist training schools. There, full advantage could be made of the potential of their body type. At the other end of the scale, an extreme endomorph would be very well suited to being a weightlifter. The large body weight, short legs and low centre of gravity are all useful to them. They can add to this advantage by following a suitable training programme, thus enabling them to increase in muscle size and strength.

Extreme mesomorphs are very well suited to swimming, basketball and high-jumping. Their height is a tremendous advantage and it is true that all top performers in these sports are taller than 1.83 metres (6 feet).

There are still many sports for the 'normal'-shaped person who is not of an extreme body type, and there are many activities where it is possible to succeed at the highest level whatever your type. It is also worth remembering that some aspects of your body type, such as your height and weight, may change quite a lot as you grow and develop. Your true somatotype will not be established until you are fully grown.

Figure 19.2 Three athletes whose body type is suited to success in their chosen sport: Yarelis Barrios (left; Cuba, discus and shot-put – an endomorph); a jockey (middle; an ectomorph); and an athlete with a Y-shape body type (right; a mesomorph)

Rugby is a good example of a sport where all different body types can play and each can use their somatotype to advantage. An endomorph could be in the pack, possibly as the hooker, where their bulk and shortness could be an advantage. A mesomorph could be one of the forwards, as one of the main lineout jumpers where their height would be a great advantage and an ectomorph would be well suited to the scrum-half position where being small, quick and agile would be an advantage.

Hints and Tips!

The three somatotypes are very specific sporting terms. An easy way to remember them is to use specific letters in their names: **ecTomorph** (**TALL + THIN**); **enDomorph** (**DUMPY, Fat**); **Mesomorph** (**MUSCULAR**). Remember they are extremes, and that body type can affect suitability for certain sports and activities.

Key questions

1. Define what is meant by somatotype.
2. Name three different somatotypes. For each one, suggest a sport that might suit this particular body type.
3. Identify a sport or activity where a particular somatotype would make it very difficult for an individual to take part. Justify your answer.

20 Individual differences

All people are different. These differences can be a very important factor when taking part in physical activity. They can affect the amount of success you are likely to have. All of the following will vary in individuals:

- strength
- flexibility
- endurance levels
- speed and power
- age
- somatotype
- the senses (sight, hearing, touch)
- physical ability
- experience
- motivation
- environment and culture
- gender or sex (male or female).

Some of these factors have been dealt with earlier as factors of fitness, but the others may be equally important.

The senses

One of the most important factors related to the senses is the quality of your eyesight. Having poor vision can affect your performance quite dramatically. For most physical activities, being able to see clearly is an advantage and even a slight visual impairment can lead to mistiming shots or strokes, not being able to see targets properly or not picking up the flight of a ball or shuttlecock. Wearing glasses may not be the solution as even these could leave you with 'blind spots'. There may even be sports where it is impossible to wear glasses due to the degree of physical contact involved and the safety factor, e.g. playing rugby or goalkeeper in hockey.

People taking part in physical activities do not always fully appreciate the importance of hearing. A good racket-sport player can tell by the sound of the impact just how well a shot has been struck. Being able to hear other people in a team game is very important. Calls by teammates must be clearly heard and understood.

Touch can also be important. Many sports involve holding a ball, bat, racket or even a piece of specialist equipment. Holding them correctly can be dependent upon the sense of touch.

> **Key point**
>
> There are some individual differences that a person can have a degree of control over (e.g. levels of strength, flexibility and endurance) but the majority of them are factors that the individual has no control over (e.g. age) and they therefore just have to accept.

> **Did you know?**
>
> If your ears are blocked up to the point where your hearing becomes limited, then your sense of balance will also be affected. (It is all connected to the workings of the inner ear.)

Physical ability (or disability)

This can vary greatly and it is not always possible to say why one person is 'better' than another. It is often explained as one person just having a 'greater amount of natural ability'. No matter how much research is done it seems there's no scientific answer to this but, clearly, some people do find some activities easier than others.

Recently, there have been many sports geared towards maximum participation by people with physical disabilities. Blind Cricket and visually impaired football are two such initiatives.

Task 1

Try to find out about the equipment used by physically disabled sportspeople in a sport of your choice. Present your findings to the class.

Figure 20.1 Even though they are sight impaired, blind and partially sighted, football players and cricketers may still have natural ability in their sport

Did you know?

The world record for the 100 metres for men is 9.58 seconds (held by Usain Bolt) and the women's record is 10.49 seconds. This means that nearly 1 second separates the two fastest times, which would mean that the fastest woman would finish about 10 metres behind the fastest man!

Figure 20.2 Florence Griffith-Joyner, the holder of the world record for the women's 100 metres

Mental ability

There are factors that can affect your level of mental ability such as your intelligence, your levels of concentration, your perception (your awareness of things around you), and your use of reasoning and logic to solve problems that might arise.

Experience

This is something that can only be gained over time. A young or new player will often be called 'inexperienced' and may be the loser because of it.

Not all people benefit from experience. It is how you learn from experience that is important. Some people make the same mistakes time after time whereas others seem to benefit and improve.

Motivation

This is how determined you are to do well and how much effort you are prepared to put in. Some people seem able to motivate themselves very well, but some need the help of others such as teammates, managers or coaches.

Environment and culture

People living in different parts of the world obviously live in different cultures, but it is possible to live in a different environment even within the same town or street. The availability of money and facilities – or lack of them – or even the type of climate you live in can all have a big effect.

Gender

Whether you are male or female is probably one of the most influential factors there is. There are real differences between men and women, and this is not an unfair comment but a fact!

There are very few sports where women compete against men on equal terms. Horse riding is the main one. Other physical activities are strictly organised separately for men and women, for the following reasons.

Strength

On average, women have only two-thirds the strength of men, as men have a greater muscle mass. Because men have higher **testosterone** levels they have greater muscle growth.

Rate of maturity

Girls mature earlier than boys so competition between them when young can be fair. From the age of about 11, though, boys start to overtake girls in terms of height, weight and strength. Because of this, many sports become single sex from 11 years upwards.

Body type

Women have a flatter, broader pelvis (designed for childbearing) and have a higher percentage of fat. Women also have smaller lungs and a smaller heart, which affects cardiovascular endurance levels. **Menstruation** (monthly periods) can also affect performance.

Flexibility

Women tend to be more flexible than men since they have less muscle mass.

Discrimination

There is little doubt that women are discriminated against in terms of prize money and finance for their sport. They are also prevented from taking part against men by many of the rules and regulations of sports. Pregnancy and the birth of a child may cause a woman to miss up to a year of competing, for each child.

Figure 20.3 South African Caster Semanya rose to fame after recording the best time worldwide for running 800 metres during the 2009 World Championships

Task 2
In what sports would greater flexibility give women an advantage over men?

Task 3
a Why do you think that horse riding is a sport totally open to both sexes?
b Are there other sports that should be open to both sexes? Give reasons for your answer.

Task 4
Research the story of Caster Semanya from South Africa and make a short presentation to your class.

Hints and Tips!

It is important to be aware of the effects that individual differences can have **in relation** to both a performer and a performance. It is also important to be aware of the factors that can be influenced and controlled and those that cannot.

Key questions

1. Which of the senses is most likely to be of paramount importance in the majority of sporting situations? Explain why, giving at least three examples.
2. Describe, using an example, how levels of experience can affect a performance.
3. What is motivation and how might it affect a performer?
4. Explain two factors that are clearly different between males and females and explain how these could affect levels of performance.
5. Give an example where women might experience discrimination purely because of their gender.

21 Factors affecting performance

Physiological factors

Physiological factors are things that can affect you physically and will, in some way, have an effect on your body. Like the individual differences covered in the previous chapter, these factors also vary between people, and they can have important effects upon performance.

Illness or medical condition

An illness is often temporary but a medical condition could be something that a performer has to cope with permanently. If they are taking some sort of medicine or receiving some form of treatment it will affect how well they perform, even if it does not stop them taking part altogether. The following are some of the most common conditions.

- **Asthma** – a disease that causes difficulty in breathing. Unfortunately, it is becoming more and more common. It can be brought about by allergies, infections or even emotional situations and it causes an involuntary contraction around the **bronchioles** (see Chapter 26) that makes the sufferer wheeze and struggle for breath. It can be controlled by drugs and medicines, the most common of which is an inhalant spray. However, a person suffering from asthma is likely to be less successful at endurance events because of their condition. The effects of asthma do tend to decrease with age so there is a chance of the condition improving.

- **Hay fever** – this also affects the breathing system but more directly affects the nose. It is caused by an allergy, often to the pollens of grasses. It causes an inflammation of the membranes in the nose, which causes sneezing and watery eyes. This condition only affects people during the time the pollens are produced (spring and summer), but it can be extremely uncomfortable and can actually stop a sportsperson performing. There are medications available that ease the condition but they will not stop it completely and some of the drugs may cause drowsiness.

- **Colds and flu** – these are infectious diseases because they can be passed from one person to another. The common cold affects the nose and throat, and causes sneezing, a sore throat, running eyes, coughing and sometimes headaches. It usually lasts just a few days but some of the symptoms can last longer. Flu (or influenza) mainly affects the respiratory system but it can affect the whole of the body causing fever, headaches and general weakness.

- **Blood disorders** – many of these are very serious (especially leukaemia, which is cancer of the blood cells) but there are other less serious ones (e.g. anaemia and fainting) that can also have an effect.

- **Anaemia** – this occurs when there is a shortage of oxygen being transported through the blood. This can be treated with iron tablets.

Key point

The factors affecting performance can be considered to fall into two categories – psychological and physiological – and can have a very serious and marked effect. As with other factors, some of these can be controlled but some just have to be dealt with.

Did you know?

There is a condition called 'exercise-induced asthma' where sufferers have to take their medication before activity to avoid the onset of this type of asthma.

Task 1

Choose **one** sporting activity and describe the ways that a bad cold or flu could affect a player's performance.

- **Fainting** – this is sudden unconsciousness which happens when a lowering of blood pressure causes lack of supplies of blood to the brain. It is only temporary but can be quite dangerous if a player is performing at the time of the faint.
- **Menstruation** – the menstrual cycle affects some women quite seriously, causing vomiting, headaches and anxiety. The extreme hormonal changes may affect performance and the fact that it happens on a 28-day cycle can certainly affect training.

Lack of sleep

Tiredness can have a negative effect on performance, as it reduces levels of concentration and co-ordination. Movements become sluggish, thoughts can often be confused and speech can sometimes become slurred.

A vicious circle can occur if someone is nervous or worried before an important event. Sleepless nights caused by worry means the sportsperson is tired during the day, which can affect a performance.

Did you know?

Depriving people of sleep has been used as a form of torture. Deprivation can cause a very confused mental state and, if prolonged, can result in serious illness.

Staleness

This can occur if a performer overdoes physical activity. It can lead to patches of bad form, caused by the over-exertion of either too much play or too much training.

In many physical activities now, there are opportunities to play all the year round instead of just throughout the traditional season, so it is very easy to do too much. There is continual pressure to improve, so performers do not take enough breaks or rests from their sport. They just have to hope that a stale patch will not occur.

Fatigue

This is one of the most serious and damaging factors that can affect performance. It occurs when the athlete's body, or parts of it, becomes so tired because of the training or competition workload and inadequate rest periods that the athlete is unable to function at their optimum level.

We have already seen that fatigue can occur in the muscles so that they will not be able to carry on whatever work they are doing. As fatigue sets in, it will lead to a decrease in skill levels, and the performer will not be able to move the extra distance to intercept a pass or play a shot. More mistakes will be made because of tiredness and the effects get worse, not better. If the performer tries to keep going without a rest they may be forced to stop completely. There are cases where this has happened even at the top levels of sport.

This can be a dangerous condition. Injuries are more likely to occur because of the performer's inability to carry out movements properly. Techniques can also start to suffer.

The only solution if fatigue has set in is for the performer to stop before they do themselves harm. It is important that coaches and managers of teams can recognise the signs of fatigue and substitute a player if possible.

Figure 21.1 West Indies cricketer Dwayne Bravo being assisted from the field

Task 2

List, in order, the signs of fatigue. Choose **one** physical activity and describe how fatigue could affect a performer.

Did you know?

The majority of professional sportspeople are likely to be extrovert personality types due to the fact that they have to perform in front of large crowds and audiences.

Task 3

Describe a sporting situation where you have felt anxious. Explain how you felt and what caused you to feel this way.

Psychological factors

Many trainers and coaches feel that the physical boundaries of performance are stretched nearly to their limits and that the main boundaries that need to be broken through are psychological barriers, taking account of:

- personality type
- tension
- anxiety
- boredom
- stress
- pressure
- motivation
- psyching up (preparing for competition).

There is often a great link between these factors. They can have an enormous effect on performance and skill levels. All of these factors can affect the actual acquisition of skills too.

Personality type

People can be divided into two identified types:

- **introverts** – these are people who are quiet and reflective, not high in confidence, not looking to lead
- **extroverts** – confident and outgoing people with high opinions of themselves; they tend to be leaders.

An extreme introvert is unlikely to fit well in a team game and would probably be far more suited to an individual sport or activity.

Tension

A performer can experience tension personally in anticipation of an event.

Tension is also an atmosphere that can be generated (or felt) by spectators. It can also exist between two players or teams. Tension is related to excitement or suspense. It is easy to see how these feelings can be transferred from performers to spectators and back again.

Tension does not always have a bad effect on performance. Some competitors find that they cannot compete properly unless there is some tension, and they respond to it positively. Others find that tension makes them nervous and uncertain, and this may result in a poor performance.

Anxiety

A person who is anxious is uneasy or troubled. Clearly this is not a good state for a performer to be in. All performers experience some level of anxiety before or during a performance and, to some extent, this is not only normal but can actually help. However, when a player becomes over-anxious, or nervous, their performance can get worse – especially if they are already in a tense situation.

The main reason why someone feels anxious is that they are worried about losing or performing badly, and this can be made worse if people they know are watching.

Boredom

When you are bored you are totally uninterested in what you are doing, your concentration lapses and the chances are you will not try as hard as you could. You may not even try at all.

It is unusual to choose to be in a sporting position that is boring, but boredom can set in if you are being unsuccessful and can lead to a decrease in the standard of performance.

Stress

In a stressful situation, you feel extreme tension or pressure. A certain amount of stress can be a good thing, as it can make you more alert and ready to perform your best. However, if your stress level rises too high it can cause problems. Different people react in different ways to high levels of stress. Some seem to cope very well, even to the point of enjoying it, while others find that their performance can be ruined.

Stress will almost certainly increase if there is an audience or a crowd watching. Top performers usually respond very well to this situation and actually look forward to it, being disappointed if there are not many people watching. It is very unlikely that anyone would reach the top level of their sport if they could not cope with this situation.

Pressure

This is something that others, usually opponents, bring to a physical activity. If a player is unable to cope with it ('cracking under pressure' is a common term), it will certainly have a bad effect on the way they perform.

Players, or competitors, are always trying to put their opponents under pressure by the way they play the game. If they find a weakness they make the most of it.

Being able to keep going when under pressure is vital for a player to be successful. This is what is meant by the expression 'soaking up the pressure'.

Motivation

This is the amount of determination a player has to do well. Highly motivated players are more likely to cope with anxiety, tension, boredom, stress and pressure because they are positive about what they are doing and they want to succeed.

Some people can be motivated just by the desire to win. For others, it is the rewards that go with winning (e.g. money and fame) that are most important.

It is probably more difficult to motivate people who are used to winning because of this. They have become used to being the best and it can then be difficult for them to motivate themselves sufficiently to stay at the top in their sport. This is why top sportspeople often employ a personal coach or trainer to help, not only with their physical preparation but also with their mental preparation and motivation.

Task 4

Describe the ways a crowd can influence a player or team. Explain the differences between how a 'home' team and an 'away' team might respond.

Figure 21.2 These netballers have to perform in front of large crowds; this can be quite stressful for some but stimulating for others

Psyching up

This is how players prepare to perform well. Different approaches are used, from calmly talking through the game or match, to arousing an emotional state of excitement and commitment to winning.

Hints and Tips!

It is important to be aware that physiological and psychological factors can have different effects on different individuals and that some of the factors can have both good and detrimental effects. Be aware of the ones that will clearly only have a bad effect on a performance.

Key questions

1. What effects can lack of sleep have on the body? How could that affect a sporting performance?
2. What is fatigue? What are the problems that can occur if someone is suffering from fatigue? What could be done to deal with it?
3. Explain how the following factors may affect a sporting performance:
   (a) tension; (b) anxiety; and (c) boredom.
4. Define motivation. How can it help a performer to do well in a sporting situation?
5. Explain what is meant by extrovert and introvert personality types. What types of activities would each be most suited to?

22 The skeletal system

Functions of the skeleton

The human skeleton has five functions:

- support
- protection
- movement
- shape
- blood cell production and storage of mineral salts.

These functions contribute to the skeletal system helping with a performance, most notably in allowing movement.

Support

The skeleton provides support for muscles and many delicate vital organs. It is the framework around which the body is constructed. Without it our bodies would collapse.

Protection

The skeleton provides a protective cover. The skull protects the brain, and the ribs protect the heart and lungs. Without this protection injuries would be far more common and serious.

Movement

Where two or more bones meet there is a joint. This is the point at which movement occurs, with the help of muscles (see Chapter 23). The amount of movement differs between different joints (see page 85).

Shape

The skeleton is the basic framework of our bodies and, as such, it gives us our shape. Muscle size and the amount of body fat also contribute to this.

Blood cell production and storage of mineral salts

These are lesser-known functions of the skeleton. Red and white blood cells are produced in the bone marrow, and mineral salts such as calcium are stored in the bones.

> **Key point**
> Although the skeleton is a very important body system and gaining knowledge regarding it is important, it is also important to realise how it inter-relates with the other body systems.

> **Hints and Tips!**
> The skeleton contributes to movement during physical activity. However, the actual movement occurs as a result of the combined effort of the nervous system (which sends the command to the brain) and the muscular and skeletal systems all working together.

> **Task 1**
> Name some other vital organs that are protected by parts of the skeleton. Name the bones that protect them. (Try using the scientific or technical names for these bones.)

Did you know?

The longest bone in your body is the femur, or thigh bone.

Task 2

Work in pairs. Take turns to identify as many bones in your body as you can, using just their scientific (or technical) term. See how many you each get right.

Task 3

Identify which of your joints has the greatest range of movement.

Task 4

With a partner, see if you can identify the **five** different regions of each other's vertebral column.

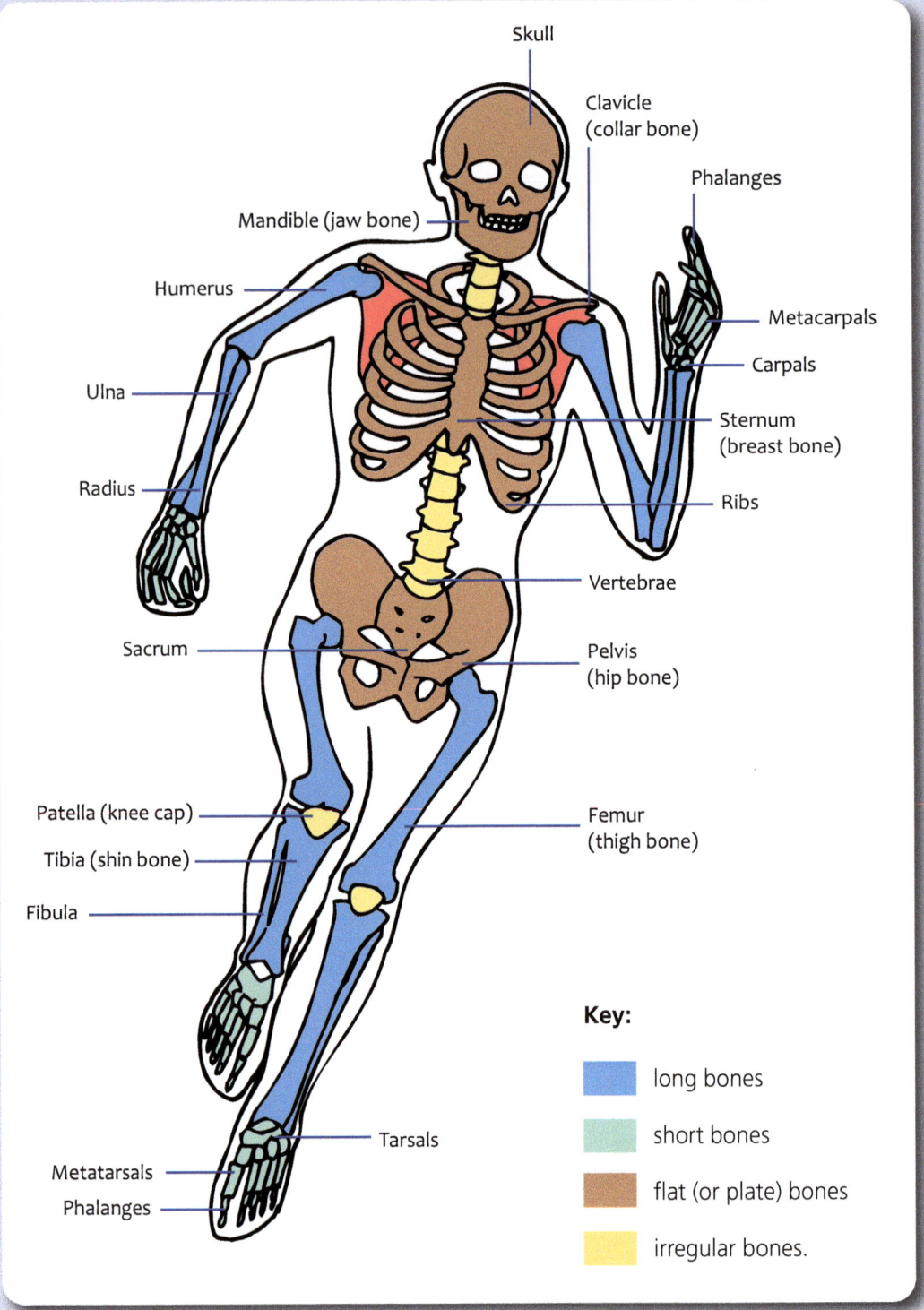

Figure 22.1 The human skeleton

Classification of bones

Figure 22.1 shows and names the bones that make up the skeletal system. The four types of bone are:

- long bones
- short bones
- flat (or plate) bones
- irregular bones

84 The skeletal system

Long bones

These are coloured blue in the diagram. They include the femur, humerus, tibia, fibula, radius and ulna. These bones are used in most of our movements, including any type of running or throwing. The greatest ranges of movement occur at the joints of these bones. These are the main points of flexibility (see Chapter 15).

Short bones

These are coloured green in the diagram. They include the wrist and ankle bones (carpals and tarsals). They are used to help you grip things and to enable you to balance and perform fine movements.

Flat (or plate) bones

These are coloured brown in the diagram. They include the skull, ribs, pelvis and scapula and are very important for protection. They are also the bones to which the larger muscles in the body are attached.

Irregular bones

These are coloured in yellow in the diagram. Most of these are in the face and the vertebrae in the spine (also known as the **vertebral column**). There are a total of 14 bones in the face. There are 33 bones in the vertebral column.

Joints and movement

All bones are solid and rigid, and do not bend, so movement has to occur in areas where the bones are connected by joints. Examples of these joints are shown in the diagrams opposite. The types of joints (or areas of articulation) are:

- immovable (**fibrous** or fixed) – e.g. the skull bones and the pelvic bones
- slightly movable (**cartilaginous**) – e.g. the vertebrae of the spine and the pubic bones
- freely movable (**synovial**) – these are the majority of joints that allow the greatest amount of movement; there are different types of freely movable (synovial) joints.

Freely movable (synovial) joints

The six types of joints are shown in Figure 22.2. These joints all have things in common, although the type and range of movement they allow is quite different. Common characteristics are as follows.

- **Hyaline cartilage** – this is a shiny, smooth and white covering on the surface and ends of the bone. It serves two purposes, as it protects and reduces friction (rubbing) between the bones at joints.
- **Ligaments** – these are bands of fibre attached to each of the bones and linking the joints. They keep the joints stable and control the amount of movement.

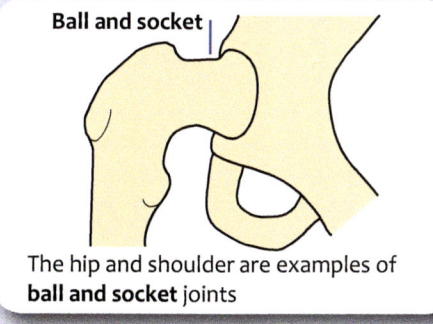

Ball and socket joint

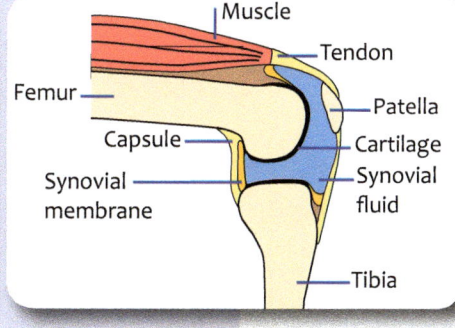

Knee joint

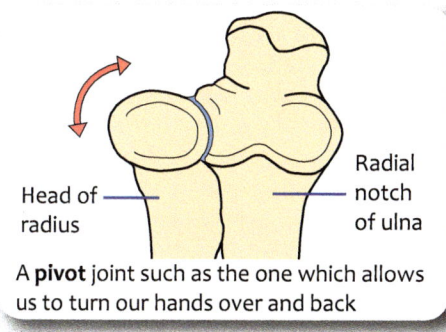

Pivot joint

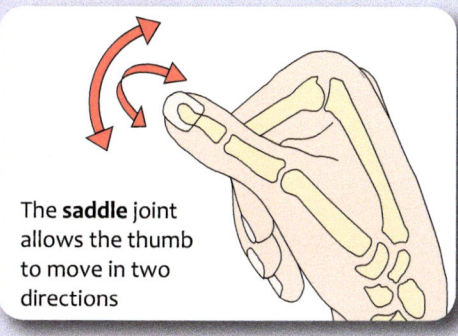

Saddle joint

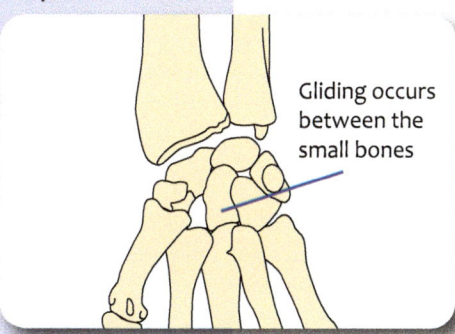

Gliding joint

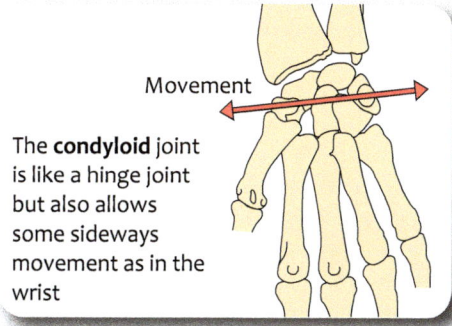

Condyloid joint

Figure 22.2 The six freely movable types of joints

> **Task 5**
>
> Work in pairs. Take turns to ask your partner to perform a movement, describing it by its technical (scientific) term only. See how many you each get right.

- **Synovial membrane** – this is a thin layer of tissue that is on the inside of the **articular capsule** (tissue that surrounds the joint). It produces synovial fluid that is like a type of oil, as it lubricates the joint and allows smooth movement.
- **Articular discs or menisci** – these act like shock absorbers and are attached to the capsule on the outside edges of the joints.

Connective tissue

We have already seen that bones need to be connected to each other in order to allow movement. The various forms of tissue that allow this to happen are as follows.

- **Cartilage** – like the hyaline cartilage in the synovial joints, this is a tough but flexible tissue that acts as a buffer between the bones at joints. There is quite a complicated arrangement of cartilage in the knee joint (as can be seen in Figure 22.3) and many injuries result in damaged cartilage. Your ear flaps and nose are almost all cartilage.
  - **Tendons** – these are very strong, non-elastic cords that join muscles to bones. Some are flat and broad. There can be one or more tendons, depending on the size of the muscle.
  - **Ligaments** – see above.

The vertebral column

The general functions of the vertebral column (spine) are to:

- keep the body upright
- help posture and movement
- act as a shock absorber
- protect the spinal cord.

The vertebral column can be divided into five separate regions, each with its own specific functions.

The five regions of the spinal column and their functions are as follows.

- **Cervical vertebrae** (or neck) – seven vertebrae make up this region. The top two are known as the atlas and axis. This region allows head movement such as nodding and shaking, and bending and twisting of the neck. The neck muscles are attached here.
- **Thoracic vertebrae** (or chest) – 12 vertebrae make up this region. These vertebrae are attached to the ribs and support the rib cage. There is some movement here allowing some bending and turning of the trunk.
- **Lumbar vertebrae** (or lower back) – there are five vertebrae in this region and they are the largest of all the vertebrae. The back muscles are attached here.
This is where there is the greatest amount of movement for bending forwards, backwards and from side to side. This is the most common area for back injuries due to the amount of movement and it is an area that should be especially worked on for flexibility exercises.
- **Sacral vertebrae** – there are five vertebrae in this region that are fused together to become one. This is where the spine is joined to the pelvis and where body weight is transmitted to the hips and legs.

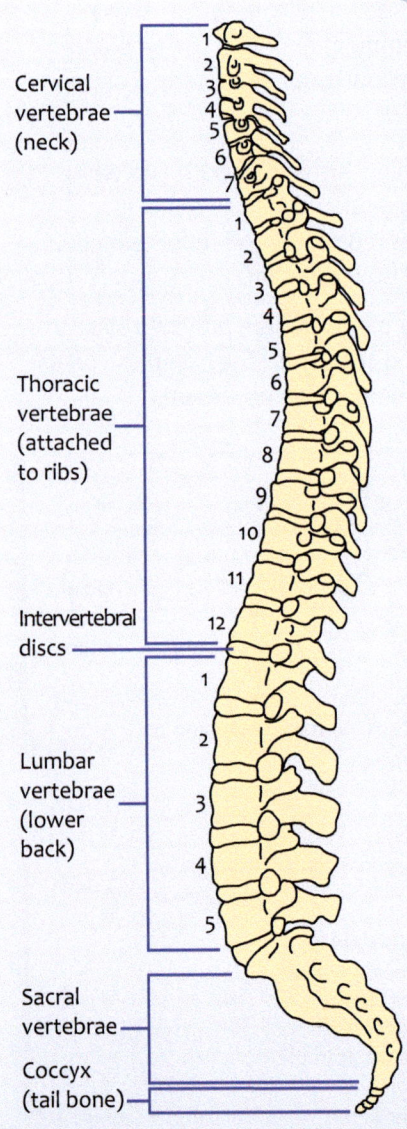

Figure 22.3 The spinal column

- **Coccyx** (or tail) – this is the very base of the spine and is made up of four vertebrae fused together.

It is very important to protect the back during any physical activities. Any injuries to the back should be treated as serious and with caution, as it possible that the spinal cord could be damaged. In extreme cases, back injury could lead to paralysis.

Types of movements at joints

Joints allow us to move in different ways. These different movements have technical names to describe them.

- **Flexion** – this is the decreasing of an angle between two bones, such as bending the leg at the knee or bending the arm up at the elbow towards the shoulder. This is the movement needed for a bicep curl, for example.
- **Extension** – this is when the angle is increased between two bones (the opposite of flexion), such as straightening the leg at the knee or lowering the arm from the shoulder. Kicking a ball requires extension of the leg.
- **Rotation** – this is when a bone may move round freely in a curve, such as the movement of the arm at the shoulder. Bowling a delivery at cricket is an example of this.
- **Abduction** – this is the movement of a bone or limb away from the body. Lifting your leg up and outwards sideways from the hip is an example of this.
- **Adduction** – this is the movement of a bone or limb towards the body (the opposite of abduction), so returning the leg back down to its straight position after lifting it up would be an example of this.

All movement involves one or more of the types mentioned earlier. It is no coincidence that most of the movements have opposite movements to counteract them. We shall see in Chapter 23 that muscles are always arranged in pairs so that movement can take place in both directions.

Movement and levers

A lever is something solid or rigid that can be used to apply force. In human movement this is brought about by the action of the muscles moving the bones. The central point of this movement is always the joint around which the movement is taking place.

If you do a chin-up on a chin bar the muscles and bones of your arms are acting as levers, and the central point (known as the fulcrum) is your elbow joint. It is an advantage to have short levers (a short overall arm length) for performing chin-ups.

If you want to add more strength to a movement you can make your levers shorter by bending. For example, pushing in a rugby scrum with bent legs is more efficient than trying to push with straight legs. You can get more power into a tennis volley with a bent arm than you can with a straight one.

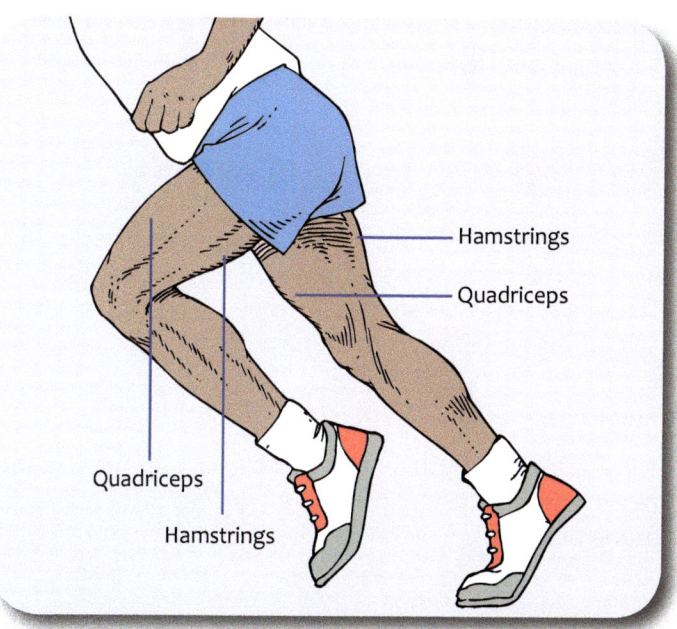

Figure 22.4 Muscles are arranged in pairs, e.g. quads and hamstrings

Key questions

1. Name five functions of the skeleton.
2. Name the four different bone classification types. Give an example for each type.
3. Choose five different bones in the body and describe exactly where they are located.
4. Name three different types of joints and give an example of each.
5. Name three different types of movement and give an example of each.
6. Explain (a) what cartilage is; and (b) what ligaments are.

23 The muscular system

A human has more than 600 muscles in their body. Muscles make up half of our total body weight. The muscles and muscle groups (when specific groups of muscles work together) combine with the skeletal system (see Chapter 22) to allow movement. Just how effective this movement is able to be through the combined actions of the body systems will have a great effect on the levels of performance you are able to achieve.

There are three particular types of muscle:

- voluntary (or skeletal) muscle
- involuntary (or smooth) muscle
- cardiac muscle.

Voluntary or skeletal muscle

These are sometimes called striped or **striated muscle**. They make up the majority of the muscles in the human body (see Figure 23.4). They also help to give the body its shape. They are called voluntary because they are under your control (through the nervous system) and only move when you want them to.

Involuntary or smooth muscle

These are muscles you cannot control. They are found in the walls of the intestine and in the blood vessels. Even though you cannot control these muscles at all, they work automatically all the time that you are alive.

Cardiac muscles

These are also involuntary muscles as they work constantly and automatically. They are a special type of muscle found only in the wall of the heart. The beating of your heart is a muscular action that goes on all the time. As you will see (Chapter 25), your heart beats approximately 72 times a minute, so cardiac muscles work very hard.

Muscles and movement

Muscles can only pull. They cannot push, so they have to work in pairs in order for any movement to take place.

As one of the muscles contracts (becomes shorter), the other one of the pair has to relax (it lengthens). This causes movement at the joint around which the two muscles are attached.

> **Key point**
> Muscles are always arranged in pairs because they only pull and cannot push.

> **Did you know?**
> There are around 150 muscles in your head and neck alone!

> **Task 1**
> Look at the image below and discuss with a partner how the biceps in this image may look if it was a weightlifter's arm.
>
>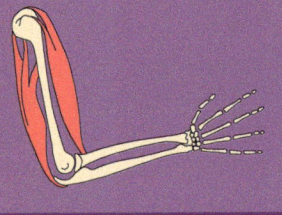

> **Task 2**
> Bend and straighten your arm. As you do so, use the fingers of the other hand to press gently on the triceps and biceps muscles. See if you can feel the movement taking place. Try to feel the location of the origin and insertion of each of the muscles at the elbow and shoulder.

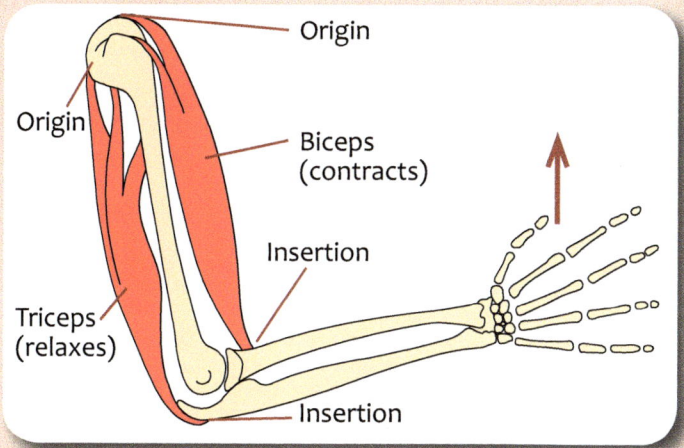

Figure 23.1 Example of how muscles need to work in pairs – here the biceps and triceps

An example of this is shown in Figure 23.1 where you can see how the arm can be moved around the elbow joint. If the biceps contracts, the triceps relaxes and the arm bends at the elbow. If the tricep then contracts and the bicep relaxes, the arm straightens back up.

The muscles involved in these movements are called:

- **prime mover (agonist)** – this is the muscle that contracts to cause the movement (in our example of bending at the elbow the prime mover is the biceps)
- **antagonist** – this is the muscle that relaxes and lengthens to allow the movement to take place (in the example of bending at the elbow it is the triceps).

The action of the muscles working together to enable movement is often referred to as antagonistic movement.

The way in which the muscle is actually attached to the bone is also very important and there are terms used to describe this.

- **Origin** – this is the end of the muscle that is actually fixed to the bone by **tendons** (see page 86).
- **Insertion** – this is the part of the muscle that actually moves the most. It is at the opposite end of the muscle to the origin.

In our example of the bending of the arm at the elbow, the origin of the triceps and biceps is at the shoulder and the insertion of both of them is at the elbow.

Types of muscle contraction

We have seen that muscles need to contract so that movement can take place. There are two different types of muscle contraction, called:

- isotonic
- isometric.

Isotonic contractions

There are two types of isotonic contractions.

- **Concentric contractions** – when the muscle shortens. In the elbow bending example the biceps muscle undergoes a concentric contraction because it shortens as the arm bends. This is also sometimes known as a dynamic contraction.
- **Eccentric contraction** – when the muscle gradually lengthens and returns to its normal length and shape. The biceps muscle undergoes an eccentric contraction when the arm straightens back up after it has been bent. This is sometimes also known as a static contraction.

Isometric contractions

In these contractions, there is no actual movement of a limb or a joint so the length of the muscle is not affected. The muscles are working although they are actually stationary – for example, when a gymnast performing a handstand holds the position by isometric contraction of the muscles in the arms. Once again, the triceps and biceps would be working but this time they would be undergoing an isometric contraction.

Categories of muscles

While all the different muscles in the body have different names they can also be put into categories depending upon the type of job that they do.

When the muscles are working as pairs to allow a movement at a joint, the muscles involved are known as:

- prime movers – the main muscles that contract to produce the movement
- antagonists – the muscles that work against the prime movers and relax to allow the movement to take place
- flexors – the muscles that bend a limb at a joint by contracting
- extensors – the muscles that work against the flexors and straighten a limb at a joint by contracting
- adductors – the muscles that move a limb towards the body
- abductors – muscles that move a limb away from the body.

Figure 23.2 shows a dual-use specialist weight-training machine which works on the adductors and the abductors of the legs.

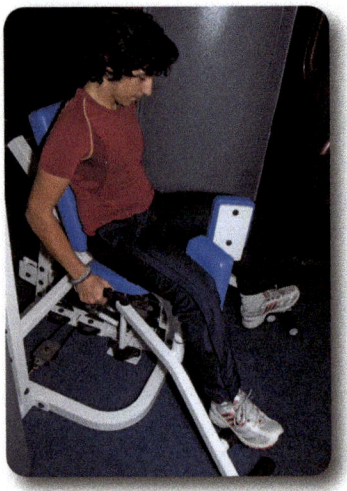 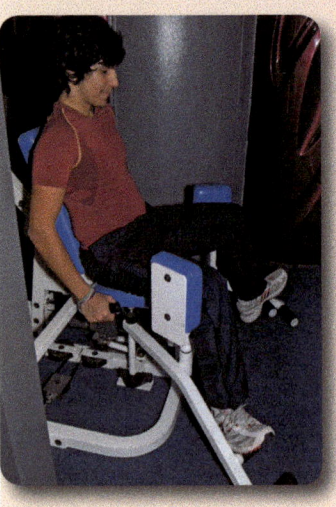

Figure 23.2 Equipment for working and strengthening adductor and abductor muscle groups

Muscle tone

Muscles are not usually completely relaxed, but keep some tension in them. It is very difficult to relax any of your voluntary muscles completely, no matter how hard you try.

The tension that remains in the muscle is known as **muscle tone**. It is important because it makes contracting your muscles for a movement to take place, easier. It means that the body is in a state of readiness as the muscles are prepared to do their job.

When you are asleep you lose body tone, whereas if you are particularly agitated or anxious your body tone will increase.

This is often called 'tightening up' or 'stiffening up', which is exactly what your body is doing!

Body tone affects your whole appearance as it helps you to maintain posture.

Did you know?

The adductor and abductor muscles in your leg can be strengthened by trying these two exercises:
- squeeze a medicine ball between your knees while sitting on a chair
- wrap a resistance band around your legs just above the knees during squats.

Posture

This is the way you hold your body. It is very important, not just so that you can look good (this could be especially important in some physical activities such as dance or gymnastics, where body shape and position are important), but also so that you can maintain good health. Poor posture can put a strain on certain parts of your body and cause muscular and skeletal damage. It can also cause damage to some of your internal organs so they become unable to operate properly. The two types of posture are:

- **static posture** – when you are sitting, standing or even lying down
- **dynamic posture** – when you are walking, running or moving more actively.

In both cases it is important that your posture is correct and that you are carrying or supporting your body correctly.

There is obviously an important link between the muscular system and good posture. There are some important rules to remember.

- Sit, stand and walk correctly.
- Exercise your muscles regularly.
- Wear sensible clothing and footwear.
- Lift and carry correctly; always lift with a straight back and bent legs.

Task 3

Put your hands flat against a wall and push hard with both arms straight. Feel the muscles contracting in your arms. Now work with a partner and feel how their biceps and triceps are both contracting.

Task 4

Work with a partner. Try to relax your arm or leg completely so that your partner can raise it easily and let it fall freely. Is it completely relaxed and moving freely?

Muscle fatigue

This occurs when the muscle – or a group of muscles – is unable to carry on contracting, and the movement you would like to make simply will not happen. If you would like to experience, or see the effect of muscle fatigue, try Task 6 on page 92.

Muscle cramp

This occurs when the muscle is locked in a contraction and is in **spasm**. It is really an involuntary contraction of the muscle and often follows a period of intensive exercise where the muscles have been overworked.

The way to relieve the cramp is to massage or rub the muscle with an ice pack and straighten the limb or affected area. Cramp can be extremely painful and the effects can last for some time, leaving a dull pain in the affected muscle. It can quite easily stop a performer from continuing or taking part in a physical activity.

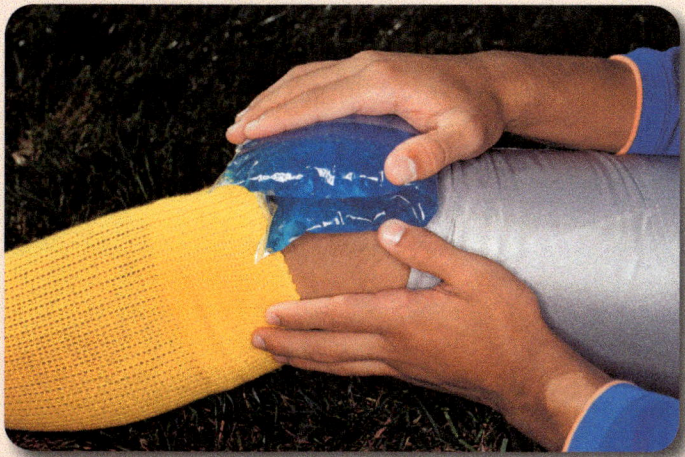

Figure 23.3 Cramp can be relieved by massaging with an ice pack

Muscle atrophy

This is a wasting, or a decrease in size, of a muscle. It can occur through a reduction of blood supply to the muscle over a long period of time. It may be due to inactivity or lack of use.

If someone has a broken leg that has to be placed in a plaster cast to immobilise it, the muscles of the leg can't be used to their full extent to contract and relax. There will therefore be a reduced amount of blood flow to them due to their inactivity, which will result in a certain amount of muscle wastage. This can be corrected by a programme of exercises to increase the activity of the muscles and build them up to their previous state.

Muscle structure

Muscles are made up of a mass of fibres that are wrapped in bundles. The middle, or belly, of the muscle usually bulges out (the biceps is a good example of this) and the muscle narrows at the ends where the tendons (see page 86) attach it to the bones.

Major muscles – location and their function

The major skeletal muscles are listed below with a description of where they are found in the body and the movements they help with. On some occasions their common names have been added in brackets.

- **Triceps** – located at the back of the upper part of the arm, between the elbow and the shoulder; they allow the arm to straighten.
- **Biceps** – located at the front of the upper arm, between the elbow and the shoulder; they allow the arm to bend and also to rotate slightly.
- **Deltoids** – located on the back of the shoulder joint; they allow the shoulder to move in all directions, up, down, backwards, forwards and to rotate.
- **Pectorals (pecs)** – located on the front of the upper chest; they help movement of the shoulders.
- **Trapezius** – located by the neck on the upper back; they help with shoulder movement as well as keeping the shoulder in position.
- **Abdominals (stomach)** – located at the front on the side of the stomach (external oblique abdominals) and across the front (rectus abdominus) of the stomach; they allow bending and turning of the trunk and also assist with breathing (see Chapter 27).
- **Latissimus dorsi (lats)** – located on the back from the armpit to the lower back; they allow movement at the shoulder backwards, forwards, up and down.
- **Gluteals** – located at the lower back around the bottom region at the back of the hips. The medius assists with walking and the maximus with climbing and standing up, as well as some rotation at the hips.
- **Quadriceps (quads)** – located at the upper front of the leg in the thigh region between the knee and the pelvis; they allow the leg to straighten.
- **Hamstrings** – located at the upper back of the leg between the knee and the pelvis, they allow movement of the hips and the knee, mainly the bending of the knee.
- **Gastrocnemius (calf)** – located at the back, bottom rear of the leg between the knee and the foot; they assist in walking, running and jumping movements and the pointing of the toes.

Task 5

Either check yourself or observe a partner sitting, standing and walking. Is the posture good or bad? What makes it good or bad?

Task 6

Hold your textbook with both arms straight out in front of you (at 90 degrees to your body). Keeping your arms straight, see how long you can hold the book for. You will eventually reach the point where the contraction of the muscles (the biceps and triceps) cannot be sustained any longer and you will have to lower your arms.

Task 7

Either on your own, or with a partner, perform a movement from a physical activity and try to identify the major muscles you have used. Try to use the correct terms for movement to describe what the types of movement were.

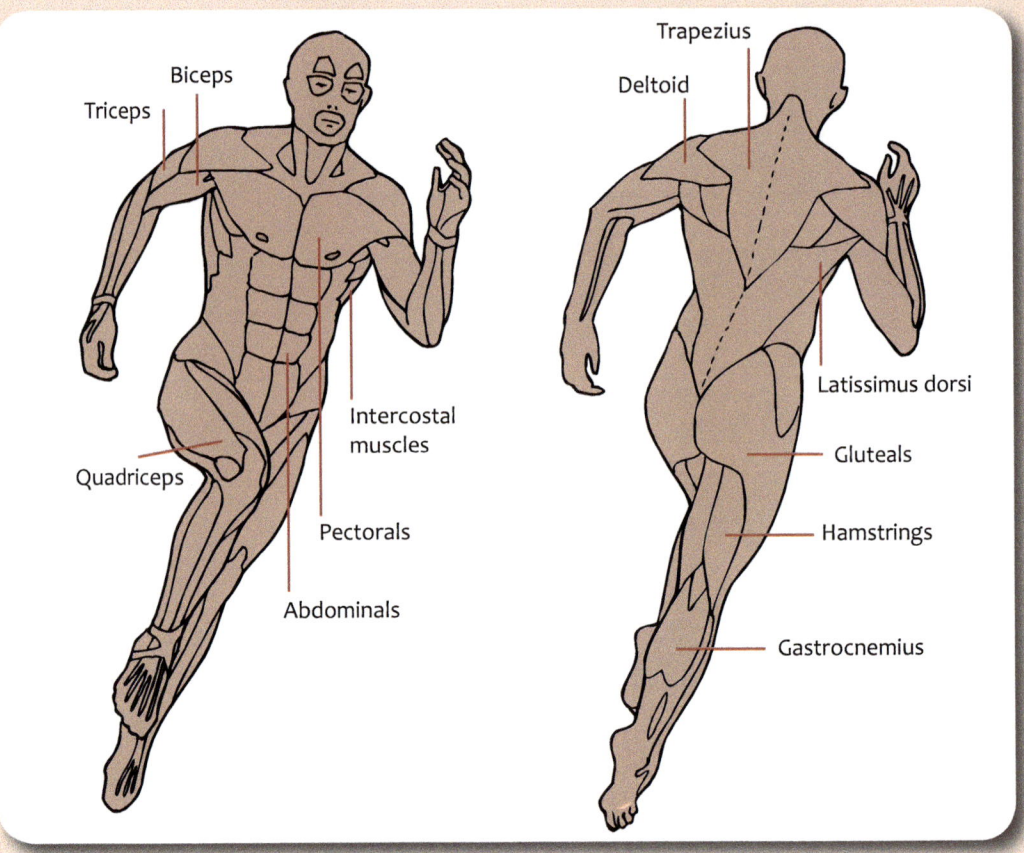

Figure 23.4 Front and rear skeletal muscles

The muscles listed above do not perform all of the movements on their own. Instead, they work together with other muscles to allow all of the complicated movements your body is capable of, especially when you are performing physical activities.

Hints and Tips!

It is important to be able to identify where certain muscles are and their basic actions. You should therefore know the main muscles (or muscle groups) that allow you to run, jump, throw and bend.

Key questions

1. Why are muscles arranged in pairs?
2. Describe the combined actions that take place between muscles and bones to allow physical movements to take place.
3. Name three different types of muscles.
4. How are muscles attached to bone?
5. Name four different muscles and describe exactly where they are located on the body.
6. Find a picture of an athlete in action. Label the major muscle groups as identified in the list on pages 91 and 92.

24 The nervous system

The muscular system (see Chapter 23) is controlled by the nervous system. This is how messages are sent from the brain to the muscle when movement is required. The nervous system is made up of two parts:

- **the central nervous system** – the brain and the spinal cord
- **the peripheral nervous system** – the nerves and the nerve centres that come from the spinal cord and branch out into the body.

Figure 24.1 shows the various parts of the nervous system.

Sensory organs

The nervous system first receives all of its messages through the sensory organs, i.e. the eyes, ears, nose, mouth and skin. These **original receptors** of information do not actually allow us to see, hear, move and so on. Instead, there is a complicated system of processes that takes place before the various functions of the nervous system come into play. These functions:

- control and co-ordinate our body movements
- allow us to see, hear, smell, taste, touch and experience physical sensations
- allow us to be aware of unseen things such as emotions and atmosphere as well as the environment
- enable us to think and act, and to use our memory or experience.

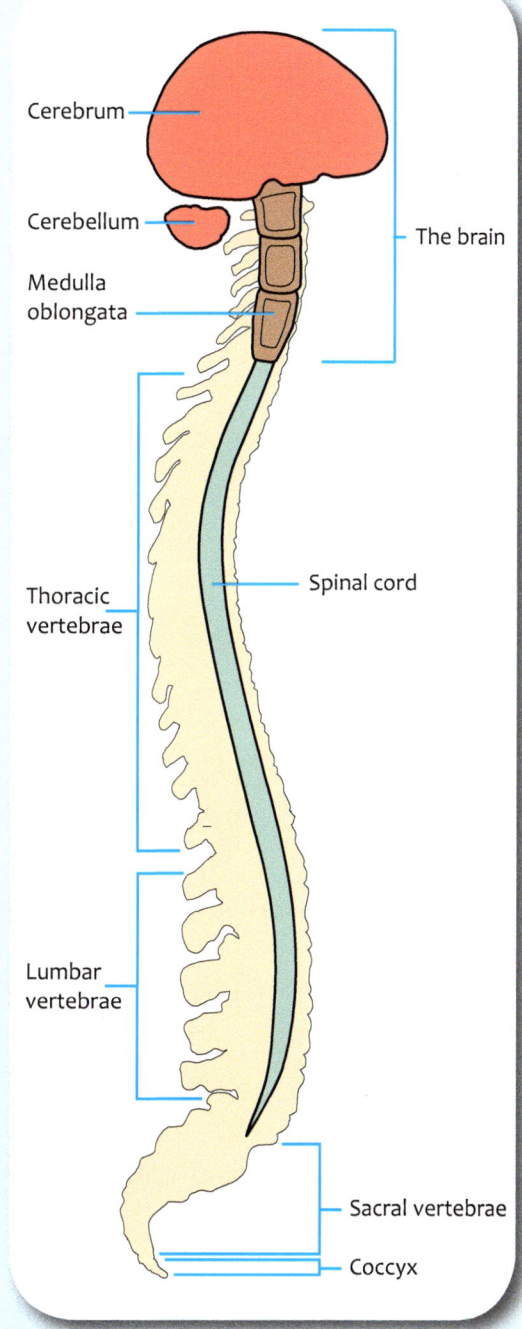

Figure 24.1 How the nervous system works

Key point

The nervous system must always be considered the link system with the other body systems, as it effectively controls them all. It integrates the information it receives and co-ordinates the activity of all parts of the body.

Task 1

Test how much you rely on your sight. Balance on an upturned bench and close your eyes. How long you can hold your position for?

Performer profile

Chris Gayle (born 1979 in Kingston, Jamaica) made his first-class debut for Jamaica at the age of 19. He played his first 1-day international 11 months later and his first test match 6 months after that. Not only is he a very successful batter (as a left-hander) but also a right-arm offbreak bowler. In 2009 Gayle hit the fifth fastest century (100 runs) in test-match history off just 70 balls. In 2010 he became the fourth cricketer to score two triple centuries in test cricket. He holds the record for the highest innings in a Twenty20 International, having scored 117 against South Africa in the 2007 World Twenty20.

Nerves (or neurons)

The **nerves**, or **neurons**, are the basic cells of the nervous system. They are made up of three parts:

- **nucleus** (**or soma**) – the main cell body
- **dendrites** – the thread-like fibres that pick up and receive impulses (messages)
- **axons** – the fibres that transmit the impulses (or messages) away from the nucleus.

The dendrites in a nerve are not connected like one long thread. They actually have gaps (called **synapses**) between them. For impulses to get from one dendrite to another they have to cross the synapse. They do this by means of electrical impulses released at the tip of the axon, and it is this constant relay between dendrite, axons and synapses that passes messages through the system at very great speed.

There are also two types of neurons:

- **sensory neurons** – these carry impulses from the sensory organs to the brain
- **motor neurons** – these carry impulses from the brain to muscles or any other body parts (e.g. glands).

Did you know?

The length of the vertebral column is an average of 71 centimetres for males and 61 centimetres for females with the spinal cord being 45 centimetres for males and 43 centimetres for females. A serious back or neck injury can result in a damaged, or even severed, spinal cord. Paralysis occurs when messages are no longer able to get through to the brain.

Figure 24.2 Cricketers like West Indies captain Chris Gayle wear specialist helmets when they are batting to protect their heads, and therefore their brains, from any dangerous blows from the cricket ball

Task 2

Work with a partner. Sit down and cross one knee over the other. Let your partner check your knee-jerk reflex by gently tapping your knee, just below the patella (knee cap) with the outside edge of their hand.

The brain

The brain has three main parts:

- **cerebrum** – the largest part of the brain, responsible for all conscious control such as movement, thoughts, speech, memory, etc.
- **cerebellum** – helps in body movement, as it controls such things as balance and co-ordination
- **medulla oblongata** – controls the automatic functions of the body such as breathing, the heart and digestion.

The brain is a very delicate organ and it is vital that it is not damaged in any way. It is protected by the skull and floats in a fluid. Any injury to the head can be very dangerous, as there is always a chance of damaging the brain. This is why any blow to the head must be treated very carefully. If a person loses consciousness they should always be checked by a doctor.

The spinal cord

This is attached to the base of the brain and runs down the body, encased in the vertebrae of the spinal column. It is the system that carries messages from the brain to other parts of the body as the nerve fibres branch out in all directions.

The autonomic nervous system

This is an involuntary system over which we have no control. It is this system that controls our reflexes such as knee-jerks and the dilation of the pupils of the eyes. Reflexes can be very useful as they can act as a protection system for the body.

Hints and Tips!

It is important to be able to identify when there is conscious use of the nervous system and when there is automatic use of it. This is why there is a link with voluntary and involuntary muscle movement (see Chapter 23), and being able to both describe these and give examples of them occurring is essential.

Key questions

1. Identify the two parts of the nervous system.
2. What is meant by original receptors? Give at least four examples of these.
3. Name the three parts of the nerves (or neurons).
4. Name the three different main parts of the brain. For each one briefly describe what function they each perform.
5. Describe the function of the spinal cord.

25 The circulatory system

The blood carries the body's 'fuel supply' and the circulatory system makes sure that it gets to all parts of our body, not only to keep us alive but also to ensure we function properly.

The circulatory system must be considered very closely with the other body systems because its efficiency can be greatly affected by the type and amount of training you do. Just as training affects it, the efficiency of this body system also affects how much training you are able to do!

The main functions of the circulatory system are:

- **transport** – carrying blood, water, oxygen and nutrients throughout the body, and transport and removal of waste
- **body temperature control** – the blood absorbs body heat and then carries it to the lungs and to the skin, where it is then released
- **protection** – it helps to fight disease, e.g. antibodies that fight infection are carried in the blood and the clotting of blood seals cuts and wounds.

The circulatory system has four main parts:

- the heart
- the blood vessels
- the blood
- the pulmonary and systemic circuits.

> **Key point**
> The circulatory system is very closely linked with the respiratory system, as it gets the oxygen to the vital organs and removes carbon dioxide as the waste product.

> **Did you know?**
> Your heart beats over 100,000 times each day!

The heart

Figure 25.1 shows a fully labelled diagram of the heart.

The heart is a muscle and, like any other muscle, it contracts and relaxes. Each time it does this it performs a **heartbeat**. We have seen before that your heart beats about 72 times a minute and this is increased a great deal when you exercise or take part in physical activity.

A typical human body has about 5 litres of blood (about 10 pints). This amount of blood is pumped by the heart in less than a minute.

The heart has four parts: two chambers at the top of the heart, called the **atria**, and two chambers at the bottom called the **ventricles**. The ventricles have thicker walls than the atria.

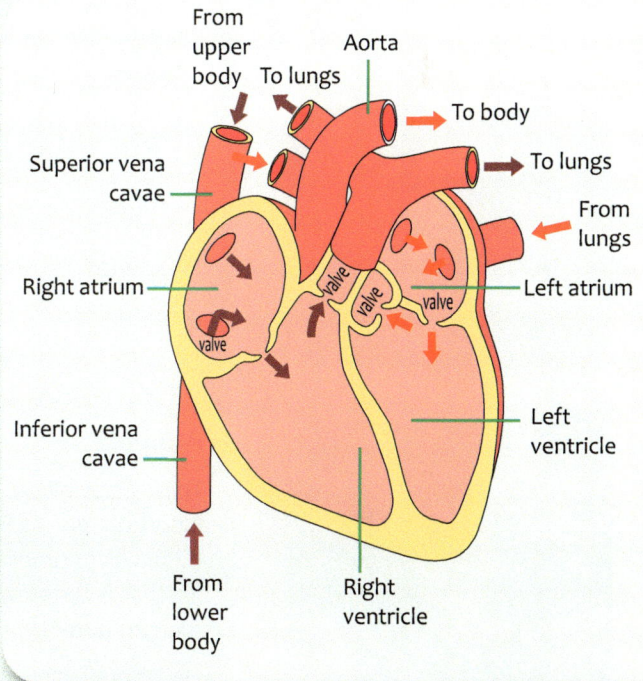

Figure 25.1 The heart

Task 1

What is the name of the device that a doctor uses to listen to a person's heartbeat?

The main function of the heart is to act as a pump, so that it can move the blood around the body. This is how the pumping action works.

- The blood enters the right atrium. At this time the blood is dark red because it does not contain much oxygen, but it does have some waste products, including carbon dioxide. (In Figure 25.4, blue has been used to represent deoxygenated blood.)
- The right atrium pumps this blood into the right ventricle, through the valve.
- The right ventricle pumps the blood through the **pulmonary artery** to the lungs where oxygen is picked up and carbon dioxide is deposited. The blood is now bright red due to the extra oxygen.
- From the lungs the blood returns to the left atrium through the **pulmonary vein**.
- The left atrium pumps the blood into the left ventricle and the blood leaves here through the **aorta** to be distributed to the rest of the body.

As the blood moves through the body, it loses its oxygen which is used by muscles and for other body functions. Then it returns to the right atrium and the cycle takes place all over again. This means that your heart works very hard. Chapter 16 showed just how important monitoring your heart rate is for assessing levels of fitness and particularly endurance.

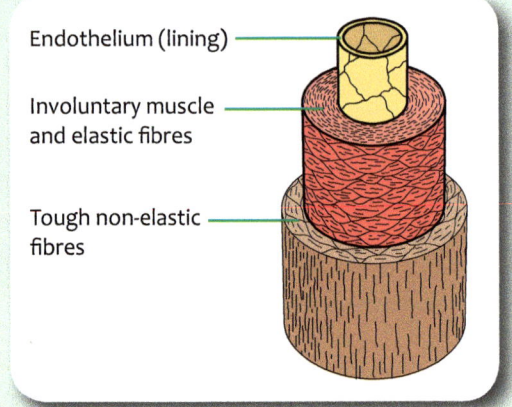

Figure 25.2 Vein   **Figure 25.3** Artery

Blood vessels

The three types of blood vessel are:

- arteries
- capillaries
- veins.

Arteries

These carry blood, at high pressure, away from the heart and they are the thickest of the blood vessels. As Figure 25.3 shows, the artery has an inner lining called the endothelium, then a layer of involuntary muscle and elastic fibres which control the diameter of the artery (so that it can expand and contract depending on the amount of blood flowing through), then an outer layer of tough fibrous tissue.

The aorta is the largest artery in the body and the arteries divide into smaller arteries known as **arterioles** and then into even smaller vessels known as capillaries.

Task 2

Explain why arteries are the thickest of the blood vessels.

Did you know?

You have about 5 litres of blood (about 10 pints) in your body and the heart is able to pump it all round your body in less than a minute!

Capillaries

These are subdivisions of the arteries and are fed by the arterioles. They are so small that they are only one cell thick. Because they are so thin they are **semi-permeable**, which means that they allow carbon dioxide, oxygen, nutrients and waste products to pass through their walls.

Capillaries are found in clusters where they feed the muscles, organs and body tissue and at the end of the capillaries the blood flows into the **veins**.

Veins

These are thinner than arteries although their structure is the same. The two outer layers of involuntary muscle and tough fibrous tissue are much thinner but the central layer (endothelium) is much the same (see Figure 25.2). The veins transport the blood back to the heart. One important feature that the veins have is a system of **valves** (also known as pocket valves), which stop the blood from flowing backwards.

The veins also receive some help pumping the blood. Muscles near to the veins help by their muscular contractions (this is known as the **skeletal pump**). These press on the veins and have a squeezing, pumping action. Arteries nearby push against the veins when there is a surge of blood through them. This action causes a pumping effect. Gravity assists blood flow in the veins above the heart, although it cannot help below. The action of breathing causes pressure changes which have a sucking effect on the blood.

As the heart pumps blood out it also causes a sucking action, which affects the veins close to the heart.

The blood

Cells

Cells make up 45 per cent of the blood and are its 'solid section'. There are three types.

- **Red blood cells (erythrocytes)** – these are extremely small but there are so many of them that they give the blood its red colour. They are produced in the bone marrow and contain **haemoglobin**. It is this that transports the oxygen and carbon dioxide. Production of these cells is very high.
- **White blood cells (leukocytes)** – there are not so many of these as red cells but they are also produced in the bone marrow and in the lymph tissue. Their main function is to fight against infection. They engulf foreign

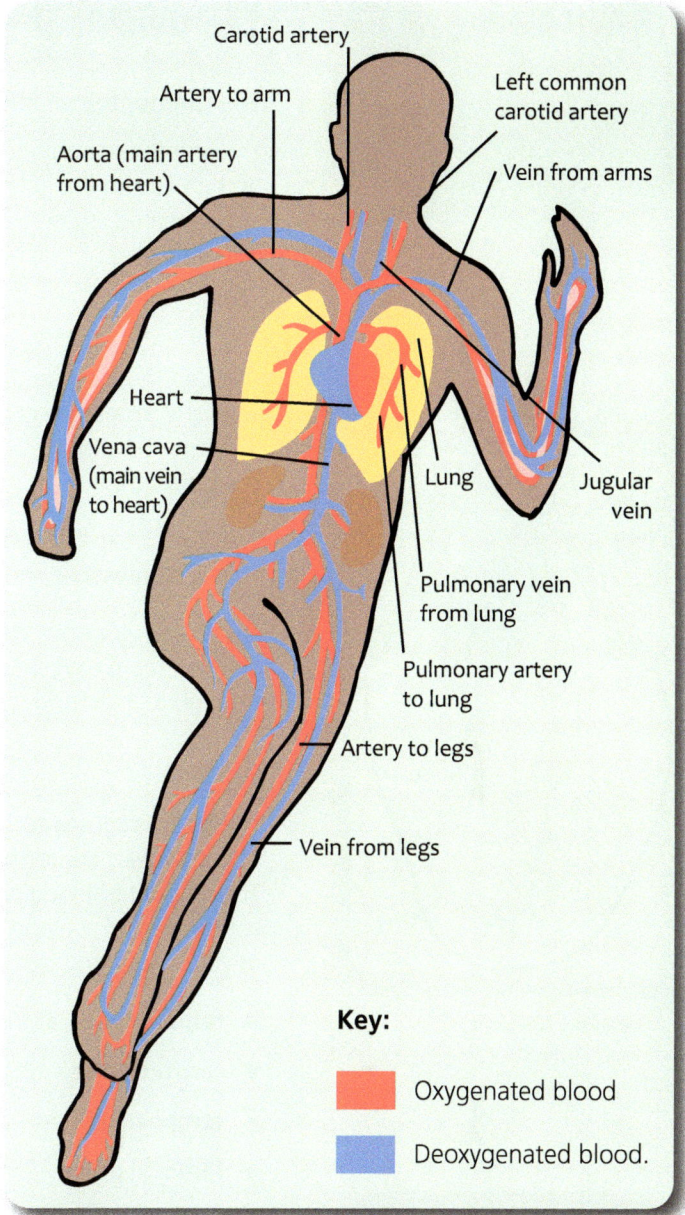

Figure 25.4 Circulation of oxygenated and deoxygenated blood around the body

bodies or bacteria. The pus in wounds is formed from dead leukocytes.

- **Platelets** – these help to clot the blood and are small fragments or particles of larger cells. They help to clot and seal the skin but also do the same job on small blood vessels that are damaged.

Plasma

This forms the remaining 55 per cent of the blood. It is the 'liquid section' and is mainly composed of water. It also contains fibrinogen protein (which helps in clotting), nutrients such as glucose and amino acids, waste products such as urea and carbon dioxide, and oxygen.

> **Did you know?**
> Up to 2 million red blood cells are produced and destroyed every second!

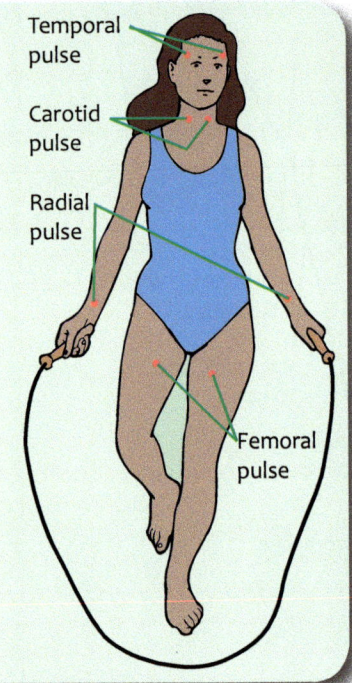

Figure 25.5 Pulse points

> **Task 3**
> Use Figure 25.5 to help you locate your pulse in each of the different areas. Make a note of the area in which you can locate it most easily, as this is useful for certain types of fitness testing.

The pulmonary and systemic circuits

The pulmonary circuit

This carries the deoxygenated blood (via the pulmonary artery) from the right ventricle of the heart to the lungs where it exchanges the carbon dioxide for oxygen, to become reoxygenated. Then the pulmonary vein transports the oxygenated blood to the left atrium of the heart.

The systemic circuit

Through this, the aorta carries the oxygenated blood from the left ventricle of the heart to all of the various body tissues, through the capillaries. The blood then flows back through the veins, having deposited the majority of the oxygen, and into the right atrium through the vena cava.

The main areas that the blood visits on this circuit are the cardiac muscle of the heart, the stomach, intestines and liver, the muscles and the skin.

The oxygen transported through this system is vital for physical activity. Because the muscles demand more oxygen when they are being used, the supply of oxygen has to be increased, through a greater flow of blood.

Pulse

The pulse is caused by the action of the heart as it pumps blood around the body. Every time the heart beats (this is the heart, or cardiac muscle contracting) it registers as a pulse. The amount of blood being pumped through the arteries makes the artery wall expand and contract and the blood rushing through the arteries causes the pressure wave that you feel as your pulse. You can check your pulse in any of the following places (see Figure 25.5):

- **radial pulse** – at the base of the thumb on the inside of the wrist
- **carotid pulse** – on either side of the neck
- **temporal pulse** – just over the temple at the side of the forehead
- **femoral pulse** – in the groin.

Blood pressure

The blood in the circulatory system is always under pressure. This is how it is pumped around the body. The pressure has to be higher in the arteries than in the veins because this is where the blood starts its journey.

Blood pressure is a measurement of how much pressure the blood flowing through the artery puts on the artery wall. It can be measured very accurately using a **sphygmomanometer**, which puts pressure on the artery wall by squashing it and then gives readings of the pressure exerted. Two readings are always taken:

- **systolic pressure** – the pressure of the blood in the arteries when the left ventricle contracts
- **diastolic pressure** – the pressure of the blood in the arteries when the left ventricle relaxes.

The final reading is like a fraction, with the systolic pressure at the top and the diastolic underneath.

Blood pressure readings should be taken when you are resting, not exercising, and should range from 100 over 60 (that is 100 systolic pressure over 60 diastolic pressure) to 140 over 90. The average for a young person is about 120 over 80.

Your blood pressure reading is taken in any medical test you might have as it is a very good indicator of ill health and a measure of how efficient your heart is. Blood pressure can be affected by:

- **age** – blood pressure is usually lower in young people than in adults
- **sex** – blood pressure readings vary between males and females
- **exercise** – exercising increases the blood pressure
- **stress and tension** – both can increase blood pressure
- **circulatory system condition** – if the heart or blood vessels are not in good condition, blood pressure will increase.

Blood pressure does vary but there is only cause for concern if it is consistently high. High blood pressure may indicate that the heart is finding it more difficult to pump blood around the body. This could be caused by narrowing or blocked arteries, and would mean that the heart has to work harder to maintain circulation. This may lead to a state where the heart muscle temporarily gets starved of oxygen, which can result in a sharp pain in the chest which is known as angina. The situation may become even more serious and can result in a **heart attack** (where the heart stops because it is starved of oxygen) or a **stroke** (where the brain is starved of oxygen). Both are very serious life-threatening conditions.

Blood pressure can be reduced by:

- increasing regular exercise
- following a sensible diet to reduce or control weight
- stopping smoking
- taking medications
- avoiding stress (or 'managing' stress).

Diseases associated with the heart are the most common cause of death in the Western world. Keeping your blood pressure under control and within acceptable limits is one of the most effective ways of avoiding these diseases.

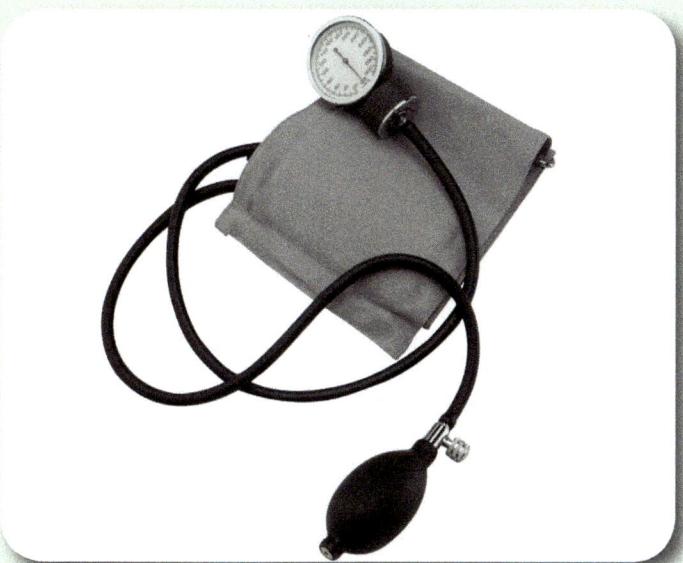
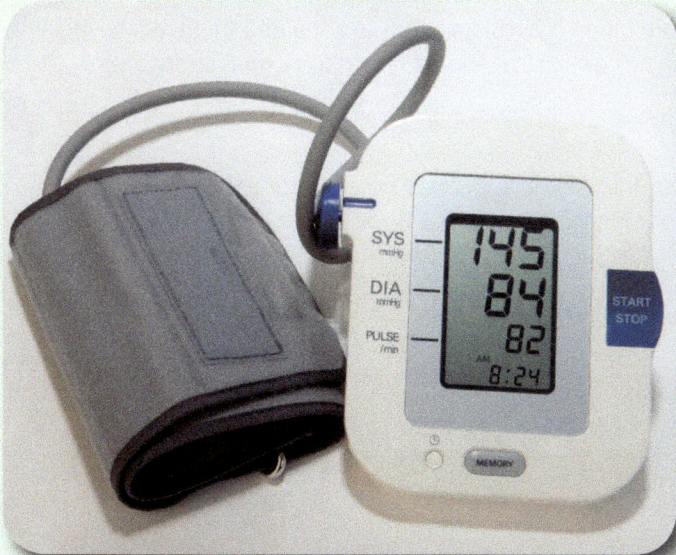
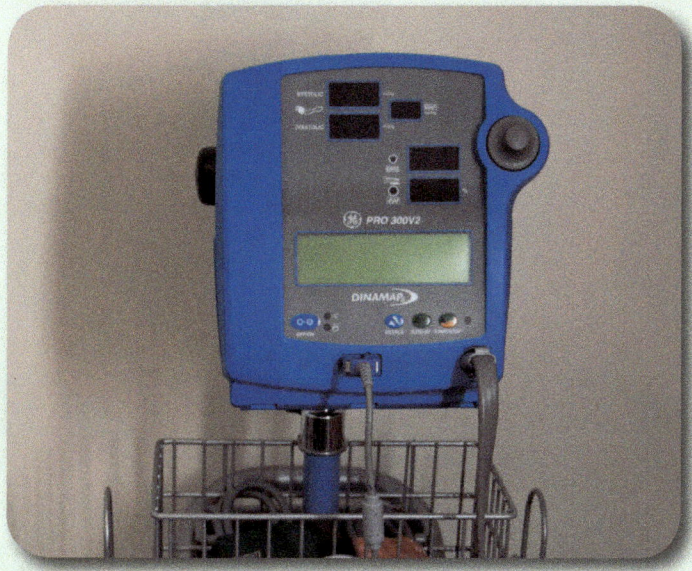

Figure 25.6 Examples of blood pressure monitors

The circulatory system

Task 4

Design a promotional poster entitled 'Exercise can seriously improve your health', based on the information here.

Exercise and the circulatory system

Exercise affects the body in several ways.

Heart rate (pulse rate)

This increases greatly during exercise and can easily double. The reason for this is the increased demand for oxygen as the muscles, in particular, need increased amounts to be able to work at the increased rate. There are certain areas or zones you should be aware of and work to when exercising.

Heat production

Exercise causes an increase in body temperature and heat is produced. Extra water and salts in the capillaries need to be removed as waste products. This is achieved through sweating. Waste is dispersed through the skin via the blood capillaries and pores in the skin surface.

Blood pressure

This increases with exercise as more blood is circulated. This is not a bad thing, as the increase is only temporary during the period of exercise. It should return to normal afterwards.

Skin colour

The blood vessels at the surface of the skin have to open up or dilate to allow the heat to escape. This causes the 'flushed' or reddening effect. It is usually most clearly seen on the face.

There is clearly a strong link between the circulatory system and the respiratory system, which is responsible for initially drawing oxygen into the body (see Chapter 26).

Hints and Tips!

It is important to be aware of the functions of the circulatory system and to be able to link the way in which this function is achieved. The transport function would be the most important of these and it is this system which links closely to the circulatory system.

Key questions

1. List the three main functions of the circulatory system.
2. Which is the most important of the three functions in your opinion? Why?
3. What is the link between the circulatory system and the respiratory system?
4. Identify the main function of the heart.
5. Name the three different types of blood vessels and briefly describe the function they perform.
6. Name the three different types of blood cells and for each one describe what they do.
7. What is plasma and what is it made up of?
8. Describe the way in which you could make the circulatory system more efficient and also describe the effects that exercise has on the system.

26 The respiratory system

The respiratory system consists of:
- the air passages
- the lungs
- the diaphragm.

Together, these are responsible for bringing air into the body, circulating it and then expelling it (see Figure 26.1).

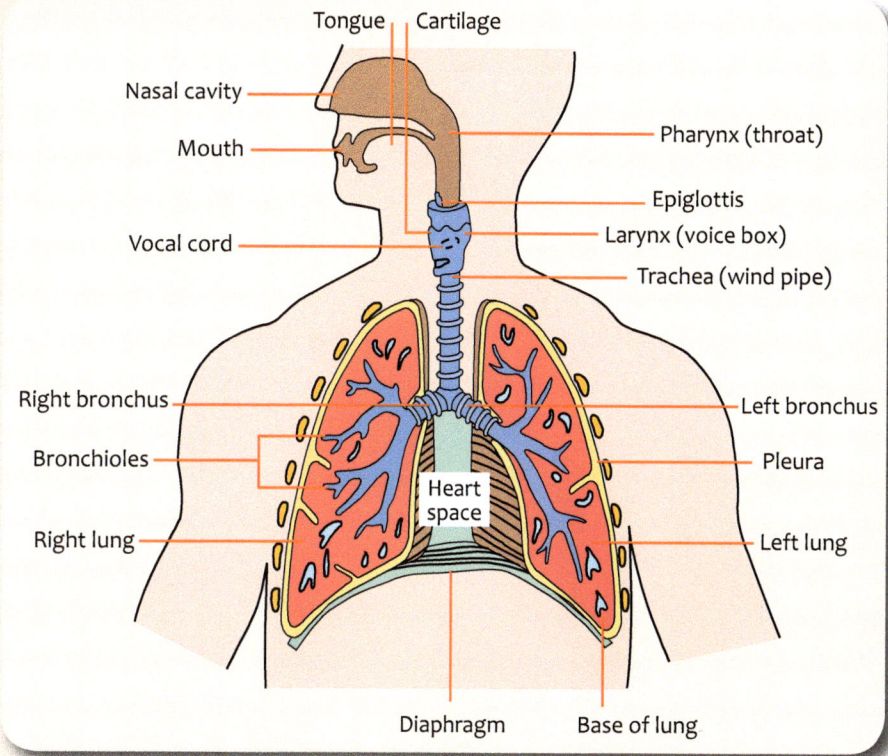

Figure 26.1 The respiratory system

The air passages

These are made up of the following parts.

Nasal cavity

Air enters through the nostrils. In each of these two cavities there are three ridges that are covered in a thick, mucous membrane that filters the air and warms and moistens it. The filtering is done by the cilia, which are small hairs that trap dust, pollen and any other airborne impurities.

Mouth

Air also enters here. The mouth is separated from the nasal cavity by the palate, which allows you to chew food at the same time as you breathe.

Pharynx

This allows both food and air to enter; the food goes into the **oesophagus** and the air travels through the larynx.

Epiglottis

This is a flap at the back of the throat that prevents food from going down the trachea or windpipe when you swallow.

Larynx (or voice box)

The epiglottis is at the upper opening of the larynx and the air passes through here to the trachea. It is in the larynx that the voice is produced, as air moves over the vocal chords.

> **Key point**
> Breathing and respiration are very closely linked, as respiration is what happens as we are breathing.

> **Task 1**
> Pinch your nose tightly and breathe only through your mouth. What difference does it make to your breathing?

> **Did you know?**
> The condition known as bronchitis gets its name from the bronchus where it occurs.

Trachea (or windpipe)

This is a large tube consisting of rings of cartilage. It is flexible but the cartilage rings are rigid and keep it open.

Bronchus

These are at the base of the trachea where it branches out into two smaller tubes known as the left and right bronchus or bronchi.

Bronchioles

The bronchi, in turn, branch out into smaller tubes known as bronchioles and these sub-divide into tiny air sacs, which are called **alveoli**. There are millions of these and they make up the majority of the lung tissue. It is here that the exchange of oxygen and carbon dioxide takes place. This will be dealt with in more detail later.

The lungs

These are the main organs of the respiratory system. They are inside the chest cavity protected by the ribs at the back, sides, front and the diaphragm at the bottom. The lungs are like two balloons. There is a slight difference between the two as the right lung is slightly larger, with three sections (or lobes), while the left has only two sections.

The lungs are surrounded by a double layer of membranes called the **pleura**. This acts like a lubricant, as it is smooth and moist and contains fluid. This protects the lungs from any friction as they get bigger and smaller during breathing.

> **Did you know?**
> The illness known as pleurisy is named after the area of the lungs, the pleura, where it occurs.

The diaphragm

This is a large muscle sheet that seals off the chest cavity from the abdominal cavity. Also, by contracting and relaxing, it is responsible for the action of breathing.

Training

The respiratory system is greatly affected by the amounts and levels of training you do. Endurance training (see Chapter 16) is specifically linked to the respiratory system, which is why knowledge of how the system works and functions is important.

> **Task 2**
> Check your resting breathing rate by counting how many breaths you take in 1 minute. Now check your breathing rate when you are taking part in strenuous exercise.

The action of breathing

Breathing involves two types of movement:

- **inspiration** – breathing in
- **expiration** – breathing out.

Inspiration

When we breathe in, the chest cavity changes shape and size. The diaphragm changes from a dome shape, flattens and moves downwards. At the same time the **intercostal muscles** raise the ribs and push out the sternum, which makes the cavity larger. This reduces the pressure inside the chest cavity and causes air to be sucked into the lungs.

Expiration

When we breathe out, the reverse procedure takes place. The diaphragm relaxes and so do the intercostal muscles. Because of this the chest cavity returns to its normal size and the pressure on the lungs is increased, which forces the air out.

When our bodies are at rest we breathe between 14 and 16 times a minute. If we increase our activity or movement by taking part in physical activity this rate increases greatly. This type of breathing is called **forced breathing** and the rate can increase to anything up to 50 a minute!

In Chapter 25 we saw that during exercise the body needs more oxygen to be supplied via the blood so the breathing rate has to increase as well.

Types of lung volume or capacity

- **Tidal volume** – the amount of air you breathe in and out, normally. It increases with exercise.
- **Inspiratory capacity** – the amount of air taken in after a normal expiration when forced breathing is taking place. It increases with exercise.
- **Expiratory reserve volume** – the amount of air that can be forced out after a normal expiration. There is a slight decrease in this during exercise.
- **Vital capacity** – the largest volume of air that can be expired after the deepest possible inspiration. There is a slight decrease in this during exercise.
- **Residual volume** – the amount of air that remains in the lungs after the maximum expiration. There is a slight increase in this during exercise.

The total lung capacity is worked out by adding the vital capacity to the residual volume.

It is possible to measure the lung capacity but this is not always a good indicator of either fitness or levels of endurance, although the greater your capacity, the more likely you are to be successful at endurance events. It will show up any abnormalities that could be caused by asthma or excessive smoking but it is the efficiency of the respiratory system that is most important.

Inhaled air and **exhaled** air are completely different. Inhaled air is high in oxygen and nitrogen, low in carbon dioxide. Exhaled air is high in nitrogen and oxygen but has much higher levels of carbon dioxide.

It is a misconception that we simply breathe in oxygen and breathe out carbon dioxide, as neither of these makes up the highest proportion of the air we breathe. Nitrogen has the highest level, at approximately 79 per cent for both inspiration and expiration. The oxygen levels are 21 per cent for inspiration and 16 per cent for expiration. The levels for carbon dioxide are 0.004 per cent during inspiration and 4 per cent during expiration.

The exchange of these two gases occurs in the lungs.

Gaseous exchange

This is the process that allows oxygen to be taken in from the air and for it to be 'exchanged' for carbon dioxide. This is how it happens.

- Oxygen, which has been breathed in, passes through the minute alveoli (air sacs) and into the red blood cells.
- The oxygen combines with the haemoglobin to form **oxyhaemoglobin**.
- An enzyme in the red cells breaks down the carbon dioxide, which is being transported in the blood (in the form of sodium bicarbonate), and turns it into a gas.
- The carbon dioxide gas then passes back through the alveoli and is breathed out through the lungs.

This process is vital for our bodies because it is the combination of food and oxygen acting together which produces the body's energy. The carbon dioxide and water are the waste products that must be removed.

Exercise and the respiratory system

An increase in the activity of the body, such as vigorous exercise, will have the following effects.

Breathing rate

This will increase greatly, up to three times the resting rate. The breathing becomes noisier and more obvious, especially to someone watching. The rate can increase so much that you can literally be left gasping for air.

VO$_2$ (or oxygen uptake)

This will increase greatly (see Chapter 16 for details). The body will need more oxygen as energy so the uptake will have to be increased to cater for this. Quite simply, the more activity you do, the more oxygen you need, but this can only go up to certain levels, so when you are at your limit you have achieved your VO$_2$ maximum.

Oxygen debt

You will develop oxygen debt after about 5 minutes or more of constant exercise. This is the point when the exercise becomes **anaerobic** (without the use of oxygen, which has to be paid back later – hence oxygen debt). If the exercise is just aerobic (with oxygen) then there will be no oxygen debt (see Chapter 16 for details).

Vital capacity

This will increase, as the volume of air required has increased.

Residual volume

This only increases slightly, and so does the **tidal volume**.

Figure 26.2 Runners at the end of a race are often left gasping for air

Task 3

List **three** activities that would be anaerobic and three that would be aerobic.

Hints and Tips!

The respiratory system is very closely linked to the circulatory system as it is the blood which transports the oxygen and removes the carbon dioxide (gaseous exchange).

Key questions

1. List the organs of the breathing system.
2. What is the trachea and what is it constructed of?
3. What are the alveoli? What important function do they perform?
4. Define the terms tidal volume and vital capacity.
5. Explain what is meant by oxygen debt.

27 The digestive system

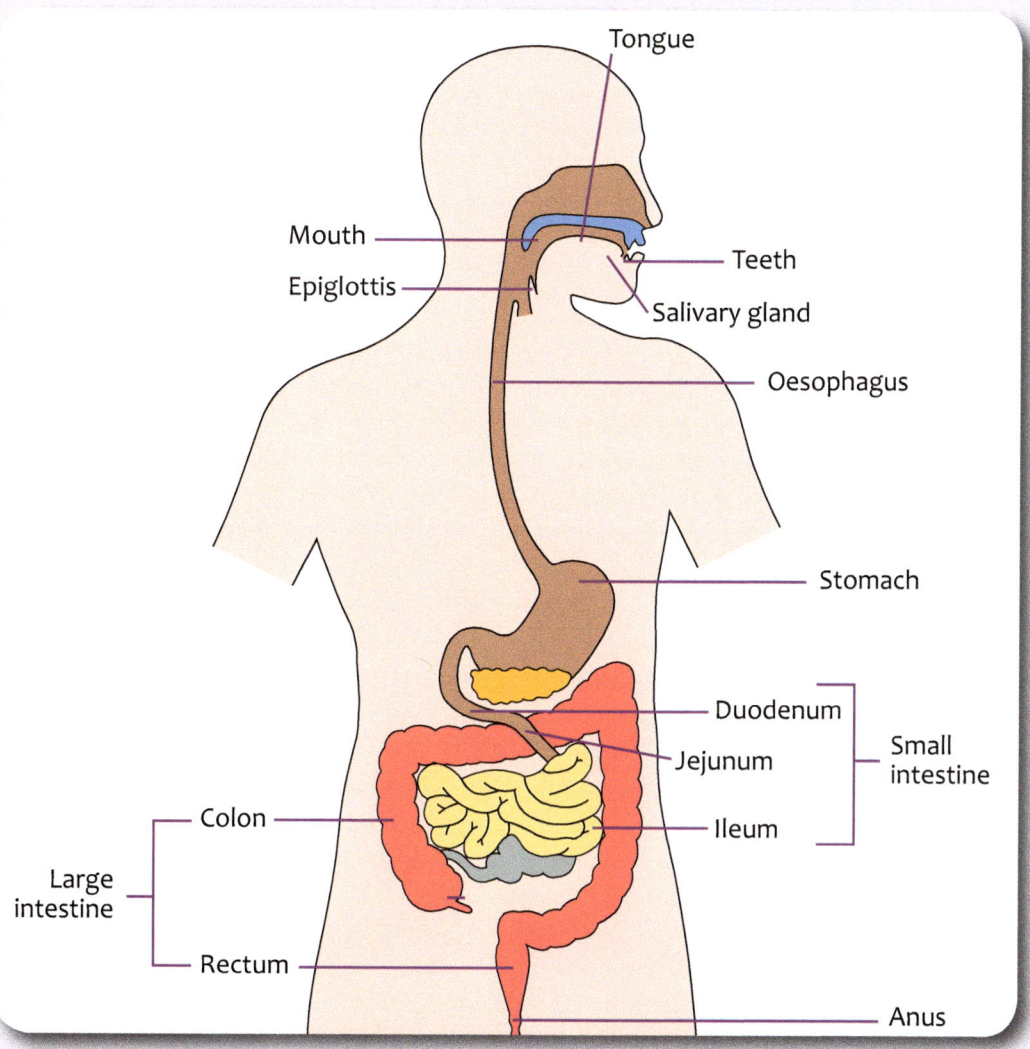

Figure 27.1 The digestive system

The digestive system is shown in Figure 27.1. Food is our main source of energy, so the process through which it passes, in order for the nutrients to be absorbed by the body, is very important. The stages in this process are:

- ingestion
- digestion
- absorption
- egestion.

Being able to digest and process food efficiently is vital to any sportsperson.

Key point

The digestive system performs a very specific function but it must also be considered in relation to the requirements for a balanced diet and nutrition intake and the specific demands from physical activity (see Chapters 10 and 11).

Task 1

Sometimes people suffer an uncomfortable condition when they are having trouble digesting food. What is it called? Try to find out what causes it.

Did you know?

There are 43 muscles in the face. Many of these are used in the action of chewing because the jaw, cheeks and tongue all move in order to help the movement. This is why anyone who breaks their jaw can only eat liquid food, which they have to ingest through a straw.

> **Task 2**
>
> How are some types of aspirin made even more effective than those in tablet form?

The mouth

This is where ingestion begins as food first enters your body. Inside the mouth the food is chewed as the teeth chop, grind and mince it into smaller pieces. The tongue, jaw and cheek muscles all help to move the food around so that the teeth can work on it. While you are chewing, the salivary glands pour **saliva**, which is a digestive juice, onto the food. The saliva:

- softens and moistens the food
- dissolves the taste chemicals in food so that they can be tasted
- keeps the mouth damp to allow swallowing and talking
- releases the enzyme **amylase** (ptyalin) which breaks down carbohydrates, especially starches, into sugar
- helps to control levels of water in the body.

The pharynx

This is the back wall of the mouth, nose and throat and it is here that the epiglottis is situated. This is what prevents any food going into the respiratory system rather than the gullet. In Chapter 26 you saw that the airways also make use of the mouth, nose and throat.

The oesophagus

As the food is chewed, it is formed into a small, moist ball called a **bolus**. It then passes into the oesophagus (or gullet) and, as a result of swallowing, into the stomach.

The stomach

The stomach is a curved, muscular bag and it lies on the left side of the abdomen just underneath the diaphragm. It is the widest part of the food canal and at either end it has a ring of muscle called **sphincter muscle** that closes when the stomach is full. The stomach can stretch. It also:

- stores food (food stays in the stomach for up to 5 hours, so we do not have to keep eating constantly)
- churns, mixes and softens the food and melts fats
- starts the breakdown of proteins with **gastric juices**, which contain an enzyme called **protease**
- destroys certain harmful bacteria with hydrochloric acid.

Liquids pass through the stomach, as they do not have to be broken down. Some drugs such as aspirin also pass through very quickly. This is why they are so fast-acting and effective in relieving such things as headaches.

The small intestine

Digestion continues in the small intestine which is made up of:

- **the duodenum** – where the walls produce a digestive juice which finishes breaking down the food; the pancreas, liver and gall bladder also provide juices to help this process
- **the jejunum** – a small middle section between the duodenum and the ileum
- **the ileum** – the final section which leads into the large intestine.

The jejunum and the ileum both also have digestive juices and their main function is to absorb digested food through their walls and into the bloodstream, which then transports it to the cells.

The large intestine

This is wider than the small intestine and is where most of the fluid waste goes, as well as the roughage and undigested food that has been absorbed so far.

The large intestine is divided into three sections or colons, called the ascending, transverse and descending colons. The large intestine:

- prepares the **faeces** for removal from the body
- absorbs water, glucose and some salts into the bloodstream
- produces a secretion called mucin, which lubricates the rectum
- stores the faeces ready to be finally passed out of the body through the rectum.

Did you know?

The small intestine is about 6 metres (20 feet) long and the large intestine (which is wider) is 1.5 metres (5 feet) long, so the overall length is 7.5 metres!

Hints and Tips!

It is important to know what function each part of the digestive system performs and to be able to relate this to how food is processed within the body as an energy source for use by active sports performers.

Key questions

1. List the four stages of the digestive system.
2. What is saliva and what does it do to help the digestive process?
3. Identify the main function of the pharynx.
4. Describe four functions that the stomach performs.
5. What are the three sections of the small intestine known as?
6. Explain the four functions of the large intestine.

28 The principles of training

The reason for training is to improve your ability to take part in physical activity. This improvement can only come about through a physical change. You must therefore have a thorough knowledge of the various body systems and all the other factors that can affect a performance. You will need to know how and why training is able to make these changes possible and the links that exist with health and fitness.

Training has certain principles that apply no matter what type you undertake. It is important to know what they are and the effects they will have. The main principles of training are:

- specificity
- overload
- progression
- reversibility.

There are other terms that also apply to the general principles of training:

- frequency
- intensity
- duration.

If training is to lead to improvement (and therefore success), it requires a combination of all these factors.

Specificity

Any type of training must be suitable, or specific, to the physical activity or sport you are training for. It would not be wise to choose a strength-training method if you were hoping to build up to running a marathon.

You may wish to choose one particular type of training and concentrate on one particular area. This may be building strength in the legs or the arms, or increasing flexibility in the shoulders, or improving reaction times.

Specific exercise will produce specific results and this must be considered with two other points:

- individuals will respond differently to the same methods
- each activity will have different, and specific, demands.

One thing you must not forget is that most physical activities require a combination of exercises and training methods. There are very few activities where it is easy to choose just one particular method and stick to that. So it is important to plan out and analyse exactly what is required and how these requirements can be met.

When you have done this, you will have a specific programme that will meet your needs. You may even find that there is specifically designed equipment to help you achieve your goals.

Key point

It is important to know all the terms associated with training and to understand how that can be used to set an effective training programme. It is also very important to have knowledge of all of the body systems covered in Chapters 22 to 27.

Did you know?

The acronym SPORT is a useful way to remember the principles of training:
S – specificity
P – progression
O – overload
R – reversibility
T – tedium.

Task 1

Name a physical activity and state the specific training requirements for it. Name the muscles – or muscle groups – that would need most attention.

Overload

This is making the body work harder in order to improve it. You will have a 'capacity' to train that will be the normal level you work at. In order to improve you must extend that capacity by increasing your workload. This can be achieved in the following ways:

- **frequency** of training needs to be increased. To start with you may only train twice a week with a recovery period in between, but this could be increased to every other day and then up to 5 days a week. Top performers would probably train on some aspect of their activity every day. It does not necessarily help to have more than one session in a day. One session is the advisable amount

- **intensity** must be increased. You can do this by simply working harder at the training method you are using. You may want to increase your heart rate to a higher level, to increase your endurance levels (see Chapter 16) or you might wish to add more weight if you are trying to increase your strength

- **duration** may refer to the length of each training session and this should be increased. It can also refer to the amount of time you wish to spend on a particular aspect of your training. If you are working in training blocks on certain areas you may want to do these over a longer period of time.

Your body responds to overload by adapting to it. Used sensibly, it will lead to an improvement.

> **Task 2**
>
> Work out a basic training programme for a specific activity, considering all the principles that have been outlined.

Progression

The training you are doing, and particularly the amount of overload, must be progressively increased. In other words, as your body adjusts to the increased demands put on it, then that demand must be steadily increased.

Improvement will not continue if you remain at the same level of training. However, you must be careful not to do too much too soon. If you do, it may lead to injury or muscle damage that could set back your training programme.

Another factor to be aware of is plateauing. This happens when you get to a certain level and seem unable to move on. It is common and likely to occur more than once. So if it happens, you should be prepared to stay on that level for some time. Eventually, you will improve or adjust enough to progress further. To get through this difficult period, you must be mentally strong and motivated.

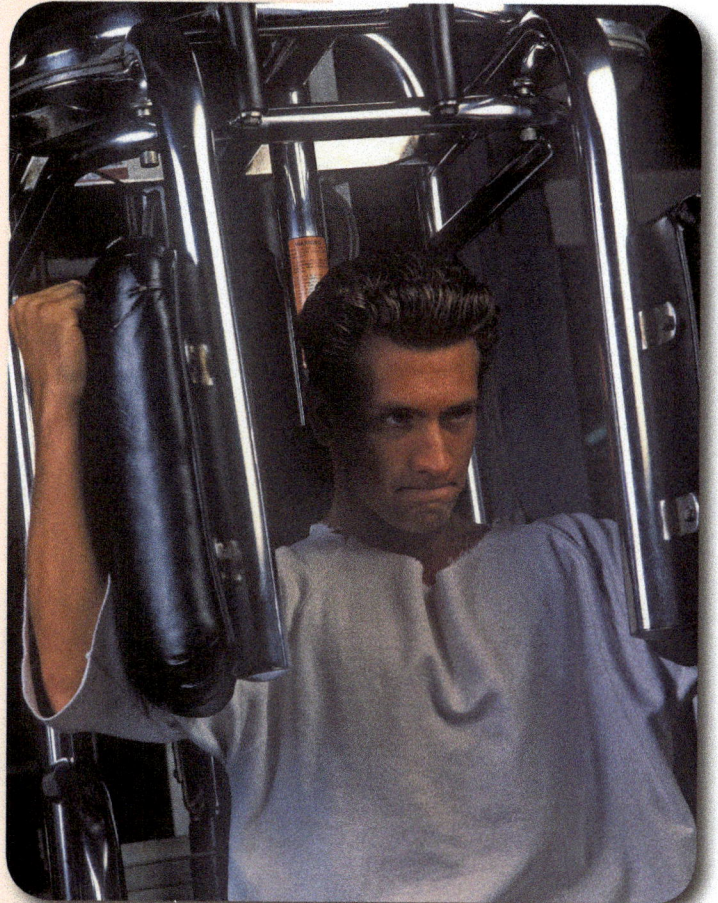

Figure 28.1 'Pec deck' training machine in use

The principles of training

Did you know?

A 3-week break in training can result in a 10 per cent loss of the effects you have gained. Some performers have claimed that having 1 month off from training takes 2 months to recover to the previous levels.

Reversibility

Just as progression can lead to an improvement, if you either stop or decrease your training you go into reverse and lose the effect. All the good you have done will be lost. Sometimes, though, you cannot avoid stopping, e.g. if you have an injury or if you are ill.

An example of the effect of reversibility can be seen if someone breaks a leg. Part of the treatment is to put the leg in a cast to immobilise it. This also prevents the muscles from being exercised properly. As we have seen in Chapter 23, muscles that are not used quickly **atrophy**, so strength is lost.

Hints and Tips!

The principles and terms in this chapter apply to all forms of training. If you are trying to improve your cardiovascular endurance levels you would still use the principle of overload but you would have to increase your heart and breathing rate progressively. If you were trying to increase muscular endurance you would overload particular muscle groups – also progressively!

Key questions

1. What do the terms specificity, overload, progression and reversibility mean?
2. Describe three ways you can achieve overload.
3. Explain what is meant by plateauing.

29 Training sessions

Once you are aware of the principles of training it is time to put them into practice with a training programme. This will consist of a number of training sessions, each with four parts (or phases):

- warm-up
- fitness or exercise phase
- skill or team-play phase
- cool-down (also known as warm-down).

These sessions may be individual but they are often more effective, and more enjoyable, if they are done in a group or at least with a training partner.

Warm-up

This is absolutely essential in any training session for the following reasons.

- It prepares the body for the activity to come. It increases the blood flow through the muscles, helping them to contract quickly. The nervous system is also stimulated, which makes you more alert and aware, getting you psychologically prepared.
- It reduces the possibility of injury, most notably muscle injury. The increased blood flow increases the temperature in the muscle and this makes it more responsive and able to contract and relax. Muscle fibres and tendons are more likely to be damaged if you fail to warm up properly.

If possible, the warm-up should be specific to the type of activity you are training for and you should aim to warm up the appropriate major muscle groups.

These are the types of things you should include in your warm-up:

- **a continuous movement activity** – something that is going to continue long enough to increase the heart rate and body temperature so that the blood flow to the muscles will be increased. You must be careful not to overdo this stage. Many training sessions are ruined by an overly energetic warm-up phase!
- **light exercises** – these should specifically work the major muscle groups to be used. Again, these must not be overdone. A couple of press-ups may be all that is required. Prolonged performance of the same exercise may lead to muscle fatigue
- **flexibility exercises** – these should really concentrate on all areas of the body and all major joints should be gently worked on to prepare them for a full range of mobility.

> **Key point**
> All training sessions must make full use of the principles of training in order for them to be fully worthwhile and effective.

> **Did you know?**
> An international standard gymnast would expect to warm up for at least an hour before competing in a competitive event.

> **Did you know?**
> At all international athletics events the organisers provide a warm-up track where the competitors can prepare for their race.

> **Task 1**
> Choose a sporting activity and write down an appropriate warm-up. Make sure you consider all the stages of the warm-up and try to relate them to the activity you have chosen.

> **Task 2**
> Choose a sporting activity in which you take part. What kinds of exercises or fitness work would be suitable for the fitness phase?

The time spent on the warm-up will vary, often with the type of activity. Many gymnasts, for example, will spend at least 15 minutes warming up and most of this would be spent on the flexibility stage. For other performers a few minutes might be all that is required. What is important is that if you do wish to emphasise one of the stages you do not ignore the others or give them too little time.

Fitness phase

During this phase you should work on the particular aspect of fitness that is most appropriate for the physical activity for which you are training. Most activities require cardiovascular fitness, so some sort of endurance exercise should be included.

One of the benefits of training is that you can get your body used to coping with fatigue, so you should try to get yourself close to fatigue in the training session. The most useful training is that which most closely resembles a game or competition, as it should then make you more effective.

You must also apply the principle of overload (see Chapter 28) during this part of the session if it is to have the full benefit.

Figure 29.1 West Indies cricket team taking part in a net training session

Skill phase

If the sport you are taking part in is a team game, it would be essential for you to use this as a team session because it may be the only opportunity you get to practise together. The whole team, or units within the team, should practise group skills and there should also be the opportunity to work on individual skills.

If your sport is an individual activity (e.g. gymnastics), then you can rehearse the various skills you need. However, it is not wise to do this alone; you should always try to have a coach or training partner with you in case of accident or injury.

It may be that the sport you are training for does not require any particular skills, e.g. a marathon run. In this case you would probably concentrate on the fitness phase and increase endurance training.

Cool-down

This is also known as the warm-down. It is often missed out in a training session.

Instead of just stopping completely after you have finished the other phases of your training, you should continue some part of the activity at a reduced rate. This can be as simple as just gently walking or performing some flexibility exercises. The reason for this is that when you stop exercising, the heart is still beating at a fast rate. If you stop suddenly the heart will not be pumping the blood back to the muscles at the previous rate, and this can cause the blood to 'pool' in the veins. This means that the waste materials such as lactic acid are not being removed. A build-up of this can cause stiffness and soreness, making it difficult for you to perform well during your next training session.

Just as your body is gradually built up to strenuous exercise by the warm-up activities, so it must also be gradually returned to its normal state by the cool-down activities.

Task 3
Choose a sport. Write down some useful skills practices you could perform for this phase.

Hints and Tips!
It is important to be aware of the different phases of a training session and also to understand the importance of each of these phases which will in turn make the session most effective.

Key questions

1. Give five reasons why you should always perform warm-up activities before taking part in a training session.
2. Describe three phases, or stages, of a warm-up. For each of these stages describe why there is a need to include it and what benefits can be gained.
3. Explain why all sporting activities do not require the same warm-up routine. Refer to at least three different sports in your answer.
4. Give some actual examples of what you would include in a warm-up. Explain each in detail and also explain what it is going to achieve.
5. Give five reasons why you should always finish a training session with a cool-down.
6. Explain briefly what you would include in a cool-down session.

30 Training methods

Weight training

Weight training is designed to increase muscle strength. Chapter 14 covers the types of strength as well as their importance.

Many activities require some form of strength and weight training. Using specialised equipment like the type shown in Figure 30.1 is becoming increasingly popular. Linked with this is the fact that there have been many recent developments in the range of equipment and its availability.

Weight training can be used to:

- increase muscle strength
- improve muscle tone.

Increasing muscle strength means following a programme designed to increase the size of the muscles and therefore increase their strength. This uses the principle of overload (see Chapter 28), which will stress the muscles, gradually making them bigger.

To improve muscle tone, performers can use:

- **repetitions** – the number of times you actually move the weights; one chest press, moving the weight up and down once, equals one repetition
- **sets** – the number of times you do a particular weight activity; so, each time you complete your repetitions of the chest press you have done one set.

Different effects can be achieved by varying the repetitions and sets and the 'load', or weight, used each time. The weights are adjustable. To increase strength (to overload) you have heavy weights with small numbers of repetitions and you may do several sets of these.

To improve muscle tone you would use lighter weights and increase the repetitions, probably somewhere between 10 and 15 times.
You would probably only do a maximum of three sets.

Additionally, there are more specific ways in which weight or strength training can be used. 'Free-standing weights' are weights that can be fixed onto long or short bars. People who want to increase their strength often prefer these traditional weights because it is easier to add more weight. One drawback of weight-training machinery is that it does not always have enough weight and it is not possible to add more.

Key point

It is important to be aware what each particular training method consists of and then to know how the training can have the particular desired effect on the body. Safety factors related to each of these training methods are also very important.

Figure 30.1 The equipment you would find in an up-to-date training room

If free-standing weights are used it is vital that you do not train alone. You should always have an instructor or training partner with you to help load and unload the weights and to help you to start and stop the weightlifting movements. At times, it will be necessary to have two people to lift the weights up for you to start and to take the weights from you when you have finished. You should also ensure that you warm up thoroughly.

Other weight-training methods are as follows:

- **isotonic training** – where the amount of weight moved, or lifted, remains constant throughout the movement. This is important as it relates to the way the muscles contract when they are exercised. In a concentric contraction the muscle shortens (e.g. a biceps curl, when the arm is bent and the wrist moved towards the shoulder) and an eccentric contraction when the muscle lengthens. For the biceps curl example, this would be the arm extending back to a straight position (see Chapter 23). The principle of isotonic training is that the weight is kept constant on both the eccentric and concentric contraction. This would be the type of training preferred by those who wished to improve strength, power or endurance
- **isokinetic training** – where specialist equipment is necessary because you need the weights to vary the effort as you work at a constant speed. These 'variable resistance' machines are expensive because they adjust the load so that the muscles are worked evenly throughout the movement. The value of these machines is that they can duplicate movements such as throwing and kicking
- **isometric training** – where a contraction is held at a particular point. This can be useful for activities such as gymnastics where you are required to hold a position, so in training you would hold the muscle in the required position for about 5 seconds, and then repeat. In this case the length of the muscle stays the same while contracting.

Circuit training

Figure 30.3 shows a typical circuit-training layout that would be useful for a general fitness circuit. One of the advantages of circuit training is that it is very adaptable. Another advantage is the variety of ways in which either an individual or group can use the circuit. The time taken, the amount of work done and the load for each area can all be varied and changed.

The various parts of the circuit are known as **stations**. It is very important that these stations work properly, following these rules.

- The stations must be clearly marked with the movement or activity to be performed.
- The activities must be demonstrated and/or practised to make sure they are performed correctly. For example, you will not get the maximum benefit from a burpee if you do not do it properly. Also you must check when the circuit is under way that all the activities are being performed properly.
- Activities must be varied around the circuit. This means that there should not be a group of stomach-muscle exercises all arranged together. They must be spread out at even intervals throughout the circuit, otherwise a performer may fatigue a muscle area by overworking it. Spreading the exercises evenly allows the muscles a little time to recover before they are exercised again, so overload can be more effective. It also makes the circuit less boring if there is a variety of exercises.

Figure 30.2 A trainer assisting with lifting free-standing weights

Task 1

Work out your own weight-training programmes. Design **one** for a specific physical activity and **one** for improved general fitness. How would they differ?

Did you know?

Many boxers train in 3-minute bursts because that is the length of one round of boxing.

- A recovery period should be allowed between each exercise so that performers recover sufficiently to do the next one. Some circuits can last up to 30 minutes and it is unrealistic to expect someone to work constantly at a high level for that long.

There are two main types of circuit – fitness and skills.

Fitness circuit

Types of exercises that could be included on a fitness circuit include:

- press-ups
- squat thrusts
- sprint starts (press-up position and with legs positioned as for a sprint start, quickly switch the right and left legs over to the front and back position)
- burpees (a squat thrust followed by a star jump and then back into squat-thrust position)
- triceps dips
- sit-ups
- trunk curls
- leg raising
- squats
- shuttle runs
- hyperextensions (lying flat on the stomach, raise the head and feet, arching the back)
- step-ups (on a bench or even a chair)
- running on the spot (this can be with high knee raising or at sprint speed)
- star jumps
- skipping
- alternate elbows to knees (arms clasped behind the head; turn the trunk and lift the knee, at the same time twisting to lower the elbows).

All of these exercises can be performed with the minimum of equipment – just a bench and a rope are required. If you have more equipment you can have an even more varied circuit.

Skills circuit

This also includes various stations but the exercises are aimed at developing particular skills needed for an activity. An example could be a basketball circuit, which might include:

- chest passes against a wall
- dribbling around cones
- continuous free-throw shooting
- continuous lay-up shots
- bounce passes against a wall
- continuous long-throw passes.

Others could be added or the circuit could cater for a combination of skills with suitable fitness exercises as well.

Running the circuit

There are various ways to run a circuit.

- **Timed circuits** – where performers work for so long at each station and then rest before moving on (for example, 30 seconds work, followed by 30 seconds rest).
- **Fixed load** – each station is labelled with the amount of work the performer must do (it could be 15 press-ups each time).

Both of these methods can be varied. The number of laps can be adjusted, or the periods of work and recovery, or the load and skills could be changed.

Interval training

Interval training consists of periods of work followed by periods of rest. The principle is much the same as for circuit training (which allows a rest period between stations) and prevents the performer from becoming too fatigued to carry on. There are several ways that interval training can be done but the following factors have to be considered.

- **Duration of the work** – this could relate to how far a performer may need to run or for how long they may work.
- **Intensity of the work** – this could be the speed at which the performer works or the load they have.
- **Repetitions** – this could be the number of work repetitions or the number of rest ones.
- **Duration of the recovery period** – this would usually refer to time but it may involve a recovery distance, such as a certain distance a performer is allowed to slow walk.

The two most important factors in interval training are the work related to the rest. When at work, the heart rate should go up to a high training-zone level (see page 61), which could be somewhere in the region of 180 beats per minute. During the rest, or recovery, periods it should drop into the aerobic zone, which is about 140 beats per minute.

The two general categories of interval training are long interval training and short interval training.

Long interval training

This is particularly good for players in team games and middle-distance athletes, as it works in bursts of from 15 seconds up to 3 minutes. Because the work periods are quite long, those taking part in it cannot be expected to work flat out so they would normally work at about 80–85 per cent maximum. The rest or recovery periods would also be quite long; after 3 minutes of work there should be 3 minutes of recovery time.

The majority of this work would consist of running, usually for a set time. It would not be possible to do this over a distance because of the times worked, as not everyone would be able to cover the same distance in 3 minutes. If shorter times were used it would be possible to use distances and ensure they were covered within a certain time, e.g. sets of 400-metre runs in less than 75 seconds.

Short interval training

This is designed more for short bursts of activity so it would suit sprint athletes or some sports, such as racket sports, where there is much stop-and-go action. The work periods are much shorter, probably no more than 15 seconds, but performers would be expected to work flat out for that time at maximum work rate. Because of this the recovery rates would be longer; up to 2 minutes would be necessary to recover sufficiently. Again, this would mainly involve running and, specifically, sprint running. In some cases the full speed running could only be for 5 seconds.

Continuous training

Chapter 16 covered the need to keep the heart rate at a high level, to improve endurance. Continuous training is a method that can achieve this because performers take part in activities that keep the pulse and heart rate high. Examples of these activities are:

- running and jogging
- cycling
- swimming
- exercise sessions (such as aerobic classes).

There are also many specialist machines that can be used for continuous training. Many of them, such as treadmills and exercise cycles, duplicate the activities mentioned above but allow them to be done indoors.

This work must be carried out within the training zone (see page 61) if it is to be effective and the performer should aim to work for at least 15 minutes at this level. This will then improve the cardiovascular and respiratory system. This type of training would therefore be suitable for anyone who wished to improve their general fitness levels.

Task 2

Devise circuits for:
a general fitness
b a specific physical activity.
Name the activity you have chosen.

Figure 30.3 Indoor exercise equipment for interval training

> **Task 3**
> Work out your own Fartlek training programme, then try it out.

> **Task 4**
> Draw up a chart and list the advantages and disadvantages of all the training methods described.

Fartlek training

This is based on a Swedish method of training. It means 'speed training' and is a form of continuous training. It alternates walking, brisk walking, running, jogging and fast steady running. This can be performed as required in a session, so the individual decides when they are ready to build up to a fast run after progressing from a walk. However, it is probably more effective to set off on a planned programme based on times and distances which will be walked, jogged and run at speed.

Altitude training

This involves performers (and these tend to be endurance athletes who take part in long-distance events) going to specific areas in the world where they can train at high altitude. The reason for this is that at high altitude the air becomes less dense and the pressure of oxygen decreases. This means that the performer is able to make some actual physiological changes occur which increase the oxygen-carrying capacity of the blood. This can make them more efficient runners by improving their endurance levels.

Continuous shuttle run

This is more correctly called the 'multi-stage fitness test', or commonly the 'bleep test'. It is covered in detail in Chapter 31 but is mentioned here because it is now often used as a method of training. Many international sports teams have adopted it as a training method and it has, as a result, been commonly accepted as such.

One important rule to remember with all training methods is that they should be carried out with care. They should be built up gradually and safely.

Hints and Tips!

Different training methods may well suit particular sports/activities but it is also likely that a combination of different training methods is likely to be used by the majority of performers. The advantages and disadvantages of each method therefore need to be clearly understood.

Key questions

1. Describe what weight training consists of. In your answer give details of the different ways that weight training can be used and the benefits. Explain specific safety rules that apply to weight training.
2. Explain the difference between a repetition and a set.
3. Describe what circuit training is. Explain how it is organised and set up.
4. Draw your own diagram of a circuit for a named sport.
5. Explain what interval training is. Describe two ways it can be used.
6. Describe what is meant by Fartlek training. Explain how it is organised.
7. What are the benefits of using the multi-stage fitness test as a training method?

31 Fitness testing

Just as specific training methods may be chosen to improve certain aspects of fitness, it is also possible to test specific aspects of fitness. This is very important when planning a fitness training programme because the testing you do before, during and after the programme will give you an idea of just how successful the training programme you followed was.

The following testing methods are linked to the specific aspects of endurance, flexibility and strength.

Progressive shuttle run

This test of fitness is often called the multi-stage fitness test or the 'bleep test' (see page 120). It is also often used as a training method, although this is not what it was originally intended to be. The test is designed to be a general test of endurance and with the use of various tables it can test a performer's VO_2 maximum (see page 62).

The test is very easy and simple to set up and administer. All it needs is a tape cassette or CD player and an area (preferably indoors) at least 20 metres long. The test consists of a tape recording that has a series of pre-recorded bleeps on it, at various intervals. The people who take part in the test line up at a start point and run to a distance 20 metres away, then run back again. However, this must be in time with the electronic bleeps on the pre-recorded tape, so they have to run at the pace the bleeps are dictating.

> **Key point**
>
> Fitness is a combination of factors so it is impossible to just test one aspect and consider that to be fitness. It is likely that a combination of factors will have to be tested to make an accurate assessment.

Figure 31.1 The progressive shuttle run, or 'bleep test' in operation

At the start this is quite easy because the bleeps are quite a long time apart, but every minute they change levels and the time between the bleeps decreases! This means that performers still have to run 20 metres but, as each level changes with each minute, they have to speed up. There are 25 levels in all but performers are at sprinting speed long before that!

The longer a performer is able to continue – and they must turn after each 20-metre run in time with the tape – the higher their score and the higher their level of endurance. If they turn after the bleep has gone on three consecutive occasions they must stop, as they are not allowed to run at a slower pace.

Figure 31.2 The 'sit and reach' flexibility test

Did you know?

Women tend to be more flexible than men. One of the reasons for this is the difference in the pelvic region: men's bones are generally heavier and rougher, whereas the women have broader and shallower hips.

Flexibility testing

Testing flexibility is quite simple and doesn't require a lot of expensive equipment. Chapter 15 dealt with flexibility and the ways it can be improved. It is quite easy to perform flexibility exercises and keep a record of the amount of movement achieved.

Even a simple exercise like bending with straight legs and trying to touch your toes with your outstretched fingers can be measured each time you do it. (You need a partner with a ruler to measure the gap between your fingertips and the ground.) This would be a test that would measure your own flexibility and any progress you might be making, but there are also tests that can be used to measure you against other set scores. The most commonly used one is the 'sit and reach test', which is shown in Figure 31.2.

The distance you can move the slide forwards is a measure of the amount of flexibility in your lower back and hamstrings.

Task 1

Work out your own flexibility test for any part of your body and regularly perform flexibility exercises while recording the progress you may be making.

Strength testing

Strength can be a difficult thing to test because it is often related to body weight and shape. Chapter 19 covers somatotypes. Body size can be a dominating factor when testing for strength.

It would be reasonable to expect a really strong person to be able to lift up, or move, a large amount of weight and to be quite big themselves with a large body weight. However, it is possible to test someone for strength by finding out how strong they are in relation to their body weight, and this is often a fairer test.

For this reason, the chin-up, or pull-up, test is often used. For this you need a bar that is suspended in the air. It needs to be above your full stretch height, as you have to hang from it. You hold the bar, with your fingers pointing away, and lift your body up so that your chin is level, or above, the bar. You then lower yourself until your arms are completely straight and then lift yourself back up again. You score one for every properly completed chin-up.

Did you know?

Men are generally stronger than women, as women have less total muscle mass than men. Women have been estimated to be only 52 per cent as strong as men in the upper body and 66 per cent as strong in the lower.

The important thing about this test is that it measures your strength in relation to your body weight. It does actually favour smaller people and being tall or heavy is a disadvantage. Chapter 20 covers the reasons for this.

Other strength movements such as press-ups, squat thrusts and dips (arm bends performed on parallel bars) can all be used as strength tests, as they all test the performer's ability to move their own body weight.

Pure strength can be tested using weights or even specialised equipment such as a **dynamometer**, which measures the strength of your grip.

Weightlifting is a test of pure strength; the more you lift, the stronger you are.

The Harvard step test

This is a test of the pulse recovery rate. It is explained in Chapter 13. It is very important when carrying out this test to be able to take an accurate pulse reading (see page 100).

The test is very easy to set up and do. All that is needed is a bench (or step or block which is about 50 centimetres high), a stopwatch, and some paper and a pencil to record the results. Before doing the test you should make a note of your resting pulse rate.

Figure 31.3 The Harvard step test being performed

To take the test you do step-ups on the bench continuously for 5 minutes, at a rate of 30 per minute. You can use a metronome to help with this or find someone to count out every 2 seconds to keep the pace constant.

At the end of the 5-minute period you make a note of your pulse rate at particular intervals as you are recovering. This should be after 1 minute, 2 minutes and 3 minutes, and you should record each of these numbers. There is a calculation you should do to give a score that you can then compare to the table on this page.

The calculation is 300 (this is the total number of seconds you worked) divided by twice the total number of pulses you recorded during the recovery period (i.e. add together your three pulse counts). The result is then multiplied by 100. Scores can be matched to Table 31.1.

Below 55	=	Poor
55–64	=	Below average
65–79	=	Average
80–89	=	Good
90 and over	=	Excellent

Table 31.1 Harvard step test results

This very common test is based on the fact that if you have a quick recovery rate after taking part in strenuous activity, you have a higher level of cardiovascular endurance.

Cooper 12-minute run

This is another test of aerobic capacity, or VO_2 maximum, so it tests the same thing as the bleep test. One of the main advantages of this test is that it is easy to set up and to do because it does not require any specialist equipment. All you need is a stopwatch and a marked-out running area.

Task 2

Perform the Harvard step test and compare your rating score with Table 31.1.

> **Task 3**
>
> Perform the Cooper 12-minute run and compare your score with Table 31.2.

The test involves running for 12 minutes around the marked-out area and making a note of how far you get in that time. The results can be used in two ways:

- you can chart you own progress by keeping a record of how far you get each time. An improvement in distance covered will show that you are improving your cardiovascular endurance
- you can compare your performance to the rating chart in Table 31.2. The distance covered is in metres so you must make sure that your course is measured out in metres.

Age	Excellent	Good	Fair	Poor
13–14				
Males	2700	2400	2200	2100
Females	2000	1900	1600	1500
15–16				
Males	2800	2500	2300	2200
Females	2100	1900	1700	1500
17–20				
Males	3000	2700	2500	2300
Females	2300	2100	1800	1500

Table 31.2 Cooper 12-minute run results (in metres)

If you don't have a running track or area that is easy to mark out, then it is best to use the first method. As long as you run in the same place or area each time you will be able to keep an accurate record of your improvement.

Cardiovascular and endurance testing

Modern technology means that there are now many ways of testing these. There are watches and monitors that can record anything from pulse rate and blood pressure to calorie expenditure as you train.

Other tests involve the use of training machinery such as running treadmills. It is possible to connect a performer up to monitoring equipment that will measure very accurately the amount of oxygen they are taking in and the amount they are expiring. Using the treadmill, they can exercise hard with all the monitoring equipment attached, so very accurate readings can be obtained. Many of these machines also have built-in monitors in hand/grip sensors that can be used.

Much of the modern equipment has programmable tests built into the readout monitors so it is quite easy to test yourself regularly. What they do not do is compare those results against set standards, which some of the other tests described do.

Nearly all of these training machine tests work on the principle of monitoring the heart rate and comparing them to training zones (see Chapter 13).

Muscular endurance

This is fairly easy to test because muscular endurance can be worked out by seeing how many times you can do an exercise – in other words, your maximum number of repetitions.

One of the easiest of these is the sit-up test. For this you just need to do correct sit-ups with your knees bent at right angles and your feet firmly on the floor. It is often easier if a partner holds your feet in place, which will keep you in position.

You perform as many sit-ups as you can and record your score. This will indicate the muscular endurance level of your abdominal muscles. You can do a similar test for arm strength by doing press-ups, or even chin-ups. The maximum repetitions you can perform for any exercise will give a clear indication of your muscular endurance. Specialised weight-training machinery can allow you to do even more specific tests on muscles, or muscle groups, so you can work out your own tests.

Power

Power can be tested by using activities that require explosive strength. The **standing broad jump** and the sergeant jump can be used to measure power.

Standing broad jump

Stand with your feet together. Bend at the knee then jump forwards, landing on both feet. Measure the total distance travelled from the start point to the landing point. If you use gym mats it is quite easy to start from behind one of the mats and mark, with chalk, where you land on the other. This has the added advantage of allowing you a soft surface to land on.

Sergeant jump

This is a vertical jump (unlike the broad jump which is horizontal). It can easily be performed just using a wall and some chalk. Stand next to the wall and reach up with your arm nearest the wall. Make a mark at the highest point your fingers can touch, with both feet flat on the floor. Then heavily chalk your fingertips, bend and jump upwards, slapping your fingers against the wall at the highest point, leaving a mark. The measurement to take is the distance between the two marks, so you actually measure how high each person can jump in relation to their own height. This makes it a much fairer test than just measuring how high they can jump.

Both of these tests measure the explosive strength, and therefore the power, of the leg muscles.

> **Task 4**
>
> Either work out – and try out – your own muscular endurance test, or test the abdominal muscular endurance in your group.

> WARNING: Be very careful not to overdo testing to the point where you are unnecessarily straining yourself. The idea is to see how many repetitions of a particular exercise you can do, not to lift one very heavy weight once; that would be a test of strength. You will find that you will not be able to continue once you have reached your maximum and it is not wise to try to carry on past this point as you could injure yourself.

Figure 31.4 Performing a correct sit-up with a partner

Agility

This can be tested by setting up any kind of obstacle course which makes you change direction regularly. It can even involve getting over and under obstacles such as gymnastic boxes or beams.

A simple test is running around marker cones over a particular course or distance and timing the run. You must make sure that you always set the course out exactly the same if you devise your own test. There is a set test for this known as the Illinois Agility Run, based on a zig-zag pattern run, with cones for the performer to run around in the middle section.

Agility tests can be devised to match physical activities so, for example, they can include dribbling tests for basketball, hockey and soccer which are very easy to set up.

Combination tests

Often, tests will be done to test a combination of factors, not just one. This is often the case when organisations such as the armed forces, police or fire service want to test the fitness levels of new recruits. They test for strength (often using the chin-up test) and endurance (usually a timed run over a particular distance such as the 12-minute run), as this is an accepted combination test for general fitness.

Another test is the JCR test, which includes a jump (the sergeant jump), chin-ups and a run (usually a timed shuttle run over a set course).

Task 5

Work out your own agility test course. It can be just a general running course or related to a physical activity. Try out your test and keep a record of the results.

Body measurements

These are often tested, or more accurately, measured. The measurements taken are:

- height
- weight
- body composition.

The first two are very easy to take but body composition requires a specialist piece of equipment known as skinfold callipers (see Figure 31.5). This device can accurately measure the amount of fat tissue in the body. Readings are taken at five body points: at the back of the arm by the triceps; at the front of the arm by the biceps; just behind the shoulder blade (this is known as a 'subscapular reading'); just above the waistband on the side of the abdomen (known as the 'anterior supra-iliac reading'); and at the back of the calf muscle.

With all these readings it is possible to calculate the levels of excess fat in the body.

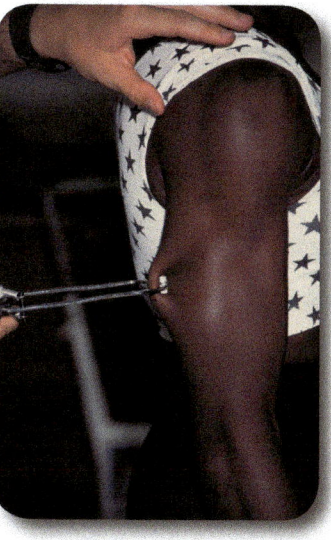

Figure 31.5 Person having body fat read with skinfold callipers

Hints and Tips!

The most important aspect of fitness testing is reliability. This is why tests that are carried out must be very carefully organised and conducted correctly so that they are clearly testing the desired aspect of fitness that they have been designed for.

Key questions

1. What is the name of the test that considers pulse recovery rate? Why is this considered to be a good indicator of fitness?
2. Name a test that can be used for flexibility.
3. What is a dynamometer and what does it measure?
4. Describe two tests that can be used to measure power.
5. What is the main advantage of using combination tests?

32 Injury prevention

Making sure that you are performing safely is one of the most important factors when taking part in any physical activity. The topics covered in this chapter all need to be considered as being potential risks and may require you to take steps to deal with them.

Injury: prevention and causes

In most cases, if you are able to spot a possible cause of injury, you can take steps to prevent it. However, you must always consider preparation, participation, equipment and environment.

Preparation

It is important to get yourself ready to take part in physical activity properly. Many people fail to do it thoroughly. You need to consider these things:

- **training** – you should not take part in any activity if you have not undergone some form of training so that you are physically prepared. Each sport makes its own demands upon your body; some put a strain on the legs, others put a strain on the arms. It is foolish to take part without at least some basic training to reduce the chance of a strain or a sprain. Your training should also include having a basic knowledge of the game, such as its rules and regulations so that you know how to participate. A player who goes onto a hockey pitch without any knowledge of the rules could be very dangerous!
- **warm-up** – this is essential in all sports (see Chapter 29) to prepare you physically immediately before taking part
- **physical state** – you should remove all jewellery such as watches, earrings and bracelets and you may even be required to make sure that your fingernails are short (netball has a rule about this). This is also the time to make sure that you are wearing the proper clothing or equipment.

Participation

While you are actually taking part or participating in a particular sport you need to be aware of the following:

- **fair play** – the rules of any activity also have a vital part to play and you should be aware of their role. You should always play fairly. Sticking to the rules ensures that you play safely. A two-footed tackle in football, for example, is against the rules as it is potentially dangerous and could result in a serious shin or leg injury
- **officials** – players have a responsibility to make sure that they respond positively to the officials in charge and also respond positively to any other instructions which others, such as teachers and coaches, might give them, as these are additional safeguards regarding safety.

Key point

Taking part safely can prevent injury. There are various safety rules that apply in all activities and situations, and there are others that are specific to a particular activity.

Did you know?

Statistically the most dangerous sport in the world is golf. More people die playing it than any other sport. However, this is not due to the dangerous nature of the game but more to the age of the players who die of natural causes when playing!

Task 1

For two named sports, make a list of the ways that injuries could happen through deliberate foul play.

Equipment

Appropriate equipment is probably one of the most important factors when it comes to injury prevention and it can also be a major cause of injuries. The following points regarding correct use and condition of equipment need to be considered.

Correctness

- The right equipment must be worn at the right time and it must be appropriate for the activity. Helmets are worn by American footballers and cyclists, but it would be inappropriate to wear one in a game of basketball!
- The equipment must only be used for protection and not in any other way. There is a rule in American football that stops players from using their helmets in a dangerous way when tackling.
- Equipment must also be worn correctly. A loose strap or fitting could be dangerous to the person playing, or to an opponent. Wearing the wrong kind of footwear, such as high-back shoes can cause Achilles tendon damage. The equipment must fit properly. An ill-fitting gum shield worn when playing hockey can be very dangerous, so it is best to have it fitted by a dentist.
- Wearing the correct sports footwear can help by giving support to the arches and cushioning the ankle joint on the impact when running or jumping.

Condition

- All equipment must be regularly checked and kept in good order. Items such as football boot studs need to be checked to make sure that there are no sharp edges that could cut an opponent. Equipment must be checked to make sure it cannot injure opponents but it is also important that it still does its job to protect the wearer. Loose spikes in a running shoe could lead to a trip or fall if they don't grip properly.
- Equipment must be regularly checked and protected. Goal posts and marker flags need to be in good condition, and rugby and netball posts should have protective coverings around them. Officials often check things like this before a game.
- Equipment used to play the game must be checked. A damaged hockey stick could break, or splinters could come from it. A worn grip on a racket can cause blisters or loss of grip and an opponent could be hit.

Environment

This is not always something you can control. Therefore you may have to be extra cautious. The environment can be considered in two ways: as being uncontrolled, and as being controlled.

Uncontrolled environment

- This would include such things as the weather. In any outdoor activity the weather may be a factor and in some outdoor pursuits it can be potentially dangerous.
- The ground conditions can be affected by the weather. Wet grounds can be slippery and dangerous as it is not possible to get a firm grip, while very dry, hard grounds can cause injuries when landing. Hard grounds can also be difficult to get a grip on if they are too dry for studs. Severe weather conditions such as electrical storms can mean that games should not be played, or even abandoned once underway.

Controlled environment

- These are things you can do something about – for example, by inspecting a pitch before a match for stones or broken glass.
- Spectators and crowds must be very carefully controlled. If they are not controlled, they can be a danger to themselves and there is a chance that they can be a danger to the participants. Excited crowds invading playing areas can cause injuries and they themselves can be injured if they are too close to the playing area and get hit by a player or a ball.

Causes of injury

There are many potential causes of injury and not all of them can be prevented. Mainly, injuries are:

- internally caused
- externally caused.

Internally caused injuries

These are injuries for which performers themselves are responsible. There are no other factors such as opponents. These injuries include overuse injuries and sudden injuries.

Overuse injuries

- These come about, fairly obviously, through training or performing too much. The pressures on performers are so great that there is a temptation to do far too much, and many sportspeople take up regular sport at a very young age. All this puts a strain on the body and the body may not always be able to cope with it.

Task 2

Choose **two** sports and, for each one, write down a list of equipment and the necessary checks.

- Performers can suffer stress fractures in bones caused through too much running, as well as tendon and muscle injuries. Cricket bowlers often sustain back and shoulder injuries caused through their bowling action, tennis players get tennis elbow (an inflammation of the elbow joint, caused by the forced straightening of the arm during play) and many soccer and hockey players get knee-cartilage damage through constantly twisting and turning.

- It is impossible to play these sports without putting some kind of strain on the body. What is important is that the performer does not overdo it and also that they cut down, or stop, if there is any sign of injury. Carrying on will only make it worse.

Sudden injuries

- These are caused instantly by such things as overstretching, or twisting or turning quickly. They may be caused by tiredness or fatigue. Many of these types of injuries happen quite late on in a game or a match.

- Obviously, lack of a suitable warm-up can also be a cause. One more cause can be trying to do something which is either too difficult or which is clearly dangerous.

Externally caused injuries

These are caused by factors other than the performers themselves. It could be the equipment used, the playing conditions or an opponent. They can be considered as impact injuries, foul play and incorrect actions, or accidents.

- **Impact injuries** – these are often injuries such as cuts, bruises and fractures. Impact can be caused by another player (many of these occur in team games where physical contact is allowed) who may be tackling or it can be the equipment used, such as goal posts, hockey sticks or soccer boots. The playing surface is also a very common cause of these injuries. It is not only outdoor surfaces that are dangerous. Indoor surfaces can be just as hard and just as harmful.

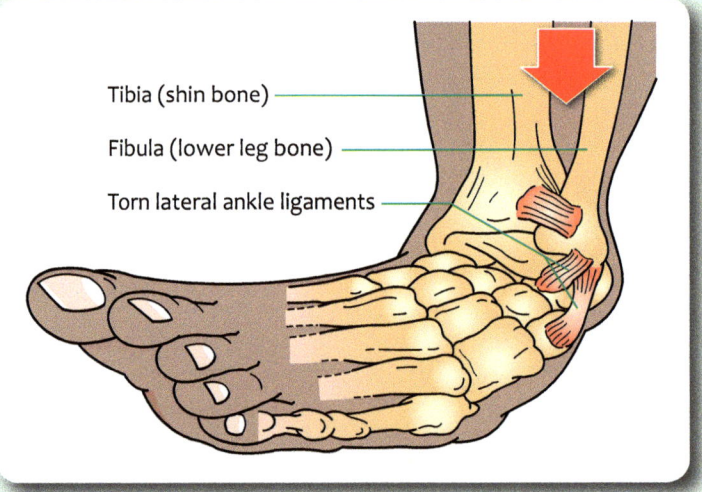

Figure 32.1 Diagram showing a very painful injury as a result of wearing loose fitting shoes on the basketball or netball court

Figure 32.2 Injuries can be minor or severe – if in doubt consult a medical professional

> **Task 3**
> Make a list of as many items of protective equipment as you can think of that are used in sports.

- **Foul play/incorrect actions** – this involves other players, usually opponents. The type of injury received may be very minor or it might be serious. Potentially, the injuries can be very serious, so there are rules to prevent them.

- **Accidents** – no matter how many safety precautions are taken there will always be accidents. They occur in all physical activities, but because some sports are more dangerous than others the accidents will be more serious.

- **Equipment** – a simple thing like a blister can be caused by the equipment. For example, tight-fitting shoes can cause blisters or even corns and bunions. However, the equipment does not have to be faulty to cause an injury. Running long distances can often leave performers with blisters on their feet and this cannot be avoided, no matter how specialist the running shoes are. Often injuries are caused by damaged, ill-fitting or faulty equipment that is not doing its job properly.

Task 4

Draw up a checklist that could be used for a particular activity to ensure that all the equipment used is safe and suitable.

In some sports the activity itself is dangerous. Boxing would be an example of this. Many boxers have died as a result of a punch that was delivered quite fairly. In certain activities, performers have to be aware of the risks they take simply by participating.

Figure 32.3 Boxing can be a dangerous sport

Hints and Tips!

It is important to be aware of the general rules that apply to safety and safe participation as well as the specific ones that apply to particular sports – especially those you are likely to be personally participating in.

Key questions

1. Explain two general safety rules that would apply in all cases of taking part in sport.
2. Choose one sporting activity and explain the various safety measures you would take into consideration before you took part.
3. Identify three ways you can prepare yourself to be able to take part more safely in a named sporting activity.
4. Explain why it might be correct to wear loose-fitting clothing for one activity and tight-fitting clothing for another.
5. Describe the correct type of footwear that should be worn for a particular sport and explain why it is appropriate for that activity.

33 Injury types and treatments

> A word of warning: This chapter will not make you an expert in first aid. However, it will allow you to have an understanding and knowledge of the types of common injuries that can occur and the basic actions that can then be taken.

When taking part in sport there is always the risk that some form of injury might occur. Many of these injuries are minor. However, you may have a responsibility to assess the level of this injury and then take the appropriate action. If in any doubt, you should contact the emergency services and let them deal with the situation.

General rules for treatment

The following rules apply in most cases where a sporting injury has occurred.

- Do not move the injured person until you are sure what the injury is. Ask the injured person to give you details of the injury and any affected areas. If the person is unconscious, or was unconscious, you must call an ambulance.

- Look at the damaged or affected areas to see if there is any sign of an injury. Cuts or wounds should be obvious but if there is any bone damage you may find a misshapen area or damage to a joint or signs of swelling. You can then gently touch the injured area and see if there are any signs of tenderness or further injury. If there does not seem to be too much damage, ask the injured person if they are able to move the area that is injured. If they cannot move it themselves, do not try to do it for them. If they can move, see how much movement there is that does not cause any discomfort.

- If you have been through all of these stages, and the injured person feels able to, then see if they can stand, then move and take their own weight. They may require help to do this, so you may need to support them. They should only continue to take part in the activity if they are clearly fully recovered. Any injury will be made worse by carrying on but a minor 'knock' or temporary damage should not prevent a performer from continuing.

- If at any time they are not able to carry on through these gradual stages they must get expert help straight away. There is a big difference between first aid and medical treatment.

Depending on the type of injury you are faced with there are various different things which you can do.

Key point

Any injury must be dealt with cautiously, as it is not always possible to know exactly how serious it might be. If there is any doubt, it must be left for the experts to deal with and the casualty must not be moved. (Know your local emergency numbers.)

Task 1

With a partner, take it in turns to practise placing each other in the coma, or recovery, position.

Head injuries

You should place the injured person in the **coma position** (also known as the **recovery position**; see Figure 33.1), lying on their side. You must make sure that they are able to breathe, so you must check that their mouth and nose (airways) are clear.

If they are not breathing you will need to give expelled air resuscitation and if there is no sign of a pulse you will need to give cardiac massage. Details of resuscitation come later in this chapter.

Figure 33.1 A person in the coma, or recovery, position

Fractures

This is the name given to broken bones. There are three main types of fracture that you should be able to identify:

- **simple or closed** – the most straightforward type of fracture where the bone is broken but it has not pierced the skin
- **open or compound** – the skin is broken so there is a wound caused by the broken bone which may even be sticking out
- **complicated** – there is serious damage to a blood vessel or a nerve; this damage could cause heavy bleeding, which could be more serious than the break itself.

These are the signs you should look for when checking for fractures.

- Has the snap of the bone been heard or felt?
- Is there pain where the injury has occurred and is there a lack of movement in the limb?
- Is the shape and outline of the limb different from normal? You can check against the other limb to see this.
- Is the limb in an unnatural position? (For example, a knee or foot facing the wrong way would show this.)
- Is there a lot of swelling around the injured area?
- Can you feel some clear damage to the bone?

If, after considering all of these points, you think there is a chance of a fracture you must be very careful not to move the injured area but to immobilise it – that is, keep it in a stable position.

You can do this by applying a splint, which is anything you can use to keep the injured person's damaged bone straight and protected. If it is a fractured leg you can splint the good leg to the bad one to give support. (You could even use cricket stumps or hockey sticks!) You might also need to pad the area. Clothing such as tracksuits and t-shirts or even towels would be good for this. If the damage is to an arm, then you can put the arm in a sling to support and protect it.

Treating a fracture is an expert's job, so as soon as you have done what you can to protect the injury and make the injured person comfortable you must get expert help and call an ambulance.

Dislocations

These occur at a joint, where one bone comes out of its normal position against another. There will be damage to the ligaments around the joint as well so this is quite a painful injury. The common places where this happens are the:

- shoulder
- elbow
- jaw
- thumb
- fingers.

It can be very difficult to tell the difference between a dislocation and a fracture, so you should treat them the same way. **On no account should you attempt to put the bone back into place; this is a job for an expert.**

Sprains

These occur where there is overstretching, or tearing, of ligaments at a joint. They are usually caused by a sudden wrench or twist and it is a very common injury at the ankle.

It can be very difficult to tell this injury from a fracture or a dislocation, so it should be treated the same way as a fracture. Often, the only way to tell these three injuries apart is to have an X-ray, so it is always best to be cautious.

Strains

These are caused by overstretching a muscle. They can also be caused by a twist or a wrench. They are quite painful and there may be some reduced or weakened movement where the injury occurred, but the symptoms would not be as serious as a sprain, dislocation or fracture.

Bandaging the area will help as this will give some support to the injury. An elastic bandage can be particularly good. Other treatment for strains is covered under the subhead 'Soft tissue injury treatment'.

Cuts

The technical name for any form of bleeding is a **haemorrhage**. Cuts can vary greatly in size and seriousness.

Any wound such as a cut should be gently cleaned and dressed. A plaster may be enough to cover and protect the cut. If not, it may be necessary to put on a bandage. Large or deep cuts may need hospital treatment as they may require stitching to close the wound properly.

If blood is pumping out of a cut under pressure, there has been damage to an artery, and this must be treated as very serious. An ambulance must be called immediately.

Bruises

These are extremely common. They are patches of blood beneath the skin. The blood vessels have been damaged just like a cut but the skin has not been broken, so the bleeding occurs beneath the skin. The first sign of a bruise is swelling. Then there will be discoloration of the area, which means it might go blue or purple first, then green or yellow.

A bruise should be treated by applying ice to it. This will reduce the swelling and relieve the pain. The ice needs to be applied quite quickly. If it is, it will limit the extent of the injury. Witch-hazel, a natural lotion, can be applied to give relief to the symptoms.

Did you know?

The correct term for a bruise is a haematoma. A very painful version of this is a 'dead leg' (also known as a Charley horse), which is where a blow to the top outside of the leg results in the muscle being crushed against the bone.

Shock

There are two types of shock, which may result from an injury.

- **Primary shock** – this is a feeling of faintness that can come on immediately after an emotional or traumatic event. This is only a temporary feeling and often passes quite quickly. Calming and reassuring the person will usually be enough to help them to overcome this. They may be able to take some liquid and might also need to be kept warm.
- **True shock** – this is a far more serious state. It will come about after a serious injury such as a very bad cut or fracture. The person affected will be close to collapse and it is very important that they are treated in hospital. You can calm and reassure them but an ambulance must be called.

One of the ways to treat shock is to move the person from the scene of the injury (follow all the safeguards outlined earlier on pages 133). It may be necessary to decide whether to treat them for shock or their injury.

It may be their own injury or someone else's that is causing the state of shock and they have to be treated accordingly. If at all possible, the person should not be left alone. Instead, try to get someone else to go for help. Your support and reassurance will be vital.

Concussion

This is a sudden loss of consciousness. It is often caused by a blow to the head, although it does not have to be a particularly hard blow to cause **concussion**. The sufferer may be unconscious for a few seconds or even for several hours. There is such a thing as **delayed concussion**, which means that the person becomes unconscious up to several hours after being injured. If there is any doubt, the person must be checked in hospital. It is a set procedure now for people to be kept in hospital overnight as a precaution if there is any chance of concussion.

Figure 33.2 A serious head wound will require hospital treatment

The signs of concussion are:

- immediate unconsciousness
- very relaxed limbs with a very weak and irregular pulse
- slow and shallow breathing
- large pupils (known as dilated)
- bleeding from the ears (this indicates a serious injury and must be dealt with as an emergency).

Like many other injuries listed here, concussion is a matter for the experts. At the scene, the important task is to spot it and get help.

Cramp

This is an involuntary contraction of a muscle and although it is quite painful it is easy to treat and to 'cure'. To do this, the sufferer needs to stretch the muscle affected as far as it will go. For example, if you get cramp in the calf you should straighten the knee and bend the foot back upwards at the ankle.

Cramp does not always stop the performer from carrying on, although serious cases can. Often it is just a slight cramp that can be put right. Remember, also, that it can be caused by loss of salt through sweating.

Skin infections

Although these are often considered to be minor, they can be very painful and uncomfortable. People who regularly take part in physical activity are very likely to suffer from them.

- **Athlete's foot** – this is a fungal infection that causes itching and broken skin on the feet, between the toes. In severe cases it causes bleeding and it is most uncomfortable. One of the causes can be not drying the feet properly. It is also highly contagious and can be passed on by sharing towels and socks. Creams and powders are available to treat it and these have to be used regularly.
- **Verrucas** – these are also known as plantar warts. They are a type of wart that occurs on the feet. These are contagious and can be painful. They may need to be treated by a doctor.
- **Blisters** – these are very common. They are caused by friction on the skin, which results in a break in the layers of the skin. The small gap between the layers then fills up with a fluid called serum and the blister forms in a bubble shape. A small blister can be left to disperse on its own and may be covered with some sticky plaster or gauze. With a very large blister, however (and therefore very uncomfortable and painful), it maybe necessary for a doctor or medical person to burst it in order to drain the fluid. The doctor/medic would do this by making a small hole with a sterile needle and gently squeezing out the fluid. It is important not to let the area become infected. Severe blisters can stop a performer from carrying on in sport.

Most skin infections are minor, but they can turn into more serious infections if they are not treated carefully. The skin is a defence barrier so performers must be very careful if it is damaged in any way.

Environmental 'injuries'

These are any disorders that can be caused by the environment. They include the following.

- **Exposure** – this can happen when a performer is in very low temperatures and the severe cold affects their body. They may not be able to keep their body temperature at the normal rate and prolonged exposure can result in death.
- **Frostbite** – this can happen if a performer is suffering from exposure where the tissue is damaged by the extreme cold and a condition called gangrene sets in. This is a decay of the tissue and is very serious. Affected areas often have to be amputated. Clearly, this is a condition that only occurs in countries where very low temperatures are a possibility.
- **Hypothermia** – this is a rapid cooling of the body where the temperature drops quickly. If it occurs, any wet clothing should be removed and the casualty should be covered with warm and dry clothing or blankets and medical help sought.
- **Heat-stroke** – this is caused by very high temperatures and can lead to vomiting and uncontrollable shaking. It is caused because the body is overheating and is not able to keep the temperature down. Exposure to very high temperatures should be avoided to prevent this.
- **Exhaustion** – this can be caused by a variety of factors, but it is a state of extreme fatigue. Excessive heat or cold can cause this because the body system is struggling to cope with the extremes of temperature.

The main cure for all of the above is prevention. If performers are exposed to low temperatures in particular, they should ensure they are dressed properly. The correct clothing is essential as a safety precaution.

Soft tissue injury treatment

Soft tissue injury is where there is an injury to ligaments or muscles. The standard treatment that can be applied to any soft tissue injury is known as the RICE treatment. RICE stands for Rest, Ice, Compression and Elevation. It is described in more detail below.

- **Rest** – stop straight away and rest the injury; carrying on can make things far worse.
- **Ice** – applying ice to the injury reduces swelling and relieves some of the pain. Do not directly apply ice; use an ice pack or wrap the ice in a towel.
- **Compression** – this can be with either a bandage or some tape which will add some support and pressure on the injured area. Be very careful not to apply this too tightly and restrict the blood flow.
- **Elevation** – try to raise the injured body part. This will decrease the circulation to the area, as it must work against gravity. It will also help to drain away any other fluid at the injury.

The RICE treatment, which is very simple and effective, should be applied to any injury to the muscles, the ligaments or the skin.

Emergency treatments

Other treatments may need to be given to a person who is seriously injured and who has either stopped breathing or whose heart has stopped beating.

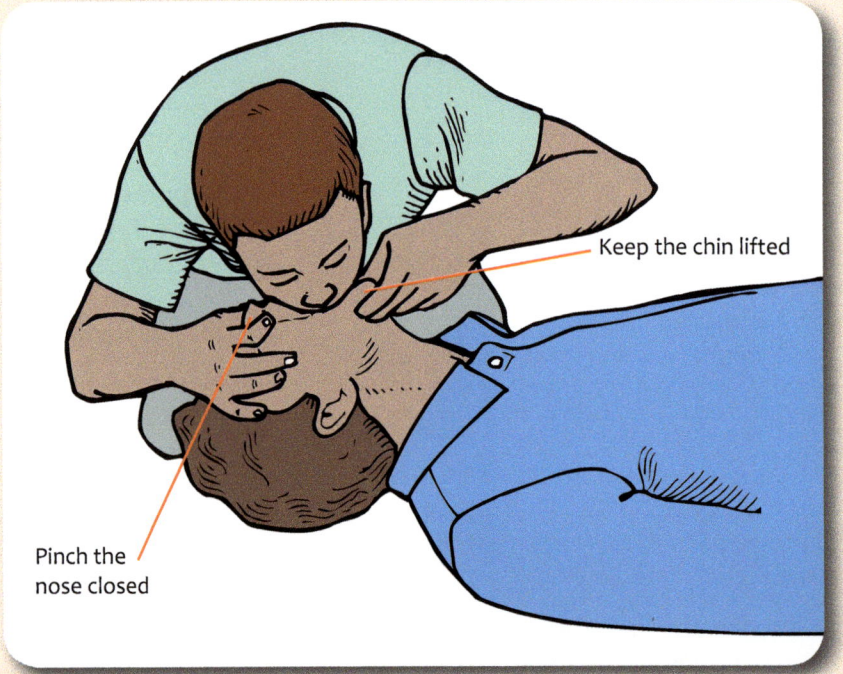

Figure 33.3 Performing expelled air resuscitation

Knowledge of the following expelled air resuscitation techniques could enable you to save someone's life. These resuscitation techniques are quite easy to do if you follow the steps described.

Expelled air resuscitation

This technique is often called 'mouth-to-mouth' resuscitation. If someone has stopped breathing, it is the most effective way to get their breathing started again.

Step 1 Before starting to treat the casualty, get someone to phone for an ambulance or paramedic.

Step 2 Tilt the casualty's chin back and check that their airways are clear.

Step 3 Carefully look/listen/feel for any signs of breathing. If there are none, then move to step 4.

Step 4 Take a deep breath, pinch the casualty's nostrils together with your fingers and seal your lips around their open mouth.

Step 5 Blow into the casualty's lungs. Look along their chest to see if their chest is rising.

Step 6 Move your mouth away and breathe out any excess air as their chest falls. Take a deep breath and blow again.

Step 7 After two inflations, spend 10 seconds checking for a pulse. If there is none then give two more inflations and check again. Do this for up to five attempts.

If you are unable to do mouth-to-mouth resuscitation, you can use mouth-to-nose as an alternative. To do this, you seal the casualty's mouth with your thumb and seal your lips around the nose.

Provided the heart is beating, continue inflations at about 12–16 per minute until the person is breathing on their own. **If there is no pulse or sign of a heartbeat, you will have to perform cardio-pulmonary resuscitation.**

> **Task 2**
>
> If you have access to a resuscitation dummy, use the seven steps to practise the resuscitation procedure.

Hints and Tips!

It is very important to know the difference between a strain and a sprain and also to be fully aware of what the RICE principle stands for, as these are the most basic forms of injury and treatment.

Key questions

1. Describe two general rules for treatment that should be applied in most cases of sporting injury.
2. List the signs to look for when a fracture is suspected.
3. Explain the difference between a strain and a sprain.
4. State the two different types of shock which can occur.
5. Explain what is meant by each of the letters in the RICE principle. What type of injury can this be used to treat?

34 The history of sport and international sport

Origins

Sport originated from hunting, fighting and the relationship of people with animals. To our ancestors, the types of activities we would consider to be sport today were the very things they needed to do to survive. In primitive cultures and early civilisations it was the fittest who survived and this meant the ones who could throw a spear accurately and powerfully, who could track, chase and catch food and who were strong enough to fight against enemies were those who lived longest.

During those times there were no nations or tribes, but this gradually changed and groups started to live together as communities. When this happened there were small settlements at first, then towns and cities, and eventually nations. As these groups formed there was a need to protect the communities they contained. This led to the formation of armies. This, in turn, led to the start of sporting activities – especially combat sports.

Armies needed to be ready for battle, and needed to be kept occupied and fit. This was achieved through practice and training. Much of this involved competition. Wrestling and boxing quite obviously developed from this time and many of the martial arts popular today also began at this time in the East.

The first stadiums to stage these 'sports' were built by the Romans. The events often involved men fighting against each other and against animals. It is interesting to note that stadiums have not changed very much from Roman times to now.

Much of the 'sport' that went on in the Roman amphitheatres was very cruel and violent. It often involved animals or men fighting against each other to the death. Five thousand animals are recorded as being killed in one day in AD 80 and there is a record of 400 bears and 300 lions being killed in one day in Emperor Nero's reign. Over the years the contests changed and became tests of skill, strength and stamina.

One of the first recorded gymnastic-type activities occurred 3000 years ago in Crete (the Minoan culture) when young men used to perform bull dances and would vault onto the head of a bull using the horns, onto the back and then somersault off onto the ground behind them. This was almost certainly performed in front of spectators and was a most important ceremony.

Horses were linked with sport early on. Originally, the horse was used for war and combat. It was essential to be a good horse-rider, and horses were trained to be used for war as long ago as 1350 BC. From this and chariot racing, the sports of racing and show jumping have evolved.

> **Key point**
>
> International sport is always closely associated with political and financial controversy as well as the problems associated with staging these major events. The Olympic Games are often the focal point for international sport in many ways.

> **Task 1**
>
> List the similarities and differences between the Roman stadium or amphitheatre and modern stadiums.

Figure 34.1 The Coliseum in Rome, Italy, where gladiators fought in front of huge numbers of spectators

Contests between men (at this point in history it was only the men who were involved) began many years ago. There are drawings on the walls of Egyptian tombs dating from 2300 BC that clearly show some moves and holds in wrestling. Interestingly, one of the most popular of the martial arts, judo, only started in the late 19th century.

There is no doubt that sport in some form has existed in all cultures throughout the world for thousands of years. Cave paintings that are 20,000 years old depict hunters with basic weapons and clearly show the movements made.

Organised sport

Organised sport is not so old, although it does originate from all the various types of combat, competition and festivals that went before.

The ancient Greek Olympics are probably the best and earliest example. The different states that made up Greece were almost constantly at war with each other. However, they would stop fighting at intervals to have a contest of athletics, wrestling and combat between contestants from the various states. The contest was held at the Temple of Zeus, at Olympia. The first time this contest is recorded as taking place was 776 BC and it lasted for 7 days.

The Greeks were also responsible for the start of another very famous contest, the marathon. In 490 BC the Greek army defeated the Persians at a place called Marathon and a runner, called Pheidippides, ran from Marathon to Athens with the news. He is supposed to have collapsed and died of exhaustion just after he arrived. The marathon distance is now set at 42.195 kilometres (26 miles 385 yards) because that is the distance over which the 1908 Olympic distance was run. The actual distance from Marathon to Athens was about 35 kilometres (22 miles) and later races were run over about 42 kilometres (26 miles). The 1908 games held in London required the runners to run an extra 195 yards so that they could finish opposite the Royal Box at the White City stadium and this has been the standard distance ever since.

Sporting contests were held all over the world. There were many local customs associated with the events, some of which still take place today.

A form of football is recorded as being played as early as AD 1352. Many villages in England competed against a neighbouring one to get a ball from one village to the next. There were no rules and the 'game' was so rough that it was not unheard of for people to be killed.

Figure 34.2 The finish of the 1908 Olympic Games marathon

Ball games, and bat and ball games, were played in some form all over the world and parts of one game were copied, or adapted, to start other games. The main reason that these games were not organised other than locally was due to the lack of transport. It was not possible to play against any but local teams. Travelling between countries was quite unusual and took a very long time.

As transport improved, competitions between areas within countries and between countries could take place. Organised and international sport was possible and this led to a need for the rules and regulations to be written down and agreed on.

Origins of some sports

Athletics

This is divided up into track and field events, the origins of which can be traced right back to the Greek Games over 4000 years ago. Many of the throwing events are based on hunting skills and many of the track events are straightforward tests of strength, speed, skill and stamina.

Basketball

This game was invented by a doctor called James Naismith in 1891. He was a professor of physical education at the University of Kansas. The game was originally played with peach baskets nailed to the ends of the gymnasium walls. It is unusual to be able to trace the origin of a game as accurately as we can with basketball. It is even possible to state the day on which the first game was played: 20 January 1892.

Did you know?

Baseball was first introduced to the Caribbean via trade ships that picked up sugar from the island of Cuba in the mid-1800s. Cuba's teams played their first organised game in 1874.

Task 2

Make a list of sports in which it is possible to have a 'hat trick'.

Did you know?

Jamaica's 'Reggae Boyz' qualified for the 1998 World Cup, and Trinidad and Tobago's 'Socca Warriors' qualified for the 2008 Games in Germany.

Task 3

Find out which country has won the football World Cup the most times.

Did you know?

The game badminton originated from two English children's games known as battledore and shuttlecock. It was thought to be played by British military officers stationed in India in the mid-18th century and was officially launched as a sport in 1873 at Badminton House, Gloucestershire. This is where the sport got its name.

The game of netball (originally an indoor game) was derived from basketball (originally an outdoor game). The changes over the years are interesting because netball then became more of an outdoor game, with basketball becoming an indoor game.

Baseball

This is a version of rounders, which was introduced into North America by the early settlers in the 18th century. A great many bat and ball games were played in various parts of Britain: rounders is just one version.

Cricket

Cricket bats have been found dating back as far as 1750. In 1774 the first game was played with two stumps with a bail between them. The third stump was added in 1776.

Records seem to show that the game has existed in some form since the 13th century. Thomas Lord founded the Marylebone Cricket Club (MCC) in 1787 and the Lords cricket ground is named after him.

Underarm bowling was the original technique used, but in 1864 full overarm bowling was allowed. Many other changes have been allowed since but all have to be agreed by the MCC, which still decides all of the rules of the game.

Cricket is one of the oldest of the international games. The first test match was played between England and Australia in 1887 and an English side had toured Australia as early as 1861.

Cricket is responsible for a famous sporting term. In the early days a bowler would be given a top hat if he took three wickets in consecutive deliveries – this was the origin of the term 'hat trick'.

Figure 34.3 Old cricket bat

Football (soccer)

The ancient Chinese played a version of football/soccer, using the head of a defeated enemy, which was kicked around the battlefield. This sport in its present form has evolved to be just about the most popular sport in the world.

The Football Association (FA) was formed in England in 1863 and started to work out the agreed rules of the game. The first international match took place between England and Scotland in 1872.

Professional football/soccer was allowed from 1885, which makes it one of the oldest professional sports in existence. The first FA Cup competition was held in 1871 when there were only 15 entries.

The World Cup was first organised in 1930 and was played in Uruguay. The host country went on to win the cup on that occasion.

The international organisation that runs soccer (FIFA) has more than 160 nations affiliated to it.

Figure 34.4 Spain were the football World Cup winners in 2010

Rugby

In 1823, a pupil at Rugby school in England picked up a soccer ball during a game and ran with it. He is credited with starting the game of rugby. His name was William Webb Ellis.

In 1895 there was an argument over whether or not players should be allowed to be paid, and this caused a split in the game. Rugby union was the amateur version of the game with 15 players on each side; rugby league was the professional version with 13 players per side. The situation changed in 1995 when rugby union players were openly allowed to earn money from the game. It is now very common for rugby players to 'switch codes' from one version of the game to the other.

Rugby union took a lot longer to stage its own World Cup. The first one did not take place until 1987 when it was won by New Zealand. The cup was named after William Webb Ellis.

Tennis

A game called real tennis was played in the Middle Ages and lawn tennis started in the 19th century. In the 18th century, inmates at Fleet prison used to hit a ball against the prison wall and, in 1850, pupils at Harrow School used to practise against a wall while waiting to play rackets on an indoor court. They used a soft, slow 'squashy' ball, and from this the game of squash started to evolve.

Table tennis began as a game played between two students at Cambridge University with two cigar boxes and a champagne cork.

Hockey

There is evidence of this being played as long ago as 3 BC. The ancient Greeks, Egyptians and Romans played a version of a combination of the games hurling and shinty from Ireland.

International sport

Competing internationally is every performer's ultimate aim. It is one of the main reasons for some people taking up sport and continuing to participate in it.

The Olympic Games

The earliest recorded Olympic Games took place in 776 BC in the stadium of Olympia, which is where the Olympics get their name. They were held in honour of the God Zeus. Even that long ago, the stadium in which the Games took place was quite impressive as there was enough room for 40,000 spectators.

These Games were held every 4 years, and all hostilities and wars stopped while the Games took place. Typical events at that time were wrestling, boxing, running (the main event was over 200 yards), discus, javelin, long jump and chariot racing. Nearly all of those events still take place today.

The Games carried on in this way for many years until the reign of Emperor Theodosius in AD 394. He thought the Games had lost their religious meaning and that the performers only took part for the riches of winning, so he stopped them.

The Olympics were not held again until 1500 years later when they were re-launched in 1896 in Athens, Greece. The links with the original Olympics went further than simply holding them in the same country. Many traditions were established based on the old Games. Before each Olympics a torch is lit at Olympia using the sun's rays. This torch is carried by a relay of runners to the host city's stadium to light a flame which then burns throughout the Games.

Thirteen nations entered the Games of 1896, and the total number of athletes was 285. They were all men, as women were not allowed to enter.

The modern Olympics

The Olympic Games that have taken place since 1896 are referred to as the modern Olympics. They were started largely due to the efforts and determination of one man.

Baron Pierre de Coubertin was a French educationalist who had been very impressed with the way that sport was organised and run in England. He had made several visits and liked the way that events such as the Henley

Figure 34.5 Baron Pierre de Coubertin, 'founder' of the modern Olympic Games

> "The most important thing in the Olympic Games is not to win but to take part. Just as the most important thing in life is not the triumph but the struggle."
>
> Baron Pierre de Coubertin

Regatta (for rowing) were organised. This, together with the discovery of the ruins of the original stadium in Olympia in 1875 by some German archaeologists, led to him starting a movement to reintroduce the Games. So, in 1894 the International Olympic Committee (IOC) was formed and it set about the task of organising the Games for 1896.

Baron de Coubertin believed that the Olympic movement he had founded would promote world peace and harmony. One of his famous quotes is displayed on the scoreboard at the opening of each Olympic Games, as it is what he based his ideas on:

The IOC originally consisted of people chosen by De Coubertin himself, but it is now a very large body with representatives from all of the participating nations. It is this committee that decides where the Games are to be held. De Coubertin decided that the Games should move all around the world and be awarded to a city rather than a country. Now, cities have to make a bid to stage the Olympic Games and the final decision can be made 6 years before, to give the host city adequate time to prepare.

At one time, not many cities were prepared to host the Games because they were very expensive and usually ran at a loss. This situation changed after the 1984 Games in Los Angeles where the marketing and sponsorship of the Games resulted in a 'surplus' being made. In theory the Olympics should not run at a profit, which is why they used the word 'surplus'. Once cities – and countries – realised that there was an opportunity to promote themselves, improve facilities and standards, and make money as well, the whole business of bidding for, and staging, the Games took on more importance.

The recent Games and some hitches

The Olympic Games were the first major international sporting event and they are still the most important and successful of all of the events to take place. However, things have not always run smoothly and nearly all of the recent ones have been affected by problems of one sort or another. The following is a brief description of the major events that have affected the Games.

Berlin, 1936

The decision to award these Games to Berlin was made in 1931, 2 years before Adolph Hitler and his Nazi party came to power in Germany.

One of the main beliefs of Hitler and the Nazis was that there was a master race, known as the Aryans. These people were blond and fair skinned and were true Germans. The Nazis despised the Jews and other ethnic groups and by the time of the Olympics had started to persecute them and introduce separate laws for them.

Hitler tried to use the Berlin Games to promote all of these ideas and they were used as a propaganda exercise. One of the main reasons it failed was due to the success of a black American athlete called Jesse Owens.

Jesse Owens ended up winning four gold medals in the track and field events, much to Hitler's obvious disapproval. The American team had only narrowly voted to attend the Games, because of Hitler's well-known views on black athletes and Jews. The success of the many black athletes in the American team was a great embarrassment for Hitler and stopped him achieving what he had set out to do.

This was the most extreme case of political interference in any of the Olympic Games and it made the organisers far more careful in selecting hosts in the future.

Figure 34.6 Jesse Owens, a successful black athlete who took part in the Berlin Games

Mexico City, 1968

One of the main controversies about these Games was that they were awarded to Mexico City in the first place. This was because it is situated at a very high altitude and this helps the performance of athletes who train in these conditions. It also assists athletes in the shorter, more explosive events. There was genuine concern for performers in longer events in case the rarefied atmosphere caused them difficulties.

The cost of putting on the event was also criticised. Mexico was a very poor country with poor housing and food shortages. A vast amount of money was spent on just staging the Games. The city of Tokyo, which had held the Games 4 years earlier, had spent US$200 million and it was doubtful if Mexico could really afford the Games.

Some black American athletes gave a 'Black Power' salute during the medal ceremony, by raising a black gloved fist. The first and third runners in the 200 metres, Tommie Smith and John Carlos, plus the 400-metre relay team, were sent home for doing so. The athletes took this action to highlight the way that black people were treated in America. At that time there was a great deal of prejudice against black citizens in the United States and the athletes chose this way to make their protest and make the world more aware of the problem.

Munich, 1972

There was another Black Power protest by two Americans, Vince Matthews and Wayne Collett, during a medal ceremony in the Munich Games when they failed to stand to attention. However, these Games were completely dominated by a terrorist attack on some of the athletes.

There was unrest in the Middle East and a group of Palestinian terrorists attacked members of the Israeli team. Eight terrorists attacked the Israeli quarters, killed two of the team and took nine others hostage. After a gun battle (seen throughout the world on television), all of the hostages, five terrorists and a German police officer were killed.

The security aspect of staging the Games was highlighted and was to become a major consideration for future Games.

Montreal, 1976

South Africa had been banned from the Games since 1964 (Tokyo) because of the apartheid policy that existed in that country (see Chapter 35). However, a rugby team from New Zealand had toured South Africa and had thereby upset most of the other African nations. The African nations threatened to boycott the Games unless the New Zealand team was banned.

New Zealand took part and the African nations stayed away – a total of 30 nations did not go. This was to be the start of a long period of boycotts for various reasons.

Figure 34.7 One of the Palestinian terrorists with a member of the negotiating team during the hostage crisis in 1972

> **Task 4**
>
> See if you can find out about any controversial events that occurred in any other major international competitions.

The financial cost of these Games was very high. After the incident in Munich security had to be greatly increased and this was on top of the enormous cost of staging the Games. The city of Montreal continued to pay off the debt of staging the Games for many years.

Moscow, 1980

The choice of Moscow for these Games had been quite controversial because the Soviet Union did not have a very good record on human rights. However, they were one of the most successful competing countries in the history of the Olympics and had never staged it before.

To make matters worse, the Soviet Union invaded the neighbouring country of Afghanistan in late 1979 and still had an invasion force there in 1980.

It was too late to change the venue for the Games but many countries demanded that the Soviet Union withdraw its forces or they would boycott the Games. The Soviet Union refused to withdraw its troops and many countries had to decide whether or not to send competitors. Some countries, such as the USA, refused to send any. Great Britain advised its competitors against going but did not stop them. As a result, a total of 52 nations, including the USA and Canada, boycotted the Games and many individuals also decided not to go.

Many thought the Games were devalued because of this. The American teams were always very strong and with so many nations away the standard was not always as high as it had been.

Los Angeles, 1984

As the venue is chosen 6 years in advance, the IOC could not avoid America staging the Olympics immediately after it had boycotted the Moscow Games. There was a great fear that the Soviet Union would retaliate against the USA, and it did.

The Soviet Union, and 14 other nations, boycotted the Games. The official reason they gave was concern over security arrangements. There was still ill feeling between the USA and the Soviet Union over the invasion of Afghanistan and there were threats of demonstrations in America against Soviet performers.

There is little doubt that the worry about security was a convenient excuse for the Soviet Union to get its own back and nearly all of the other countries that boycotted were influenced by this, as they were also communist countries.

Another excuse was that the Games were being over-commercialised. The staging of the Games and its organisation followed the American tradition of showmanship and the opening ceremony was one of the most spectacular ever seen. The whole event was sponsored by large international companies and, for the first time, the Games ran at a large profit. All of this was against what the communist countries believed in.

Seoul, 1988

Seoul is in South Korea, and there had been a longstanding dispute between it and its neighbouring country of North Korea. There had been a war between the two countries in 1952 and their situation in 1988 was little improved. The IOC was criticised for awarding Seoul the Games and there was a great amount of tension, right up until the start, because it was thought that the facilities would not be ready and that North Korea would interfere. The North Koreans had already demanded that they be allowed to stage some of the events.

In the end there was very little disruption and the Games were quite successful. There was another boycott by five countries, including North Korea and Cuba. It is likely that more countries would have considered boycotting but the IOC had introduced a rule that if a country boycotted the Games all their officials would be excluded and not allowed to take part in decision-making. This clearly deterred many.

Sadly, the main controversy at these Games involved positive drug tests. In all, ten athletes were banned after testing positive for **performance-enhancing drugs**. The most famous athlete was Ben Johnson. He was a Canadian sprinter who won the 100 metres in a world record time and was then stripped of his title 2 days later.

Barcelona, 1992

After all the controversial events that had gone before, the 1992 Games were just about incident free.

A great deal of political change had occurred since the previous Games. The Eastern European communist governments had collapsed and the Soviet Union had ceased to exist. This meant that there was no longer an East and a West Germany but a unified German team. Also, the countries that had previously made up the Soviet Union all now existed in their own right and were able to compete individually. There were 12 new competing states from the former Soviet Union and some individuals, who could not be considered to be from an affiliated nation, competed under the Olympic flag.

Another 'new' face was South Africa, which was allowed to return to the Olympics for the first time since 1964. The South Africans had abolished the apartheid system (see Chapter 35) and were entering a mixed-race team.

The total number of official sports was increased to 25 with the addition of badminton and baseball, and the total number of medal events was increased by an additional 20 to 257. There were over 12,000 athletes and officials involved in the Games.

There was still some drug controversy as three British competitors – sprinter Jason Livingstone, and weightlifters Andrew Saxton and Andrew Davies – were tested positive and sent home.

One of the major changes made by the IOC in recent years was to organise the Winter Olympics to take place between the Summer Olympics. This is why the 1992 Games in Albertville, France were followed 2 years later by the Games in Lillehammer, Norway. They have since continued on a 4-year cycle in between the Summer Games.

Atlanta, 1996

The Games were scheduled to run from 19 July right through to 4 August and there had been some controversy about switching of the venue at this time of the year. Atlanta, however, had spent 6 years planning, constructing and organising the largest Olympics yet.

The high temperatures and high humidity were thought to be potentially dangerous in many of the events. One of the measures the organisers took was to have fans blowing fine mists of water. This was used in many of the cross-country horse-riding events.

There were 197 nations taking part and over 11,000 competitors took part in the opening ceremony alone. This meant that the ceremony lasted over 4 hours, and as a result it was decided to review the format for Sydney in 2000.

By Day 3 there were problems due to the large number of media and spectators who had come along for the event. There were crushes and queues at many of the venues. The IOC criticised the organisers for repeated transportation breakdowns (performers were often late getting to events or struggled to get there at all) and for computer failures that left the media unable to report properly.

Softball was introduced to the Olympics for the first time. Another new sport to be added to the Olympic events was beach volleyball. Atlanta also saw a great deal of attention focused on the 'Dream Team' of American professional basketball stars.

Irish swimmer Michelle Smith won her third gold medal by Day 6 and insisted her rapid progress was not due to any performance-enhancing drugs. By 1997, however, Smith had been tested positive and charged, and was eventually banned in 1999. There are still moves to have her medals taken from her.

On Day 9, 27 July, there was a tragedy that marred the whole event. A pipe bomb blast in Centennial Olympic Park (a nearby park that had been renamed and was a meeting point for people attending the Olympic Stadium) killed one person and injured a further 11 people who were attending a concert there. This brought new fears of terrorist attacks and although the Games continued, security was greatly increased and the park was closed for 3 days.

At the closing ceremony the IOC president Juan Antonio Samaranch invoked the memory of the 11 Israeli athletes who had been killed in Munich in 1972, and also asked for 1 minute's silence for the injured and dead from the bomb explosion earlier during the Games.

> **Task 5**
>
> What problems do you think are likely to occur at the next Olympic Games?

Sydney, 2000

This was generally thought to be one of the most successful games of recent times. The Games were very well organised and presented, and there was very little in the way of controversy or major incident.

Perhaps the most controversial aspect was the withdrawal of 27 athletes and 13 team officials by the Chinese team just before the Games. They also withdrew an entire rowing team after 'suspicious tests' were returned regarding drugs. The general opinion was that the Chinese had decided to pull out team members rather than risk them failing drug tests during the Games. As it was, there were ten positive tests during the event with athletes from 18 different countries being banned through positive drug tests. An Uzbekistan Olympic official also had two phials of Human Growth Hormone (HGH) seized at Sydney airport just before the Games began.

The drug-testing procedures for Sydney were said to be the most advanced and effective yet used. It was claimed that the low levels of performance in many of the events (such as the marathon) were evidence that less cheating had occurred.

These Games also proved to be the most successful ones for the Great Britain team since 1920. This was thought to be largely due to the vast amounts of money the National Lottery had made available to performers. A total of £53.7 million had been provided since 1997. Rowing received £9.6 million and proved to be one of the most successful, with two gold medals. One of these medalists was Steve Redgrave, who won his fifth gold medal in a row – a record for an endurance event athlete and an amazing achievement over a 20-year period!

Athens, 2004

This was the first time since 1896 that the games returned to Greece. There were real concerns about whether or not all of the facilities would be completed in time for the games to get underway. The main stadium was only completed 2 months before the start and the opening ceremony.

For the very first time women's wrestling was included as an event. One of the controversies was when the Brazilian runner Vanderlei de Lima was attacked by Irish priest Cornelius Horan and dragged into the crowd. De Lima recovered to take bronze, and was later awarded the Pierre de Coubertin medal for sportsmanship.

Figure 34.8 The excitement of Usain Bolt after his record-breaking performances at the Olympic Games in 2008

Swimmer Michael Phelps went on to win eight medals (six gold and two bronze) and to become the first athlete to win eight medals in a non-boycotted Olympic Games.

Beijing, 2008

The choice of China as hosts was controversial because of concern about the country's record on human rights but the event had the largest television audience in Olympic history with 4.7 billion viewers worldwide.

To many, the highlight of the games was Usain Bolt becoming the, 'world's fastest man' and breaking the world record in both the 100- and 200- metre sprints on his way to winning two gold medals.

It was estimated that US$40 billion was spent by China in hosting these games which would make it the most expensive Olympics by a very wide margin. There were a total of nine new events added in these games, including BMX cycling.

Despite concerns, there were no protests, no terrorist attacks, no performer protests and no issues with the poor quality – an area of great concern prior to the games.

Figure 34.9 Drummers performing at the opening ceremony of the Beijing Olympics

Figure 34.10 Trinidad and Tobago Men's 4x100 metres relay team, silver medal winners at the Beijing Olympics

Other international events

In many ways most other major international events are based on the success of the Olympics. There are several other major 'Games' that take place throughout the world.

Commonwealth Games

The idea of staging some Games for all the members of what was then the British Empire (countries previously governed and ruled by Great Britain) was first suggested by Astley Cooper in 1891. It was not until about 40 years later, in 1930, at Hamilton, Ontario, Canada, that the first such games took place.

There had been similar types of events because just after the 1920 Antwerp Olympics there was an athletics match between the USA and the British Empire, and the same thing happened after the 1924 Paris Olympics.

Originally the organisation that ran the games was called the British Empire Games Federation, but this was later changed to the British Commonwealth Games Federation. Any country that is a member of the Commonwealth may take part. The games follow the format of the Olympics very closely and are also held every 4 years, following each Olympics by 2 years. They have a reputation for being the 'friendly games' and have not been as disrupted by boycotts or scandals as the Olympics.

These have been very successful games for many Caribbean countries that regularly participate and enjoy a large measure of success. The 1966 Commonwealth Games were held in Kingston, Jamaica. This was the very first time that the games were held outside of what was known as the 'White Dominions'. Commemorative stamps were designed in honour of this occasion.

Pan-American Games

These were started in 1951 and took place in Buenos Aires. They are also modelled on the Olympic Games even down to a copy of the opening ceremony. They take place the year before each Olympics and any country in North or South America may take part.

Wimbledon

The Wimbledon tennis tournament is actually known as the All England Tennis Championships, but it is largely regarded as the most important tennis tournament of all. There is no official World Championship in tennis, but if there were the players would regard Wimbledon to be it.

Originally, Wimbledon was the home of the All England Croquet Club and the members decided to use the well-tended croquet lawns to play tennis. In 1877 the first tennis championships were held and, apart from breaks for the First and Second World Wars, they have been held every year since.

In 1968, the organisers took the very bold step of declaring the championship to be an open event so that both amateurs and professionals could play. This was the first major international competition to take this step and it paved the way for the breakdown of barriers in other sports.

> **Task 6**
> List as many other major international sporting events as you can.

World championships

Many different sports stage their own world championships that are now established as major international sporting events. Some of them have only begun fairly recently but it is unusual to find any major sport that does not have one.

Football/soccer

The world championship in football is usually simply called the World Cup. This is because it was one of the first world championships to be held in any of the major sports. The first World Cup was held in Uruguay in 1930. It took the ruling body of football/soccer, FIFA, quite a long time to organise it. When the six member countries met in 1904, they decided to organise a tournament. The principle of the cup was agreed in 1920 and the president, Jules Rimet (after whom the first World Cup trophy was named), was influential in getting it under way.

The choice of Uruguay to host the first World Cup was not unexpected. It had won Olympic gold medals in 1924 and 1928, and 1930 was its centenary year. The government also offered to pay all of the competing teams' expenses and build a new stadium for 100,000 spectators.

The tournament has continued to be very successful and is televised throughout the world. Its success encouraged other sports to start their own version, in the same way that the Olympics set the standards for other championships.

Cricket

Cricket was quite late organising a world championship due mainly to the nature of the game. At test level a game lasts for 5 days, so organising a tournament on this basis would be just about impossible. The development of the 1-day knockout games meant that cricket could be played in a format that could be used in a tournament.

Figure 34.11 Logo for the ICC World Twenty20 cricket tournament 2012 – Sri Lanka

The first Cricket World Cup was held in 1983 in England and has been played every 4 years since. The Twenty20 version of the cricket World Cup is now also very popular and, in 2010, the third event played was hosted by the West Indies.

Rugby

The Rugby World Cup started in 1987 – New Zealand beat France in the first final on home territory. The second finals were held in England and the third in South Africa. Each tournament has been bigger and more successful than the last.

Specific matches and events

Some sports become international events because of interest in a particular contest, or due to nations promoting their own interests. This is often true of boxing and, in particular, many of the heavyweight contests. One problem is that there are so many versions of the world championship that it is held several times a year.

Test match series, such as those played in cricket and rugby, are considered to be international events and command a lot of attention.

The Super Bowl is the climax of the American football season, when the final game is played between the winners of the two conferences (that is, the two separate leagues) in America. It is billed as the World Championship even though it is only open to American teams.

Hints and Tips!

The history of sport is a vast subject and questions relating directly to it are very unlikely. However, the political and financial issues linked to sport and the advantages and disadvantages of staging sporting events are very current issues.

Key questions

1. Describe the controversial issues surrounding three different Olympic Games held since 1936.
2. Describe and explain the advantages to be gained from hosting a major international sporting event.
3. Describe and explain the disadvantages of hosting a major international sporting event.
4. Choose one particular sport and give a brief outline of its origins and history.
5. Describe and explain the links that exist between sponsors and major international sporting events.

35 Politics and sport

Despite what many people would like to happen, it is almost impossible to keep politics out of sport. Sport in most countries is financed, or at least monitored, from a government level and is therefore bound to be influenced.

Most countries have a minister, or politician, who is responsible for sport and who is very influential when advising the various sporting bodies. In some other countries, especially the old communist countries, sport was a political priority area. The state was in complete control.

The degree of control was shown when, in some years, communist countries boycotted the Olympic Games and refused to send their athletes. Their political systems meant that they could do this. In a similar situation, other countries could only advise its athletes against going and could not actually stop them from taking part.

Politics assisting sport

It is often thought that politicians only influence sport in a negative way, but this is not the case. Without the backing of the governments there would be far less provision in terms of facilities and funding. Past and present governments have also ensured that sport is, by law, part of the range of educational subjects offered in schools.

If there are major problems, then the government will usually act.

Figure 35.1 Sporting regulations often require officials such as stewards to organise and oversee aspects of events

There is no doubt that in many communist countries the political systems raised the standards of sport. Sport was given a very high profile. The athletes and sportspeople in those countries would not have considered that the government was interfering with sport, but were more likely to think that it was giving valuable assistance.

Key point

It is generally considered that politics only interferes with sport, but it does make positive contributions as well. It is important to consider it in line with both the history of sport and its relationship with the Olympic Games in particular.

Did you know?

All-seater stadiums were only introduced in Britain in 1994 (and therefore for all Premiership football matches) as a result of a British government enquiry that was set up following two serious football disasters involving crowds attending football matches.

Task 1

List the boycotts that occurred at different Olympic Games.

> **Task 2**
> List any recent examples you can find of politics interfering with sport.

Political issues

- 1920 – the Olympic Games were held in Antwerp, Belgium immediately after the First World War. Germany and its wartime allies were not sent an invitation to take part.
- 1925 – the year following the Paris Olympics, the Soviet Union Communist Party made a declaration that 'sport should be used as a means of rallying the broad masses of workers and peasants around the various Party and trade union organisations through which the masses of workers and peasants are to be drawn into social and political activity'. This set the tone for the communist attitude towards sport for the next 65 years.
- 1936 – the Olympics in Berlin were used as a propaganda exercise by Hitler.
- 1949 – a New Zealand rugby team was banned from South Africa because the team included Maori players.
- 1954 – China was finally admitted to the Olympics despite it still not accepting the International Olympic Committee's decision to recognise Taiwan.
- 1956 – China withdrew from the Olympic movement, and started a boycott of sports organisations and competitions.
- 1964 – South Africa was banned from the Olympics because of the apartheid laws (see Chapter 39). This led to a long period of demonstrations and boycotts throughout the 1960s and 1970s.
- 1970 – a state of war was declared between El Salvador and Honduras after a (football) World Cup qualifying game. Also, the South African cricket team was asked not to tour England after a formal request from James Callaghan, the British Home Secretary.
- 1972–88 – many political events disrupted the Olympic Games over this period.
- 1990 – the large communist states in Eastern Europe began to crumble and many new, smaller states were formed. The communist states' dominance of many sports started to decline.
- 1992 – South Africa was re-admitted to world sport after finally abandoning its apartheid policy.
- 2000 – following their first round exit from the African Nations Cup, the Ivory Coast national soccer team players were taken prisoner by the country's military forces! The first claim by the authorities was that they were being held 'for their own security', but another official stated that they were being held 'to teach them a sense of civic responsibility because of their indiscipline'. Many of the players held were contracted players for top European clubs and this put a question mark over players being released from their clubs to play for their countries.
- 2009 – Eight people were killed and more than a dozen injured when unidentified terrorists attacked a convoy of vehicles carrying players and umpires to a Pakistan–Sri Lanka cricket match. As a result Pakistan was not allowed to host matches at home and even played a series against Australia in England in 2010.

> **Hints and Tips!**
> The relationship between politics and sport is constantly changing, so it is important to keep up to date with current events via newspapers, television and the internet. Remember also that politics can be local, national and international, and all of these can affect sport in some way and at some level.

Key questions

1. Does politics always interfere with sport? Give an example where it clearly has.
2. Can politics assist with sport? If so, describe an actual example.
3. What was apartheid?
4. What is meant by a boycott and what effects is it intended to have?
5. Describe two particular issues that highlight the relationship between sport and politics.

36 Sponsorship

Sponsorship is now a vital part of sport. Without it many sports would not be able to provide what they do, and many performers would not be able to participate at the level they do. Some top-level performers would not be able to take part at all without it.

What is sponsored?

The range of sponsorship now covers individuals, teams or clubs, sports and events. It is very rare to find any aspect of sport where there is not some form of sponsorship.

Individuals

It is not only sportspeople who take part in individual sports who are sponsored. It is increasingly common for individuals within a team to be sponsored, too. Most professional sportspeople are sponsored, often by more than one company. For example, a racing driver's overalls and car are often an ideal place for sponsors to advertise themselves and their products. Each sponsor must pay for that space. Individuals (such as basketball players and cricketers) may have their own sponsorship for some things, while their team is separately sponsored.

If the sportsperson is particularly successful they can be paid very large amounts of money and have companies queuing up to sponsor them. It can reach the stage for some that they earn far more money from sponsorship deals than they do from the sport itself.

Teams and clubs

At just about any level, from small local cricket teams to full international teams, there is a great deal of sponsorship. Particularly successful teams can attract very large amounts of sponsorship, which can have great benefits.

Sometimes local firms and businesses sponsor local teams. This is a good system, as the local teams would not be able to attract major sponsors and small firms or businesses would not be able to afford to sponsor very big clubs.

Sports

Sometimes, the actual sport itself, or its controlling association, is sponsored. This means that all the members of the association, including all the clubs and players, benefit.

Many sports with a good image are chosen by sponsors, and they are happy to help the sport nationally – not just in one area.

Key point

The issue of sponsorship in sport is a large and constantly changing one. Rules relating to it and different forms and levels of sponsorship are updated all of the time, and it is very closely linked to both sport in general and performers specifically.

Did you know?

When Usain Bolt extended his sponsorship contract with Puma in 2010 through to 2013 it was the biggest contract in athletics history. The exact figure was not disclosed but it was reported to be worth US$32.5 million!

Task 1

Find out the main sponsors for:
a a sportsperson of your choice who plays just as an individual
b one who plays as part of a team.

Task 2
Find one local small team, or club, that is sponsored by a small local company and one large local club that is sponsored by a major company.

Task 3
Find two sports that have their own sponsorship deals with firms.

Task 4
Find out the sponsor of a local event or competition. Then find out the main sponsors of at least one major international competition.

Events

Events have become very popular to sponsor because sponsors are guaranteed to be associated with success and successful teams. They do not have to take the risk that an individual, or team, might fail if they take charge of the whole event and, as long as the event or competition goes smoothly, they are guaranteed to get a lot of free advertising and publicity.

All sorts of events are sponsored, from local football and cricket competitions right through to major international events such as the Olympic Games. In the case of the Olympics, the event is so big that it can attract a large number of sponsors.

Most big events are guaranteed to be a financial success because of the sponsors alone; in the past, though, they had to rely on making money from people attending.

Types of sponsorship

Sponsorship can take many forms. It originally started in the days when there was more amateur sport and it was a way of helping a sportsperson without directly giving them money, as this was not allowed. Now it takes the following forms.

Equipment

As part of a sponsorship arrangement a sportsperson is given all their equipment for their chosen sport. This equipment would obviously be manufactured by the sponsors and could range from sports shoes to rackets, even to specialist training equipment.

Clothing

This does not even have to be the actual clothing worn by the sportsperson when taking part. It can often be extra items such as sunglasses or baseball caps with the sponsor's name on. In some sports there are even rules saying how large the sponsor's logo can be on clothing and where it may be displayed.

Accessories

Some firms are prepared to pay for their products to be worn even though they have no direct link to the sport. This is why many tennis players are sponsored to wear certain watches (which can be seen on television as the player serves) and cricketers are paid to wear sunglasses.

Transport and travel

This is often at least paid for and, in some cases, even provided. Car firms will provide free cars, often with drivers, for competitions, and air travel companies will provide free flights. Even at lower levels, coach firms will provide free transport (or at least at a reduced cost) and local garages will provide cars and/or petrol.

Money

Actual payments of money are made and the person sponsored can choose what to spend it on. If all the other aspects of sponsorship are covered (see the examples above), then this becomes an extra income for the sportsperson.

Training

This can be sponsored in several ways. The facilities can be provided, or paid for, or paid time off work can be arranged to enable training to take place. In some sports, such as tennis, personal trainers or coaches are provided for individual players.

Entry fees and expenses

These can mount up and be quite expensive and, if not paid for, could prevent a performer from taking part.

Food

This is another very common type of sponsorship. There are many examples of butchers sponsoring field athletes who need a large protein input which they get from meat.

Benefits for sponsors

Advertising

Sponsoring in any of the ways already outlined is one of the most effective ways of advertising a product or service. It can also work out to be cheaper than many other forms of advertising such as television, newspapers, billboards, radio or the internet. It has the added advantage that if the event, or performer, is shown on television wearing the sponsor's name, they will get a bonus.

Some products are not allowed to be advertised on television (e.g. cigarettes and other tobacco products), so sponsorship can sometimes be a way around these rules.

Did you know?

In the 2011 golf season, American golfer Bubba Watson was given a watch by one of his sponsors and paid to wear it. The watch was a Richard Mille RM038 worth US$525,000 and the same watch was also worn by tennis player Rafael Nadal in the previous year's tennis season!

Task 5

Find **at least one** example in sport of each of the eight types of sponsorship listed here.

Figure 36.1 The 2011 cricket test match series between the West Indies and Pakistan was sponsored by Digicel, whose logo appeared around the cricket ground and on the clothing of the West Indies players

Task 6

a Name a sport and its sponsor that are both commonly associated as having a good image.
b Name **three** sports award schemes and their sponsors.
c Name a sport that has been sponsored, resulting in an increase in interest and participation.
d Give an example of a sport where the clothing worn has been changed to suit a sponsor.
e Give an example of an event taking place at an unusual time in order to satisfy the sponsor.

Tax relief

Sponsors can claim for any of their sponsorship costs against the taxes they have to pay. This means sponsoring certain events can actually save them money.

Image

Sport generates a positive image such as a healthy, successful lifestyle. It is good for companies and products to be associated with this image.

Research and development

By getting performers to use their products, many sponsors are able to try out new developments in materials or equipment to see how well they work.

Goodwill

Although this is closely linked with image, many sponsors are prepared to help as a gesture of goodwill without any guarantee that they will gain from it.

Improved sales

This is probably the single most important benefit to any sponsor. If they have to pay money out in some form then they will wish to get as much back as possible in terms of increased sales of their product. Successful sponsorship, it has been proved, guarantees this.

Acceptable and unacceptable sponsorship

Most sports and sports performers are always on the lookout for sponsorship. However, not all forms of sponsorship are seen as acceptable.

Tobacco companies

Because of the health risks associated with smoking, any form of sponsorship from tobacco companies could be seen to encourage smoking, particularly among young people. Associating tobacco with sporting activities could glamourise the image of smoking. Governments have very strict guidelines that prohibit the direct advertising of tobacco products. There are moves to have all forms of advertising, including sponsorship, banned.

Alcoholic drinks firms

Because of problems associated with alcohol abuse, sponsorship could be seen to glamourise excessive drinking, therefore encouraging young people to drink before the legal drinking age.

Certain legal restrictions on both smoking and drinking are another reason for considering the sponsorship of these types of companies to be unacceptable. Alcoholic drinks companies often sponsor senior clubs and competitions, but often they are not deemed to be acceptable for any junior sporting situations.

The companies that benefit most from associations with sport are those that make sports goods. This is why Nike, Reebok, Puma and Adidas sponsor as many sports personalities, events and sports as possible.

Advantages	Disadvantages
Young and promising sportspeople are able to concentrate on their sport without many of the financial worries.	The sport can lose its own identity and be dictated to by the sponsors. This can happen in the following ways:
Sports can be promoted and encouraged so that participation levels increase.	Rules can be changed at the sponsors' request. This is particularly so in the case of what it is appropriate to wear and sometimes the length of time the event is to last.
The image of the sport can be improved with a link to a company that has a good image.	The timing of events is often dictated by sponsors, particularly when the sport is being televised. Times are chosen to suit an international audience and this might not be in the best interest of the performer or the sport.
More money is provided for the sport to pay for administration, facilities, coaching, training and improving standards.	Less successful sports and performers do not receive any sponsorship.
Bigger and better events can be staged and organised.	A bad product image can damage a sport.
Award schemes can be paid for and advertised.	If the sponsor has to withdraw, the sport or performer may not be able to carry on.
New and minority sports can be encouraged and financed.	The sport may become over-commercialised, reducing the fun aspect of taking part.
Competitions and leagues can be run, and prizes and money provided.	
Sponsors can get the many benefits listed on the previous pages.	

Table 36.1 Advantages and disadvantages of sponsorship

Hints and Tips!

The main thing to consider about sponsorship is that it has both advantages and disadvantages. Also, rules that relate to sponsorship need to be covered as well as keeping up to date with the latest sponsorship contracts and stories.

Key questions

1. Describe the range of sponsorship that exists in sport today including what and who may be sponsored.
2. Describe and explain what different forms of sponsorship exist for both sports performers and for specific sports.
3. What are the main advantages to a sport, or sportsperson, of being sponsored?
4. What are the main benefits to the sponsors of sponsoring sport?
5. How easy might it be for either a sport or an individual to obtain sponsorship? What factors will influence this?
6. Explain and describe some of the main advantages and disadvantages associated with sponsorship in sport.

37 The media

The media – including TV, newspapers and magazines, the internet and radio – are extremely influential in sport. One of the greatest strengths of the media is as a source of information and a shaper of ideas and views, and this can influence people to take part in sport and even to turn away from some activities.

Television

Television falls into one of two particular categories. Terrestrial television programmes are those that can be received by an ordinary television using a television aerial – in many countries you have to pay a licence fee to watch these programmes. The other category is that of satellite television, which is increasingly becoming the most common and popular option.

Satellite television

Sky launched its Sky Sports service on the Astra satellite in 1991 and you could obtain its service by subscription in 1992. In August 1994, a second Sky Sports channel was launched followed by a third one in 1996. There are currently even more dedicated channels and programmes have been developed to be broadcast in HD (high definition) and even 3D.

Viewers can watch 24-hour sports news programmes, and major football clubs such as Manchester United have even launched their own subscription channel. Additional sporting fixtures such as major boxing contests and special broadcasting events are also broadcast on a 'pay per view' system.

Television and sponsorship

The relationship between TV and sponsorship can be very complex and controversial.

All – or part – of other programmes may be sponsored, provided general guidelines are obeyed. The main rules are that sponsors must not be allowed any undue influence and that they must be clearly identified at the beginning and end of the programme. They must also be acceptable manufacturers or suppliers.

Sponsors themselves like the coverage because it is a form of advertising for them and they can be assured of large audiences. Some of the highest viewing figures for any programme in any year are for sporting events. The sponsors also have the benefit of being associated with something that may have a good and healthy image.

Key point

This is one of the most influential factors in local, national and international sport and is also rapidly changing. Although the main issues concerning the media are covered here, you will need to keep up to date with current events and developments by making use of the various forms of the media.

Task 1

Find out just how many specific sports channels are currently being broadcast in all of the different forms of broadcasting.

Types of programmes broadcast

There is a wide variety of different ways in which television shows and promotes sport, including:

- live sporting action
- highlights programmes
- documentaries
- quiz programmes
- news bulletins
- information services
- coverage of major sporting events
- sporting magazine programmes
- educational, schools, skills programmes
- dedicated channels (such as Manchester United TV)
- interactive programmes.

One of the main reasons for the large and varied amount of sporting coverage is that sport is relatively cheap to televise. Many programmes are far more expensive to produce and film and they do not have the uncertainty and drama of a live sports event.

Benefits TV brings to sport

Television clearly benefits from showing sport. However, it is not entirely a one-way process because sport benefits too through:

- **increased popularity** – many minority sports have greatly increased in popularity, and in the number of participants, due to TV coverage (e.g. gymnastics nearly always has a boom period immediately following an Olympic Games after there has been extensive coverage)

Figure 37.1 Most major sporting events are extensively covered by the media

> **Task 2**
> Choose **two** recent sporting events broadcast on television. Name the sponsors of the television programmes that covered these events.

Did you know?

Much of the technology used by officials such as Hawkeye and video analysis was initially used by the TV companies to improve the quality of their commentary and provide information to put before the viewers. However, this has now been taken over by many sports to enable them to have 'third officials' or 'video-refs'.

Did you know?

The tie break was first introduced to tennis partly due to pressure from TV companies to make the game more appealing to TV audiences.

Did you know?

During American football matches, the TV director can invoke a 'time-out' to allow an advertisement break to take place if they consider the play has gone on for too long!

Task 3

Make a list of the sports that now have extra officials who can advise the officials in direct control of the match through the use of any of the forms of television/broadcasting technology. What are these officials called and what technology do they use?

Figure 37.2 Highlights programmes provide a popular way to keep in touch with sporting events

- **increased revenue** – through sponsorship and endorsements
- **direct payments** – from television for the rights to broadcast events.

Conflicts between the media and sport

For the most part, the media only brings benefits to sport. However, there are some occasions when there are problems, such as:

- television may intrude on an event
- directors can even influence what we see
- sometimes rules are changed or adapted to make sports more appealing
- timings can be dictated by the TV companies, and the audience or spectators may have to wait until the broadcast is ready to start (on some occasions the entire starting time of the event is decided by TV)
- use of replays both in slow motion and from various angles can undermine officials (the official in charge does not have all of these benefits and many panelists and commentators sit in judgement on decisions)
- if particular sports are not shown on TV, they may decline in popularity and participation in them may drop off
- if a match or activity is shown on TV, this can discourage spectators from going along, which can lead to a loss of revenue for sports; also, if something is being televised, it could clash with another sporting event and reduce attendance
- the media can intrude upon a performer's privacy.

Despite the points listed above, the benefits of televised sport almost certainly outweigh the disadvantages, otherwise it is unlikely that there would be so much sport on television.

Developments are being made all of the time and television is constantly looking at ways of improving sports coverage. Interactive television is being introduced on the digital networks where viewers can choose from a variety of different options.

Information Technology (IT)

The widespread use of computers (and laptops, netbooks and 'tablets'), especially in homes and schools, now allows far greater use of information technology. Developments in mobile phone technology also make much of this accessible on these hand-held devices.

CD-ROMs can be used as either a source of information or as interactive programmes. However, the Internet has the greatest influence as a provider of information, with literally thousands of websites allowing access to a wealth of information on sport and leisure.

Radio

Most radio stations cover sport in much the same format as television. The obvious disadvantage is that they cannot broadcast pictures. However, because of this they are not regarded as rivals by TV, and particularly by the satellite companies, so they are allowed to cover all of the major sporting events. It is quite common to have these events broadcast on TV and radio at the same time.

There are even specialist radio stations that concentrate on sports coverage. This is very common with local stations that can service any particular local area.

Radio has advantages over TV because:

- broadcasting costs are much lower, as it only requires one commentator (sometimes with an expert analyst) and the basic technology to transmit the broadcast
- radios are portable, cheap and plentiful and listeners can even tune in while driving their cars, so the potential audience is bigger.

Figure 37.3 Many sports are covered on radio as well as television

Task 4

While you are watching a televised sports event, try to work out how many different cameras are being used.

Task 5

Choose any sport, or sports-based subject. Then see how many websites you can find on the internet connected with that particular subject.

Task 6

Study three different daily newspapers and find out how many sports pages are in each.

The press

The (printed) press consists of newspapers, magazines and books. All of these can be very influential and cover sports in a variety of ways.

Newspapers

All daily newspapers have sports sections, usually at the back. Some, especially the Sunday papers, have separate sports section supplements, which are newspapers in themselves.

Newspapers are very influential as not only do they print results, match reports, team news, rule changes and fixtures but they also comment on many major sporting issues – and especially about sporting personalities.

Magazines

There has been a great increase in the number of specialist sports magazines in recent years and most sports have at least one publication devoted to them. These magazines concentrate on issues connected with those sports, or on health and fitness, and often print very detailed information for readers.

Books

These can vary from novels with sporting themes to textbooks dealing with particular aspects of a sport. Some of the most controversial books recently have been autobiographies.

Hints and Tips!

The influence of the media is the most important aspect associated with it. A television (in its various forms) is such a high profile example of the media that it has become just about the most influential form as well.

Key questions

1. Explain the role of the media in sport.
2. Identify at least three types of coverage that the media can offer to the public.
3. What positive effects can the media have on sport? Give at least three examples.
4. Describe three negative effects that the media can have on sports.

38 Drugs and sport

A drug is a chemical substance that, when introduced to the body, can alter the biochemical system.

Most drugs are designed to improve an imbalance caused by a disease or illness. For example, a simple and common drug is paracetamol. If you have a headache and take paracetamol, the headache goes away due to the change the drug has caused in your body. However, when drugs are used in a healthy body they do not always have the desired effect. It must always be remembered that all drugs have some side effects.

The law and drugs

Most countries have specific laws that ban the sale and use of so-called 'social drugs'.

World Anti-Doping Agency (WADA) classifications

WADA was created in 1999 as the international independent organisation to promote, co-ordinate and monitor the fight against doping in sport in all its forms. In order to achieve this WADA has set out the following:

- a code – acceptance, implementation and compliance
- science and medicine – this includes updating the Prohibited List (see pages 166-170)
- out-of-competition testing – the rules and regulations relating to this
- anti-doping co-ordination (ADAMS)
- anti-doping development
- athlete outreach
- education.

All sports have to undertake three steps in relation to WADA: acceptance, implementation and compliance. This means that all sports organisations agree to the principles of the code, which they then have to implement, and the compliance means that they enforce all of the code as well. This world anti-doping code therefore harmonises anti-doping in all sports in all areas of the world. It is WADA that decides on the list of prohibited substances and methods.

Prohibited substances

The types and effects of each of the prohibited classes of substances are detailed overleaf.

> **Key point**
>
> The drugs most commonly associated with sport are the performance-enhancing ones. These are the ones that performers take, as they consider the effects are likely to improve their performance. Some drugs taken by people are legal (they are taken to maintain health); some are clearly illegal (such as heroin and cocaine); and some have specific rules relating to them for sporting events and sports performers.

> **Did you know?**
>
> Athletes can be banned if they are unavailable for a drug test! All athletes have to submit a diary/list of where they are going to be at any time so that the authorities can contact them at short notice to be tested. If they fail to be available three times, they are automatically banned.

Task 1

Write down some activities where stimulants might help a performance. Explain why you think they would help.

Stimulants

These substances increase alertness, reduce fatigue and may increase competitiveness and hostility. They can also produce a loss of judgement and this can lead to accidents in some sports. An overdose of stimulants can cause death. This has occurred twice in cycling events: once in an Olympic event and once in the Tour de France. Other side effects can include:

- high blood pressure and headaches
- strokes and increased and irregular heartbeats
- anxiety and tremors
- insensitivity to serious injuries
- addiction.

There is an unusual group of stimulants known as the **beta$_2$ agonists**; these are classified as being both stimulants and anabolic agents.

Many of the compounds found in stimulants are found in treatments for colds, hay fever and asthma, so it is very important to check with a pharmacist before you take any medications prior to an event.

Another recognised stimulant is caffeine (this is found in tea and coffee). There is a maximum level, of 12 micrograms per millilitre, above which it would be considered performance enhancing. Cocaine is also a stimulant and it is one of the controlled, and therefore illegal, drugs.

Narcotics

These include morphine and heroin. The main reason that they are banned is because they hide the effects of illness and injury. They suppress the feeling of pain but their side effects are:

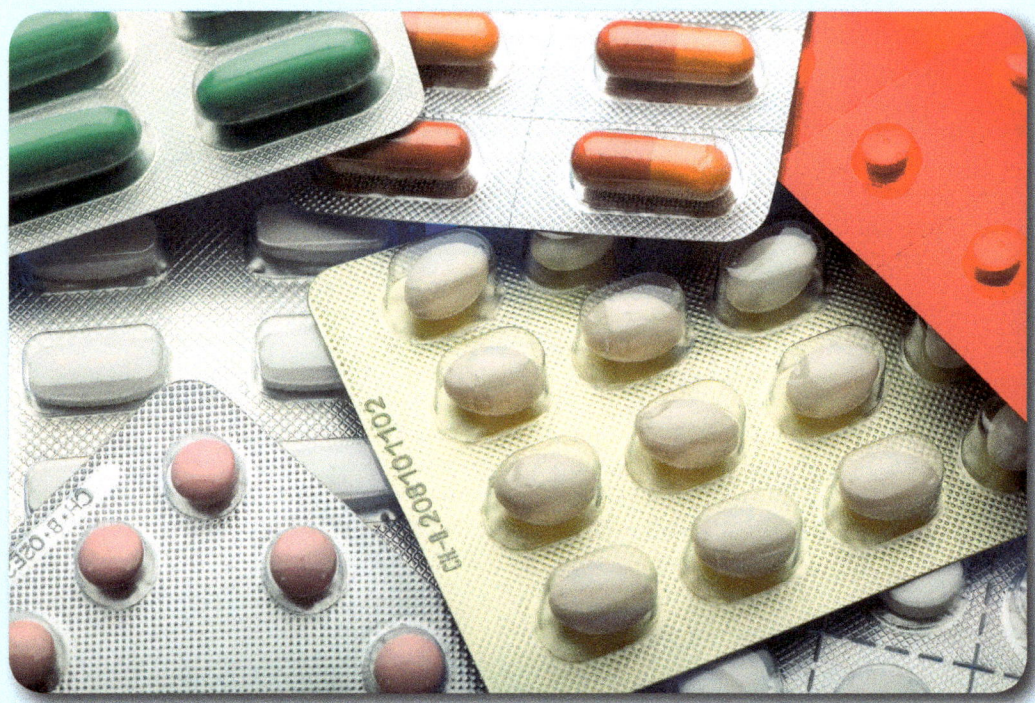

Figure 38.1 Not all drugs are harmful and banned – many have beneficial uses

- respiratory depression
- physical and psychological dependence
- exhaustion or over-training
- constipation
- extreme apathy.

Performers must be very careful to draw the line between treating an injury and actually concealing its full extent by taking narcotics. A far more serious injury could occur and an addiction to these drugs can lead to death.

Cannabinoids

These are a compound contained in the marijuana plant; they have no positive effects on performance and, in fact, can be detrimental. Prolonged use can cause 'amotivational' syndrome, which causes the user to lose focus and determination to succeed. It is their analgesic (pain relief) properties that make them prohibited.

Glucocorticosteroids

These are naturally produced steroid hormones that inhibit the process of inflammation, so they effectively stop the inflammation process.

Anabolic agents

These are probably the best known and most commonly abused drugs in sport. The main type is known as **androgenic anabolic steroids** – a group of both natural and synthetic compounds very similar to the natural male hormone known as testosterone. Testosterone has two main effects:

- **androgenic** – promotes the development of male characteristics
- **anabolic** – stimulates the build up of muscle tissue.

There are more than 100 types of anabolic steroids available. The most common ones are nandrolone, testosterone, stanozolol and boldenone. These are taken in tablet form, but some of the steroids are taken by injection directly into the muscles.

Steroids were originally developed because they helped to cure anaemic conditions, eased wasting conditions and bone diseases, and were useful in the treatment of breast cancer.

The first records of performers taking steroids were noted in the 1950s when some bodybuilders and weightlifters started to use them. This has now spread to other sports as performers feel that it can help their performance by:

- increasing muscle strength
- enabling them to train harder and for longer
- increasing their competitiveness.

There is no real evidence to back up claims that these drugs can have such a marked effect, but there is evidence to suggest that they can help with training. Taking steroids can enable a performer to have better and longer training sessions. Because of this they are often called 'training drugs'. They enable the performer to train very hard and then stop taking the drug in enough time before a competition to make sure that traces of it are not found during testing. This makes accurate testing for the use of this type of drug very difficult.

> **Task 2**
> Draw up a table listing the possible advantages and disadvantages of taking anabolic steroids.

Did you know?

Anabolic steroids are generally considered to be the main category of performance-enhancing drugs and are certainly the highest profile ones in relation to illegal drug taking by performers. If a performer can obtain a 10 per cent improvement (which is accepted to be the final result), this could make the difference between being an average sprinter and a world class one by shaving off 1 second from a 100 metres time!

Task 3

Name some activities where taking diuretics could assist a performer. Explain why.

Task 4

In what sort of sports could performers obtain an advantage through blood doping?

The risks involved in taking steroids are quite serious, and are listed below.

- **Liver disorders and heart disease** – there can be serious damage to the liver structure leading to jaundice, liver failure, liver tumours and bleeding of the liver. In one case a 26-year-old body builder who had been taking steroids for several years died of cancer of the liver. The heart can be affected by changes in its fatty substances, which can lead to an increased liability to heart attacks and strokes, as well as increased blood pressure.
- **Sexual and physique problems** – in children, growth can be affected or even stunted. Men can suffer from reduced sperm production and sterility. There can be shrinking and hardening of the testicles, impotence and even the growth of breasts. Women can have a disruption of the menstrual cycle and ovulation, changes in the sex organs, balding, acne, growth of facial hair and deepening of the voice. Steroids can also cause miscarriage, stillbirth or damage to the foetus, especially during early pregnancy.
- **Behavioural effects** – there can be quite marked changes of behaviour in some individuals. This can be seen as increased moodiness and aggression. The changes can be so extreme that they would constitute a psychiatric disorder.

All of these disorders depend on the amount of steroids being taken and the period of time over which they are taken. The effects can be reversed if their use is stopped quickly enough. It must also be remembered that beta$_2$ agonists have anabolic effects and can have similar side effects. Corticosteroids also have quite serious side effects that include:

- high blood pressure
- salt and water retention
- potassium loss
- bone and muscle weakness
- mental disturbances such as euphoria, depression or paranoia
- diabetes
- suppression of growth in children.

Diuretics and other masking agents

These are used medically to reduce excess body fluids and for the management of high blood pressure. Sports performers could misuse them to reduce:

- weight rapidly in sports where weight categories are important
- the concentration of banned substances by diluting the urine.

Because of this second effect, some authorities reserve the right to obtain urine samples from competitors at the weigh-in prior to a competition.

The following side effects can occur through injecting diuretics into the system:

- faintness and dizziness
- muscle cramps
- headaches and nausea
- dehydration.

The body needs a certain amount of fluids during exercise to perform properly and safely and diuretics can cause kidney and heart failure due to the excessive loss of water.

Peptide hormones, growth factors and related substances

Peptide hormones 'carry messages' around the body to increase growth, influence sexual and general behaviour and to control pain. This category includes the following drugs:

- chorionic gonadotrophin (hCG)
- pituitary and synthetic gonadotrophins (LH)
- corticotrophin (ACTH testracosactide)
- growth hormone (hGH)
- insulin-like growth factor (IGF-1)
- erythropoietin (EPO)
- insulin (permitted only to treat insulin-dependent diabetes; written notification of diabetes must be given by an endocrinologist or team physician).

Some of the above are already present in the human body, but drug misuse increases the levels artificially. It is these higher levels or 'abnormal concentrations' that are tested for and banned. The side effects of increasing the levels can include:

- muscle wastage through prolonged use
- enlarged internal organs
- unusual growth patterns such as enlarged hands and feet.

Beta$_2$ agonists

These result in smooth muscle relaxations and therefore dilate the bronchial passageways, so could be seen to assist in breathing.

Hormone antagonists and modulators

These are 'messenger molecules' released by endocrine glands to regulate specific body functions like blood glucose levels or muscle growth.

Enhancement of oxygen transfer (blood doping)

Some years ago, endurance athletes used this to make their blood more efficient in carrying and supplying oxygen. It involves having a transfusion of blood (this is when blood is actually added back into the bloodstream). The athlete has blood taken away, trains with depleted blood levels, then has the blood replaced before performance. This could even be someone else's blood, red blood cells or related products. This used to be tolerated, but is now banned. Possible side effects are:

- development of allergic reactions such as a rash or fever
- acute kidney damage if the incorrect blood type is used
- delayed transfusion reaction which can result in a fever and jaundice
- transmission of infectious diseases such as viruses, hepatitis and AIDS
- overload of the circulation and metabolic shock.

As well as banning the use of blood doping, the International Olympic Committee (IOC) has also banned any interference by what it calls pharmacological, chemical and physical manipulation. This covers such things as interfering with urine samples or using medical knowledge to assist performers.

Chemical and physical manipulation

The following is prohibited:

- tampering, or attempting to tamper with any testing procedures. Intravenous infusions – except for those legitimately received in the course of hospital admissions
- sequential withdrawal, manipulation and reinfusion of whole blood into the circulatory system.

Gene doping

Any of the following have the potential to enhance sports performance:

- the transfer of nucleic acids or nucleic acid sequences
- the use of normal or genetically modified cells
- the use of agents that directly or indirectly affect functions known to influence performance by altering gene expression.

Beta-blockers

These are prescribed to people who have a medical condition affecting their heart. They calm and control the heart rate. They would not be of any real benefit in some activities, but in others they have been identified as providing an advantage. Beta-blockers are therefore banned in:

- archery
- bobsleigh
- diving and synchronised swimming

Task 5

Look through the list above and say how taking beta-blockers might help the performer.

Did you know?

All performers are responsible for keeping up with the Prohibited List and to make sure they are not taking any medicines that could contain substances within it. As this is updated every year, they have to be very careful, seek advice and stay current with all information.

Task 6

Find out the penalty imposed on anyone who recently tested positive for banned drugs.

Figure 38.2 Shooting is one of the activities that specifically bans the use of beta-blockers

- luge (a form of bob sledge)
- modern pentathlon
- shooting
- ski jumping
- free-style skiing.

The use of beta-blockers in events requiring endurance would actually decrease performance, but there are cases where they have been used in sports to calm nerves and keep the performer steady.

Alcohol

This is prohibited in competition only, in the following sports:

- aeronautic
- archery
- automobile
- karate
- motorcycling
- ninepin and tenpin bowling
- powerboating.

Doping control

The use of drugs to improve a performance is clearly cheating and it can also be very harmful, sometimes even fatal. Despite all of this, some performers still use them in an effort to gain an unfair advantage.

Their use is banned and there are procedures in force to try to catch those who use drugs, and to discourage others from doing so. The procedure is called doping control and it involves obtaining a urine sample, testing it for any banned substances and following that up with any disciplinary procedures that might be necessary.

Recommended sanctions

The following sanctions can be imposed following a positive drug test.

- **Scale 1** (all the main listed doping classes) – 2-year ban for the first offence, life ban for the second offence.
- **Scale 2** (ephedrine, phenylpropanolamine, etc.) – a maximum 3-month ban for the first offence, 2 years for the second offence and a life ban for the third offence.

Unfortunately, these sanctions do have to be used. There are many cases where performers have used drugs to improve their performance.

> **Task 7**
> Make up a scrapbook of any recent drug controversies reported in newspapers.

Drug use in sport

The first recorded use of drugs in sport goes back as far as 1865. Here are some famous cases.

1988

In the Seoul Olympics there were ten positive doping results. Five of these were in weightlifting, two in the modern pentathlon, one each in wrestling and judo, and one in athletics.

The athlete found guilty was Ben Johnson. This was one of the most famous cases of drug abuse as he had just won the Olympic 100 metres championship. Johnson was given a 2-year ban and returned to racing with little success. He then subsequently failed another test and was banned from the sport.

There is little in sport that's more controversial than the drug situation, and several athletes have battled against the authorities after their bans.

Figure 38.3 The Canadian sprinter Ben Johnson, who failed a drugs test after winning the Olympic 100 metres in 1988

1998

In January 1998 it was revealed that there had been an organised system of drug use by athletes and performers in the former German Democratic Republic (East Germany). Files were discovered that revealed the 'Stasi' (the secret police force) had been running and organising a state-controlled drug/doping programme where sports performers were encouraged, and even forced, to take performance-enhancing drugs.

One of the GDR's Olympic swimmers, Petra Schneider, won a gold medal in the 1980 Olympics for the 400 metres individual relay. She was known on the Stasi files as 'sportsperson 137' and had been given drugs since the age of 14. In adult life she has suffered many of the side effects that the drugs can have.

Another East German performer, shot-put champion Heidi Kruger, was so badly affected by the amounts of steroids she was given that she had to undergo a sex-change operation.

In September 1998, US sprinter Florence Griffith-Joyner, who had won the Olympic gold medal in the 1988 Seoul Olympics, died of a heart attack. There were allegations that she had achieved her success with the help of performance-enhancing drugs – although she never failed a drug test. Doubts had been expressed when she was at her most successful, due to the deepening of her voice and her noticeably more muscled physique.

1999

In June 1999, triple Olympic gold medallist Michelle de Bruin (formerly Michelle Smith), the Irish swimmer, was found guilty of 'tampering with a drug sample' and banned following a 17-month case in which she had protested her innocence. There had been doubts expressed over her achievements in the Atlanta Olympics because of her swift and spectacular progress and improvement.

2003

In December 2003 Manchester United footballer Rio Ferdinand was banned for 8 months and fined £50,000. He had been found guilty of misconduct for not taking a drugs test in September at his club's training headquarters. He claimed he had forgotten about the test. He provided a sample 2 days later, which was negative, but still received a ban. This meant he missed the rest of the football season and the Euro 2004 international tournament.

Hints and Tips!

It is important to be aware of the general rules relating to drugs and also to be able to consider why some sports performers are tempted to take them. The performance-enhancing drugs are the crucial ones here and keeping up to date with recent drug scandals and controversies (which are bound to happen all too frequently) is very important.

Key questions

1. Why are some drugs legal and other drugs considered to be illegal? Give at least two examples of each.
2. What does WADA stand for and what role does it play in relation to drugs and sport?
3. Apart from anabolic steroids, name three other categories of prohibited drugs for sports performers.
4. Why would sports performers be tempted to take anabolic steroids? Describe the effects they consider would make it worthwhile for them to take these substances.
5. Describe three harmful effects that could result from taking anabolic steroids.
6. Explain what is meant by 'doping control'.

39 Discrimination in sport

Being unfair or hostile to someone for any reason is not acceptable, but there are examples where it has happened in sport and in some cases it is still happening. Any kind of discrimination clearly affects people's chances of participating fully and being able to perform to their best. Discrimination has taken place in the following ways.

Racial discrimination

This can and does occur, not only because of the colour of someone's skin but often just because of their nationality. Many countries are host to more than one race that has settled there, and there are often conflicts between the different cultures. They may even have different languages and marked-out areas within a country, so their access to sporting facilities may be completely different.

In this sort of situation, the racial groups are often referred to as 'sub-cultures'. This has also been the case with black and Asian sports performers and athletes. In America, and in many parts of Great Britain, the minority groups had been denied access to clubs, schools and organisations because of the colour of their skin. Changes in the law were necessary and were introduced to prevent this.

Until quite recently it would have been most unusual to find a professional black soccer player, or international athlete or cricketer in some mixed race countries. Now it is very common as the barriers are being broken down.

Apartheid

This was an extreme example of racial discrimination that existed in South Africa. A system was introduced that put people into different classes, based entirely on the colour of their skin. This **segregation** meant that they had totally separate schools, cinemas, living areas and even transport. Sports facilities and opportunities were also separate, which meant that black and coloured people were only allowed very limited sporting opportunities.

This system finally ended in 1994, but many generations suffered because of it. The political effect of apartheid is dealt with in more detail in Chapter 34.

> **Key point**
> Discrimination can take many forms and no one form is any more or less acceptable than another. It is probably true to say that discrimination is now far less acceptable than it was in the past when many forms of it were simply accepted without challenge.

National rights

Not all nations give equal rights to their citizens. There might be discrimination against some members of a society.

In some of the Eastern European countries many potential sports performers are selected, often at a very young age, and either put into special training schools or placed on specific coaching and training courses. One of the famous sprinters of the past, Valeri Bortzov, was supposed to have been selected and specifically trained, using computer technology.

In Cuba, there was a period when only eight sports were made available. This was so that they could achieve a high international status in the sports on which they concentrated.

These forms of selection are known as **elitism**, because not all the same opportunities are made available to all people.

Religion

Many individuals – and countries – have been victims of discrimination on religious grounds.

Many committed Christians will not compete on a Sunday – so if there is a tournament or event that takes place on that day, they will not take part. Many competitors have withdrawn from Olympic events because they have taken place on Sundays.

Jews were discriminated against in Germany in the 1930s when they were treated as second-class citizens.

In some Islamic countries it is not permitted for women to wear certain types of clothes. For example, it would be unacceptable for women to wear athletic running clothing or swimming costumes.

Hassiba Boulmerka, who won the 1500 metres Olympic gold medal in 1992, caused controversy in her own country by training and performing in shorts, because cultural practice in Algeria is for a woman to keep her legs and arms covered.

Sex

Sexual discrimination, notably against women, can take many forms in sport.

- **Fewer events** – many events are held for men only and in many professional sports there are no organised women's events.
- **Lower prize money** – nearly all events have lower prize money for women than for men.
- **Lower profile** – events are not so well promoted or publicised.
- **Women are banned** – in contact sports such as soccer and rugby, women are not allowed to compete against men. Show jumping is one of the few activities where women compete against men on equal terms.

Task 1
Try to think of **three** other examples where religious beliefs clash with sport.

Did you know?
A marathon for women was not included in the Olympic Games until 1984. This was because it was considered by many to be too strenuous a race for women to perform in. The first ever officially sanctioned International Association of Athletics Federation's (IAAF) marathon race did not take place until 1979. Women had been excluded altogether from track and field competition until 1928, and in the Moscow Olympics in 1980 the longest women's race was the 1500 metres!

Task 2
Try to identify other forms of sexual discrimination in sport.

Discrimination in sport

Social, economic and cultural

In many areas (and in whole countries) there is simply a lack of money, so the people who live there have less of everything. Even in the wealthier countries there are inner city areas that are very poor and that have few – if any – facilities. Almost certainly, the few sporting opportunities that are available will be very basic. This is why many of these areas have produced many excellent boxers, basketball players and soccer players. These sports do not require expensive facilities. Golf courses, tennis clubs and swimming pools may not be available, so these sports are not an option.

Certain cultural groups within an area may wish to have their chosen sports available, but they may be denied the facilities because of the cost or because it clashes with the choices of the majority culture.

Figure 39.1 Olympic gold medallist Hassiba Boulmerka suffered from religious discrimination

Hints and Tips!

Discrimination in sport is now mainly thought of as a historical issue, as so much has been done to make sure it does not happen. Knowing the history behind some of the issues associated with it is still important.

Key questions

1. What does racial discrimination consist of? Describe an example where it has affected sport.
2. Where was apartheid introduced and when did it finally come to an end.
3. Explain what is meant by elitism and say what connection it has with national rights.
4. In what ways might someone be discriminated against for religious reasons?
5. Identify four different ways in which women have been discriminated against in the past.

Glossary

active opposition
opponents in a practice situation who are actively involved

aerobic energy
energy expended over a long period of time that requires oxygen

aesthetic
something performed with beauty and sensitivity, pleasing performer and spectator

agility
combination of speed and flexibility

alveoli
small air sacs in the lungs where gaseous exchange takes place

amateur
sportsperson, usually part-time, who competes without receiving payment

amino acids
substances that link together to form protein molecules

anaemia
deficiency or poor quality of red corpuscles in the blood

anaerobic energy
energy expended in short bursts that does not require oxygen

androgenic anabolic steroids
commonly used performance-enhancing drugs

anorexia
eating disorder marked by insufficient intake of food

aorta
blood vessel carrying blood away from the heart, distributing it to the body

arterioles
blood vessels into which the arteries sub-divide

articular capsule
strong, fibrous tissue which surrounds a synovial joint

athlete's foot
fungal infection of the feet, usually between the toes

atria
two chambers at the top of the heart that receive blood from the veins

atrophy
wastage of a muscle marked by the muscle's loss of shape and strength

basal metabolic rate
minimum rate of energy required to keep all the life processes of the body maintained when the body is at rest

beta$_2$ agonists
group of stimulants and anabolic agents (performance-enhancing drugs) that are banned

bowel
common name for the lower intestine

bronchioles
small tubes in the lungs into which the bronchi sub-divide

bulk
size or mass (of a sportsperson)

calorie
unit that measures heat or energy production in the body

carbohydrate loading
increasing the amount of carbohydrates in the body before an endurance event

cardiovascular endurance
ability of the heart and lungs to keep operating efficiently during an endurance event

cartilage
tough form of tissue that covers and protects the ends of bones, and acts as a buffer where two bones meet at a joint

cerebellum
part of the brain that controls body movement

cerebrum
largest part of the brain, responsible for conscious control of the body

cholesterol
fatty deposit that can build up on the inner walls of the arteries, reducing blood flow

closed skills
skills performed in an unchanging environment

coma position
position in which a casualty should be placed when first aid is needed

concentric contraction (or dynamic contraction)
when a muscle shortens and gets fatter as it contracts

concussion
head injury that may cause a person to become unconscious

conditioned
game where the rules or the way a game is played is changed during a practice session to work on a particular aspect

consistency
being able to perform a skill properly, the same way each time

constitution
rules by which a club or organisation runs itself

control
being able to perform something in a regular and consistent way

convention
agreed rule or form of etiquette in a physical activity

co-ordination
ability to properly control the body when performing a physical action

creatine
food/nutritional supplement taken by performers to aid training and muscle development

decree
set statement or order, usually about a sports rule or regulation

dehydration
rapid loss of water from the body

delayed concussion
when the symptoms of concussion occur some time after the injury is received

diastolic pressure
pressure of the blood flow in the arteries when the left ventricle relaxes

dietician
someone who advises on the type of diet a person should have

differentiate
way of making a physical task easier or harder to perform

drill
set way of performing a practice or skill

dual provision
agreement whereby sports facilities are used by one or more types of users such as schools and the public

dual use
see dual provision

duodenum
part of the small intestine

dynamic contraction
see concentric contraction

dynamometer
device used to measure strength

eccentric contraction
return of a muscle to its original length and shape after a concentric contraction has shortened it

ectomorph
somatotype, or body type, where a person is relatively short with thin arms and shoulders

elitism
system in which certain groups are selected for special treatment, such as special squads who receive extra training and coaching

endomorph
somatotype, or body type, where person is basically short and rounded with short legs

endurance (or stamina)
ability of performers to keep going with a movement or activity for a relatively long period

etiquette
convention or unwritten rule in an activity that is not enforceable but usually followed

exhale
breathe out

expiration
action of the diaphragm and intercostal muscles that forces air out of the body

extra-curricular activity
activity that takes place at a school outside of timetabled lesson time

fainting
temporary unconsciousness or dizziness

fast-twitch muscle fibre
fibres that contract very rapidly but are quickly exhausted

feedback
information performers receive about their performance

fibrous
where fibres link together, such as fibrous joints

fitness
variety of factors that combine to give a sportsperson an efficient body, able to cope with a high degree of physical demand

flexibility (or suppleness)
range of movement around a joint

forced breathing
increase of the breathing rate during physical activity

form
level of performance the performer maintains or the good shape, position, presentation or manner of a performance

foul play
play that is against the rules or regulations of a sport

gangrene
infection that can set in after a fracture has occurred

glucose
type of sugar found in carbohydrates

glycogen
form in which glucose is stored

grooved performance
ability to repeat a skill consistently as a result of a great deal of practice

group skills
skills performed within a unit or group in a team

haemoglobin
substance in the red blood cells that transports oxygen and carbon dioxide

haemorrhage
when a blood vessel breaks followed by heavy bleeding

heart attack
when the heart muscle is starved of oxygen due to a blockage, causing severe chest pain and sometimes death

heartbeat
one contraction and one relaxation of the heart

hygiene
ways of maintaining cleanliness and health; good personal habits

ileum
lower part of the small intestine

immunisation
vaccination or injection that prevents disease

impartial
being fair to both sides; essential for a referee

independence
being able to do something on your own without help or interference

individual skills
physical skills performed on your own

ingrown toe nails
toe nails growing unevenly into the skin at the sides of the nails

inhale
breathe in

inspiration
air taken in when the diaphragm flattens and moves downwards

interaction
two or more people working or reacting with each other

intercostal muscle
muscles surrounding the ribs that assist breathing

invasion games
physical activities where teams have to get into their opponents area in order to score

isokinetic training
training using specialised machinery where resistance against muscles is variable

isometric contraction
muscle contraction where the length of the muscle does not change

isometric training
where a muscle is held at a particular point for approximately 5 seconds

lactic-acid system
breakdown of carbohydrates to provide energy, usually functioning during activities lasting between 1 and 3 minutes

leukocyte
white blood cell

ligaments
strong fibrous bands that stabilise joints and control movement

linear progress
fairly level and consistent skill acquisition

lineout
in a rugby match, a restart situation on the sideline

linesman
official who checks whether the ball has stayed in play; also known as referee's assistant

link player
team member who connects the units in a team game

malnutrition
poor physical condition due to a lack of nutrition

medulla oblongata
part of the brain that controls automatic functions of the brain such as breathing, heart rate and digestion

menstruation
monthly discharge of blood from the womb

mesomorph
somatotype, or body type, basically a 'Y' shape, well-muscled, with wide shoulders, long arms and narrow waist

movement replication
ability to copy exactly and repeat a physical movement

muscle tone
tension that remains in the muscles, even at rest

muscular endurance
amount of dynamic strength in a muscle; its ability to keep working for long periods

muscular fatigue
state of a muscle when it can no longer contract

negative acceleration
where a performer first learns a skill quite quickly and their rate of progress then slows down

nerves
state of anxiety that can affect a performance, or another name for neurons (see below)

neurons
basic cells of the nervous system

neutral
impartial, not taking sides

nucleus
main cell body of the nervous system

obese
extremely fat or overweight

oesophagus (or gullet)
canal from mouth to stomach, along which food passes

open skills
skills that exist in a situation that is constantly changing

open sports
sports events in which both amateurs and professionals can compete

oxygen debt
state where the body has used more oxygen than it can supply

oxyhaemoglobin
compound in red blood cells that carries oxygen from the lungs to the tissues

passive smoking
where someone who is a non-smoker inhales someone else's cigarette smoke

passive stretching
flexibility exercise where a performer stretches by pushing against something

peak physical condition
(athlete who is) at the best of their ability

penalty
punishment for breaking a rule or regulation in an activity

penalty move
set way of making use of a penalty that has been awarded

performance-enhancing drug
type of unlawful drug that can help to improve performance

physiology
study of the function and processes of the human body

physiotherapist
specialist who treats someone by using exercise or massage

plate competition
separate competition for losers in a main competition

plateau
situation in which a performer stays at the same level of skill, at least temporarily

platelet
small fragments of blood cells that help to clot the blood

pleura
double membrane surrounding the lungs, which contains fluid and acts as a lubricant

positive acceleration
where a performer finds mastering a skill difficult at first, then improves rapidly

posture
position in which a person holds their body

power
combination of the maximum amount of speed with the maximum amount of strength

practice
frequent repetition of an act, skill or physical activity

prescription
medical treatment that a doctor must authorise

professional
full-time sportsperson who gets paid for competing

psychiatrist
someone who helps people to psychologically prepare or psychologically cope

pulmonary artery
blood vessel that carries deoxygenated blood from the right ventricle of the heart to the lungs

pulmonary vein
blood vessel that carries oxygenated blood from the lungs to the left atrium of the heart

pulse raisers
exercises designed to increase the heart rate

pulse rate
rate per minute at which the heart beats

reinforcement
going over a movement or skill many times to ensure it is correct

relegated
being put down to a lower division or league in a sporting event

routine
regular and repeated procedure often of rehearsed and set moves

saliva
digestive juice found in the mouth that helps to digest food

scout
person who watches, finds and recommends players for sports teams

sedentary
sitting down or being physically inactive for long periods of time

seed
one of the acknowledged top players in a competition or event

segregation
keeping people or teams apart

self-esteem
feeling of being pleased with, proud or confident of oneself

semi-permeable
type of membrane that allows the passage of some substances but not others

set play
pre-arranged and practised move in a physical activity

skeletal pump
muscle action that helps the veins to pump blood around the body

skill
ability to perform certain activities or movements with control or consistency to bring about a desired result

slow-twitch muscle fibre
red fibres in skeletal muscles that contract slowly and repeatedly for long periods

somatotype
body types (see ectomorph, endomorph, mesomorph)

spasm
sudden involuntary muscular contraction

sphygmomanometer
device for measuring blood pressure

standing broad jump
two-footed jump forwards, starting from a squat position

static opposition
opponents in a practice situation who does not get actively involved

station
place or area that is part of a circuit used in circuit training

stimulus
something (such as music) that influences or assists a performance

striated muscle (or voluntary or striped muscle)
skeletal muscles of the body

stroke
sudden attack when the blood supply to the brain is cut off

sucrose
type of sugar (e.g. white table sugar)

synovial joint
joint that has a large range of mobility

systolic pressure
pressure of the blood in the arteries when the left ventricle contracts

tactics
pre-arranged and rehearsed strategies or methods of play

teamwork
ability of a team to work together as a single unit with a common aim

technique
manner in which someone performs a skill

tendon
fibrous tissue that joins a muscle to bone

testosterone
one of the banned types of androgenic anabolic steroids

tidal volume
amount of air breathed in and out during normal breathing

training
method of practising or preparing for physical activity

transfer of skills
skills that are common between different physical activities and that can be performed in them

travelling
moving forwards in an activity such as trampolining; can also be a basketball infringement

undernourished
lacking in certain nutrients

unit
group or number of players within a team

vaccinate
injection or inoculation with a vaccine

valve
structure that permits the flow of blood in only one direction

vein
thin blood vessel that transports blood

ventricles
two bottom chambers of the heart

vertebral column
groups of vertebrae that make up the spine

vitamin deficiency
lack of the necessary level or intake of vitamins

vitamin supplement
means of correcting a vitamin deficiency

VO_2
total amount of oxygen the body needs and takes in at any time

VO_2 maximum
maximum amount of oxygen the body can take in

warm-down
period of gentle exercise after taking part in physical activity to allow the body to recover safely and return to its normal state

warm-up
preparation period before taking part in physical activity

Index

abdominals 92
abduction 87
abductors 89
accessories 156
accidents 131
active contraction 59
active opposition 176
activity levels 38
adduction 87
adductors 89
advertising 156
aerobic capacity 124
aerobic energy 63, 176
aerobic zone 61
aesthetic 176
age 42, 68–70, 101
agility 49, 65, 176
agility tests 126
agonist 89
agonists 166, 169, 176
air passages 103–4
air quality 34
alcohol 32, 50, 158, 170
allergy 78
altitude training 120
alveoli 104, 105, 176
amateur 15, 176
amino acids 39, 176
amylase 108
anabolic agents 167–8
anaemia 78, 176
anaerobic energy 63, 106, 176
androgenic anabolic steroids 167
anorexia 44, 176
antagonists 89
anterior supra-iliac reading 127

anxiety 80
aorta 176
apartheid 173
arms 57
arteries 98
arterioles 98, 176
articular discs 86, 176
asthma 78
Athens Olympics 149
athlete's foot 35, 137, 176
athletics 141
Atlanta Olympics 147–8
atria 97, 176
atrophy 112, 176
autonomic nervous system 96
axons 95

back 57
badminton 13, 147
balance 67
ball games 141
bans 20
Barcelona, 1992 147
basal metabolic rate (BMR) 38, 176
baseball 142, 147
basic skills 1
basketball 12, 141
beach volleyball 147
Beijing, 2008 149–50
Berlin, 1936 144–5
beta$_2$ agonists 166, 169, 176
beta-blockers 169–70
biceps 91
Black Power protests 145
bleep test 121
blind spots 74
blisters 137

blood 97, 99
blood disorders 78
blood doping 169
blood pressure 100, 102
blood vessels 98–9
BMR see basal metabolic rate
body measurements 127
body shape 64
body temperature 97, 102
body tone 90
body type 76
Bolt, Usain 149
bolus 108
bones 84–5
books 164
boredom 81
bowel 176
boycotts 146
brain 96
breathing 104–5
breathing rate 106
bronchioles 78, 104, 176
bronchus 104
bruises 135
bulk 42, 176

caffeine 166
calories 38, 176
cannabinoids 167
capillaries 99
carbohydrate loading 39, 176
carbohydrates 38
cardiac muscle 88
cardiovascular endurance 60–1, 176
cardiovascular testing 124–5
carotid pulse 100
cartilage 86, 177

cartilaginous joints 85
central nervous system 93
cerebellum 96, 177
cerebrum 96, 177
cervical vertebrae 86
chin-up test 122
cholesterol 177
circuit training 117–18
circulatory system 97–102
cleaning 35
closed fractures 134
closed skills 6, 177
clothing 156
cocaine 166
colds 78
coma position 134, 177
combination events 29
combination tests 126
Commonwealth Games 150–1
competition 50
competitive events 16
complex skills 1
complicated fractures 134
compound fractures 134
concentric contractions 89, 177
concussion 136–7, 177
conditioned 177
connective tissue 86
consistency 177
constitution 177
continuous feedback 6
continuous shuttle run 120
continuous training 119
control 177
convention 177
cool-down 115
Cooper 12-minute run 124

co-ordination 1, 67, 177
correctness 129
de Coubertin, Pierre 144
cramp 137
creatine 177
cricket 11, 19, 142, 152
culture 76
cuts 135

decree 177
dehydration 41, 43, 177
delayed concussion 136–7, 177
deltoids 91
dendrites 95
dental care 36
diaphragm 104
diastolic pressure 100, 177
diet 37–41, 42–4, 50, 69
dietary needs 43
dietician 177
differentiate 177
difficulty 22, 23
digestive system 107–9
disability 75
discrimination 77, 173–5
disease 69
disease prevention 36
dislocations 135
diuretics 168–9
doping control 170–1
drills 25, 27, 177
drugs 50, 165–72
drug tests 147, 148, 171
dual provision 177
dual use 177
duodenum 109, 177
duration 64, 111
dynamic contraction 59, 177
dynamic posture 90
dynamic strength 54
dynamometer 123, 177

earrings 36
eccentric contractions 89, 177
ectomorph 71, 177
elitism 174, 177
emergency treatments 138
endomorph 71, 177

endurance 49, 54, 60–3, 177
endurance testing 124–5
energy 38
entry fees 157
environment 76, 129
environmental injuries 137
epiglottis 103
equipment 18, 129, 156
erythrocytes 99
etiquette 19, 178
evaluating 22
events 156
exercise 45–7, 101, 102, 105–6
exhale 178
exhaled air 105
exhaustion 137
expelled air resuscitation 139
experience 76
expiration 105, 178
expiratory reserve volume 105
explosive strength 53, 65
exposure 137
expulsion 20
extension 87
extensors 89
external/extrinsic feedback 6
extra-curricular activity 178
extroverts 80
eyesight 74

faeces 109
fainting 79, 178
fair play 128
family life education 31
Fartlek training 120
fast-twitch muscle fibres 60, 178
fatigue 79
fats 38, 39
fat-soluble vitamins 40
feedback 6, 178
femoral pulse 100
fibre 41
fibrous joints 85, 178
fines 20
fitness 33, 48–50, 178
fitness circuit 118
fitness phase 114

fitness testing 121–7
fixed load 118
flat bones 84–5
flexibility 46, 49, 56–9, 68, 77, 178
flexibility testing 122
flexion 87
flexors 89
flu 78
fluids 43
food groups 37
football
    diet 42
    etiquette 19
    formations 12
    history 141, 142
    world championship 151
forced breathing 105, 178
form 2–3, 178
formations 11–13
foul play 18, 131, 178
fractures 134–5
free weights 55, 116–17
frequency 111
frostbite 137

game plan 8
game situation 26
gangrene 178
gaseous exchange 105
gastric juices 108
gastrocnemius 92
gender 76–7, 101, 174
gene doping 169
glucocorticosteroids 167
glucose 38, 178
gluteals 92
glycogen 39, 178
goals 110
goal setting 7
goodwill 158
grooved performance 27, 178
group skills 178
growth factors 169
guidance 6
gullet see oesophagus
gymnasts 4, 25, 42, 56

haemoglobin 99, 178
haemorrhage 135, 178

hamstrings 92
Harvard step test 123
hat trick 142
hay fever 78
head injuries 134
health 31
health-related exercise 31
hearing 74
heart 88, 97
heart attack 101, 178
heartbeat 97, 178
heart rate 102
heat-stroke 137
height 50
hips 57
hockey formations 13
hormone antagonists 169
hyaline cartilage 85
hygiene 31, 35, 178
hyperextensions 118
hypothermia 137

ileum 109, 178
Illinois Agility Run 126
illness 50, 78
immunisation 36, 178
impact injuries 130
impartial 178
independence 178
individual differences 74–7
individual skills 178
information technology (IT) 163
ingrown toe nails 35, 178
inhale 178
inhaled air 105
inheritance 64
injuries 50, 69, 129–32
injury prevention 128–32
injury types 133–9
insertion 89
inspiration 105, 178
inspiratory capacity 105
intensity 111
interaction 178
intercostal muscle 105, 178
internal/intrinsic feedback 6
international governing bodies 19

international rules 19
international sport 143
interval training 118
introverts 80
invasion games 8, 10, 178
involuntary muscle 88
irregular bones 84–5
isokinetic training 117, 179
isometric contractions 59, 89, 179
isometric training 117, 179
isotonic contractions 89
isotonic training 117
IT *see* information technology

JCR test 126
jejunum 109
Johnson, Ben 147, 171
joints 57, 83, 85, 87
Joyner, Florence Griffith 172

knockouts 29
knowledge of performance 6
knowledge of results 6
Kruger, Heidi 173

lactic acid 63, 179
large intestine 109
larynx 103
latissimus dorsi 92
lawn tennis etiquette 19
leagues 29
learning 68
legs 57
leukocytes 99, 179
levers 87
ligaments 85, 86, 179
linear progress 5, 27, 179
lineout 179
linesmen 15, 179
link player 179
local governing bodies 19
long bones 84–5
Los Angeles Olympics 146
lumbar vertebrae 86
lungs 104

magazines 164
malnutrition 39, 179

Marathon 141
maturity 76
maximum pulse 61
media 160–4
medical conditions 50, 78
medicines 33
medulla oblongata 96, 179
menisci 86
menstruation 77, 79, 179
mental ability 76
mental rehearsal 7
mesomorph 71, 179
Mexico City Olympics 145
minerals 40–1
minor officials 16
monounsaturates 39
Montreal Olympics 146
Moscow Olympics 146
motivation 76, 81
motor neurons 95
mouth 103, 108
movement 89
movement replication 179
movement time 64
Munich Games 145
muscle atrophy 91
muscle contraction 89
muscle cramp 91
muscle fatigue 91
muscles 60, 88, 105, 178
muscle structure 91
muscle tone 90, 179
muscular endurance 60, 124–5, 179
muscular fatigue 60, 179
muscular system 88–92

nails 35, 178
narcotics 167
nasal cavity 103
national rights 174
negative acceleration 5, 27, 179
negative feedback 6
nerves 95, 179
nervous system 93–6
netball 11, 142
neurons 95, 179
neutral officials 16, 179
newspapers 164

nucleus 95, 179
nutrition 31, 37–41

obesity 38, 44, 179
oesophagus 108, 179
officials 15–17, 128
oils 39
Olympic games 141, 143–50, 154, 169
open fractures 134
open skills 5, 179
open sports 179
origin 89
original receptors 93
overload 110
overuse injuries 129–30
Owens, Jesse 144
oxygen capacity 69
oxygen debt 63, 106, 179
oxygen uptake (VO_2) 62, 106, 124, 181
oxyhaemoglobin 105, 179

Pan-American Games 151
passive contraction 59
passive smoking 33, 179
passive stretching 179
peak physical condition 179
pectorals 91
penalties 20, 179
penalty move 179
peptide hormones 169
performance, factors affecting 78–82
performance enhancing drugs 33, 180
performing 21
peripheral nervous system 93
personal hygiene 31
personality type 80
pharynx 103, 108
physical ability 75
physical activity 42–4, 69–70
physical handicaps 50, 75
physiology 180
physiotherapist 180
planning 21, 28
plantar warts 137
plasma 99
plateau 5, 27, 180

plate competition 180
platelets 99, 180
playing career 70
pleura 180
politics 153–6
pollen levels 34
polyunsaturates 39
positive acceleration 5, 27, 180
positive feedback 6
posture 45, 90–1, 180
power 65, 67, 126, 180
practice 2, 26, 68, 180
practice sessions 5, 25
prescription medicines 33, 180
pressure 81
primary shock 136
prime movers 89
professional 5, 180
progression 111
progressive shuttle run 121
promotion 29
protease 108
proteins 39
psychiatrist 180
psyching up 82
pull-up test 122
pulmonary artery 98, 180
pulmonary circuit 100
pulmonary vein 98, 180
pulse 100
pulse raisers 180
pulse rate 47, 61, 102, 180
pulse recovery rate 62, 123

quadriceps 92
quality 22, 23

racial discrimination 173
radial pulse 100
radio 163
reaction time 64, 69
recovery period 118
recovery position 134
red blood cells 99
reinforcement 27, 180
relegated 180
religion 174
repetitions 116

replays 162
residual volume 105, 106
respiratory system 103–6
restarts 10
resting pulse rate 61
reversibility 112
RICE treatment 138
risk assessment 29, 33
Romans 140
rotation 87
round-robin 29
routine 180
rugby 12, 73, 143, 152
rules 18–20

safety 31, 33, 74
saliva 108, 180
satellite television 160
saturates 39
Schneider, Petra 171
scout 180
sedentary 45, 180
seed 180
segregation 173, 180
self-esteem 35
semi-permeable 99
senior officials 16
senses 74
sensory neurons 95
sensory organs 93
Seoul Games 147, 171
sergeant jump 126
set play 10, 180
sets 116
sex education 31
shock 136
short bones 84–5
shoulders 57
show jumping 174
simple fractures 134
sit-up test 125
skeletal muscle 88
skeletal pump 99, 180
skeletal system 83–7
skeleton 83–4
skill phase 115
skills 1, 5–6, 180
    age 69
    practice 3, 25
skills circuit 118

skill transfer 5
skin colour 102
skin infections 35, 137
Sky Sports 160
slow-twitch muscle fibres 60, 180
small intestine 109
SMART target setting 21
smoking 32–3, 50
smooth muscle 88
soccer see football
softball 147
soft tissue injury 135, 138
soma 95
somatotype 50, 71–3, 180
spasm 91, 181
specificity 110
speed 49, 64–7
sphincter muscle 108
sphygmomanometer 100, 181
spinal cord 96
sponsorship 155–9, 160
sports 18
    events 28–30
    origins 140–1
sprains 135
sprint starts 118
staffing 29
staleness 79
stamina see endurance
standing broad jump 126, 181
starches 38
static posture 90
static strength 51
stations 117, 181
steroids 167, 172
stimulants 166
stimulus 181
stomach 108
strains 135
strategies 14
strength 49, 51–5, 69, 76
strength testing 122
stress 81, 101
stress fractures 130
striated muscle 88, 181
striped muscle see striated muscle

stroke 101, 181
subscapular reading 127
substance misuse 31
sucrose 38, 181
Super Bowl 152
suppleness see flexibility
suspension 20
Sydney Games 148
synapse 95
synovial joints 85, 181
synovial membrane 86
systemic circuit 100
systolic pressure 100, 181

table tennis 143
tactics 8, 181
tax relief 158
teamwork 9, 181
techniques 7, 181
television 160–2
temporal pulse 100
tendons 86, 89, 181
tennis 143
tension 80, 101
terminal feedback 6
terrorist attacks 145, 148, 154
test match series 152
testosterone 76, 181
thoracic vertebrae 86
throwing events 15
tidal volume 105, 106, 181
timed circuits 118
tiredness 79
tobacco companies 158
toe nails 35, 178
touch 74
trachea 104
training 2, 104, 110–12, 128, 157, 181
training methods 116–20
training sessions 113–15
training zone 61
transfer of skills 5, 181
transport 156
trapezius 91
travelling 156, 181
treatment 133, 138
triceps 91
true shock 136

undernourished 181
unit 181

vaccines 36, 181
valves 99, 181
variable resistance machines 117
veins 99, 181
ventricles 97, 181
verrucas 137
vertebral column 86–7, 181
vital capacity 105, 106
vitamin deficiency 181
vitamin supplement 40, 181
VO_2 maximum 62, 106, 124, 181
voice box 103
volleyball formations 13
voluntary muscle see striated muscle

WADA see World Anti-Doping Agency
warm-down 181
    see also cool-down
warm-up 2, 25, 113–14, 128, 181
warts 137
washing 35
water 41
water-soluble vitamins 40
weight 50
weightlifters 42
weightlifting 123
weight-training 55, 90, 116–17
white blood cells 99
Wimbledon 151
windpipe 104
witch-hazel 135
World Anti-Doping Agency (WADA) 165
world championships 151–2
World Cup 19, 142, 151
wrestling 149